CW00923861

London Calling

The projection of Britain abroad was an important part of BBC programmes overseas during the Cold War. In June 1950, a BBC Yugoslav Section reporter introduces listeners to the sounds of London, and the chimes of Big Ben.

London Calling

Britain, the BBC World Service and the Cold War

Alban Webb

Bloomsbury Academic
An imprint of Bloomsbury Publishing Plc

B L O O M S B U R Y

LONDON • NEW DELHI • NEW YORK • SYDNEY

Bloomsbury Academic
An imprint of Bloomsbury Publishing Plc

50 Bedford Square
London
WC1B 3DP
UK

1385 Broadway
New York
NY 10018
USA

www.bloomsbury.com

BLOOMSBURY and the Diana logo are trademarks of Bloomsbury Publishing Plc

First published 2014
Paperback edition published 2015
Reprinted by Bloomsbury Academic 2015

© Alban Webb, 2014

Alban Webb has asserted his right under the Copyright, Designs and Patents Act, 1988, to be identified as Author of this work.

All rights reserved. No part of this publication may be reproduced or transmitted in any form or by any means, electronic or mechanical, including photocopying, recording, or any information storage or retrieval system, without prior permission in writing from the publishers.

No responsibility for loss caused to any individual or organization acting on or refraining from action as a result of the material in this publication can be accepted by Bloomsbury or the author.

British Library Cataloguing-in-Publication Data
A catalogue record for this book is available from the British Library.

ISBN: HB: 978-1-4725-1501-8
PB: 978-1-4742-2749-0
ePDF: 978-1-4725-1503-2
ePUB: 978-1-4725-1502-5

Library of Congress Cataloging-in-Publication Data
A catalog record for this book is available from the Library of Congress.

Typeset by Deanta Global Publishing Services, Chennai, India
Printed and bound in Great Britain

For Willow

Contents

List of Illustrations viii
Acknowledgements ix

Introduction 1

Part 1 From Total War to Cold War

1 Planning for Peace 13
2 The Home Front 26
3 The Cold War Challenge 35

Part 2 Through the Iron Curtain

4 The Imagined Audience 53
5 The Radio Arms Race 75

Part 3 Global Reach

6 A World Service 91
7 Austerity 101

Part 4 Battlefields

8 The Soviet Challenge 119
9 Hungary 133
10 Suez 157

Reflections 185

Notes 189
Select Bibliography 235
Index 243

List of Illustrations

Frontispiece	The projection of Britain	ii
Figure 1	William Haley, BBC Director-General, February 1952	16
Figure 2	Ian Jacob, Controller, BBC European Services, July 1946	27
Figure 3	Ralph Murray, BBC Governor, July 1968	39
Figure 4	Listener Research, BBC European Service, Bush House, April 1948	54
Figure 5	Hugh Carleton Greene, BBC German Service Director, January 1946	61
Figure 6	Christopher Cviic of the BBC's Yugoslav Section, September 1955	70
Figure 7	Bush House canteen, November 1960	92
Figure 8	BBC European Service News Room, Bush House, February 1945	139
Figure 9	Ivone Kirkpatrick, Controller, BBC European Services, February 1943	167
Figure 10	Bush House, The Aldwych, London, April 1948	184

It is with gratitude that I would like to acknowledge the kind permission given by the BBC for the reproduction of these photographs.

Acknowledgements

The enjoyment I have derived from writing this book is as much about the people it has brought me into contact with as the treasure trove of sources and fascinating stories that have come to life during the course of its research. To these people I owe a debt of gratitude for their help, guidance and invaluable insight. Chief among these is Peter Hennessy, my doctoral supervisor and the person who showed me what joy and excitement there was to be had in explaining history. This is also true of Jean Seaton, the official historian of the BBC and great chronicler of modern media, whose infectious appetite for understanding is a constant source of stimulation. Much of the primary research for the book was conducted as part of a PhD funded by a scholarship from the BBC and administered by the University of London through Queen Mary College. I am grateful to the family of Austen Kark (former Managing Director of BBC External Services) and his wife Nina Bawden for the honour the title of Austen Kark Memorial Scholar bestowed on me. Although facilitated by the BBC in its funding of the PhD, this work is academically independent and at no point have I, or the work, been subject to any external editorial influences.

It was at Queen Mary that I came alive to the possibilities of researching history and I would particularly like to thank James Ellison for his support and guidance in this, as well as John Smele, John Ramsden, Gary Magee, Philip Ogden, Virginia Davis, Matthew Grant, Catherine Haddon, and Gabriella Gera. My subsequent work at the Open University in the Centre for Research on Socio-Cultural Change has greatly benefited from collaboration and friendship with colleagues such as Marie Gillespie, Francis Dodsworth, Kath Woodward and Sophie Watson. A number of others in academic and related fields require special mention for the significant part they have played in supporting and enhancing my work. I am particularly grateful to Asa Briggs, David Cannadine, Nicholas Cull, Daniel Day, Anne Deighton, Michael (M.R.D.) Foot, Robert Fox, Suzanne Franks, David Hendy, Keith Kyle, Anthony McNicholas, Martin Moore, Michael Nelson, Barbara Parry, Lowell Schwartz, Tony Shaw, Heather Sutherland, and Bela Szombati. In addition, I am obliged to those whose tireless work behind the scenes in vital archives has made my research possible. In this regard, I would especially like to thank Jacquie Kavanagh, James Codd and Erin O'Neil at the BBC Written Archive Centre, and Sarah Tyacke and Stephen Twigge at the Public Record Office of The National Archives of the United Kingdom. I also want to thank Robert Seatter, Robin Reynolds, Katherine Schopflin, and John Escolme of the BBC Heritage department for their considerable assistance in facilitating the research project and supporting it through to publication.

In the course of researching this book it has been the greatest pleasure to encounter a wide range of programme and policy makers who made the BBC World Service what it is today. Their generosity of time and spirit has been invaluable, offering insight, understanding, and vital context. In particular, I would like to express my gratitude to, Marie Anthony, David Wedgwood Benn, Noel Clark, Christopher Cviic, Dimiter Dimitrov, Leonid Finklestein, Christopher Graham, John Gray, Brian Hanrahan, Viola Huggins, Peter Johnson, Laszlo Jotischky, Tania Kelim, Dora Lavrencic, Hugh Lunghi, Jessica Macfarlane, Malcolm Mackintosh, Zdenka Mastnik, Graham Mytton, Antoni Pospieszalski, Hugh Saxby, Efim Slavinsky, Vania Smith, Dianko Sotirov, Andrew Taussig, Peter Udell, John (J.G.) Weightman, Wilf Weston, Charles Wheeler. They, among others, have illuminated and enriched my research. Any errors or mistakes in the book, however, are my own. Finally, and most importantly, I would like to thank Willow Grylls for her support at all stages in the preparation of this book. Her penetrating eye for detail, sharp wit and companionship have made its completion possible.

Introduction

The Overseas Services of the BBC provide one of the most effective instruments for use by this country in maintaining the stability of the free world in the present struggle with Russian Communism. This struggle, often called the "Cold War", seems likely to be long. It cannot be won quickly, though it might quickly be lost.

BBC Memorandum for the Cabinet Committee on Colonial Information Policy, June 1950[1]

From 1 January 1947, the third successive Charter of the British Broadcasting Corporation (BBC) was intended to mark not only the continuation of the BBC as the monopoly broadcaster in the United Kingdom but also denote the transition from the wartime activities of its overseas services to the broadcasting requirements of peace.[2] Emerging from 'six long, weary and perilous years', as the BBC's Director-General William Haley put it in his Victory in Europe Day message to staff, broadcasting was considered as having a vital function to perform as 'the newest of the great instruments of peace'.[3] However, it was not long before fissures in post-war international relations plunged the world into a 'cold war'. Once again, radio was pressed into service by the British government, this time as an adjunct to its non-shooting war with the Soviet Union, providing the opportunity to directly engage the hearts and minds of populations behind the Iron Curtain.

Broadcasting overseas by the BBC had begun on 19 December 1932 with transmissions in English to the Empire on shortwave but it was not until January 1938 that programmes in other languages were inaugurated, with an Arabic Service, followed quickly by Spanish and Portuguese Services for Latin America. Transmissions to Europe began in September 1938 with German, Italian and French news broadcasts started at the time of the Munich crisis, in a deliberate attempt to counter the propaganda of Italian and German radio stations.[4] It was this competitive impulse to ensure that people in other countries should be made aware of the British interpretation of events that became a founding principle of broadcasting in other languages and lay at the heart of the subsequent massive expansion of the BBC World Service, not just in Europe but to all continents, during the Second World War. In this way, Britain's geopolitical concerns and the intricacies of international diplomacy were dynamically and irrevocably knitted with the existing purpose of the BBC's Empire Service, which had been to transmit the core values of the British way of life to the imperial outreaches and create a tangible (as well as metaphorical) border-defying community of interests, held together by an imperceptible network of wavelengths with London at its heart.[5]

At its peak, in 1943, the BBC was making regular programmes in over 45 languages (not including English) and by the end of the war, the number of hours beamed abroad exceeded that of domestic broadcasting.[6] This explosion in the overseas activities of the BBC during the war, affecting the scope of its transmissions and the scale and multinational character of its workforce, altered the nature and remit of the BBC to a point where Haley was able to assert that in the ten years since the BBC started its previous Charter in January 1937, 'the horizons of broadcasting [have] immeasurably widened. The BBC's field is now the world'.[7] This was indeed the case by 1947, when the threat of a Cold War was being defined not just in the minds of policy makers and military planners but also in terms of a wider public perception. The 1946 White Paper on *Broadcasting Policy*, the precursor to the Royal Charter, argued that 'other Powers intend to continue to use the broadcasting medium to put their point of view . . . and we cannot afford to let the British viewpoint go by default'.[8] To this end, the BBC was charged with the task of ensuring that the voice of Britain remained a force overseas at a time of intense economic uncertainty at home and high anxiety abroad, as post-war reconstruction gave way to a recrudescence of deep international schisms, which posed a grave threat to the recently achieved peace.

The character, reach and editorial practice of the BBC World Service, as we know it today, owe a very great deal to this critical post-war period of recalibration. The peacetime establishment of a publicly funded, editorially independent, multilingual global broadcast operation was a considerable leap of faith in the austere context of post-war Britain. It produced a model of international public service broadcasting that has been an important part, albeit a relatively unheralded one, of British civil society ever since. Without it, the capacity of the BBC's domestic services to provide news and analysis on an international scale and of a genuinely global nature would have been severely diminished. It opened a window on the world while at the same time introducing audiences abroad to British culture, politics and institutions. Yet, the name 'World Service' itself is a relatively late addition in its more than 80-year history. Known as the Empire Service until November 1939,[9] the Second World War recast both the context and the purpose of its output, partitioning the world between its European and other Overseas operations. These organizational entities were, after the war, finally brought together under the umbrella of the Corporation's 'External Services', with respective Controllers reporting to an overall Director. It was not until May 1965 that the English-language General Overseas Service was rebranded as the World Service and another 33 years before this title was given to the collective overseas broadcast effort of the BBC, both in English and other languages, in 1988. For the majority of the period covered by this book, the 'BBC External Services' is the name that contemporaries would have recognized and is, therefore, the term that will predominate here.

Despite the high-profile roles to which it has been assigned by government and global public familiarity with it as an institution (with a current weekly audience in excess of 190 million),[10] the political, diplomatic and cultural impact of the World Service over eight decades has not been matched by a similar appetite to explore its significance both as a broadcaster and as an agent of public diplomacy. In part, this is a problem of assimilation: as Philip Taylor noted, the academic community has generally failed to integrate the media and other forms of cultural exchange into mainstream political and administrative histories.[11] Similarly, Nicholas Cull has pointed out that 'Historians have been slow to pay serious attention to the details of the cultural components of the Cold War.'[12] In this way, the story of international broadcasting has traditionally appeared in the margins of other historical narratives. Nevertheless, the cultural Cold War has become a subject of increasing activity in the last couple of decades. The end of the Cold War had the twin effect of opening up previously inaccessible archives (if only temporarily, in some cases) while at the same time loosening curatorial attitudes to Cold War-related materials.[13] This has precipitated a 'new wave' of publications and a concurrent widening of the investigative landscape as the societal impact of the Cold War attracts an increasingly interdisciplinary approach.[14] While this was initially a factor in the liminal presence of culture in Cold War narratives, requiring a complex pulling together of political, media, diplomatic, artistic, technological, sociological, geographic and cultural expertise, this interdisciplinarity is now a driving force behind an expanding literature.[15] This in turn has revealed the extent to which governments competing in the geostrategic context of the Cold War were themselves implicated in establishing, fostering and sometimes funding these cultural battlegrounds.[16] As David Caute notes, 'the cultural cold war was shaped by the new primacy of ideology', and between 1945 and 1989–91, argue Jessica Gienow-Hecht and Mark Donfried, 'cultural productions became the most powerful tools for the promotion of ideological goals and strategies'.[17] Amid the conventional stalemate of the Cold War, the result was 'the continuous pursuit of victory by other means'.[18]

Radio was one such method that occupied the minds and activities of an army of policy and programme-makers on both sides of the Iron Curtain. In the case of the BBC External Services, the planning for and execution of this battle of the airwaves can be found in the reports and memoranda that passed within and between the BBC and Whitehall. Invaluable though these sources are, it is an unfortunate reality that very little remains of actual broadcast output, thereby placing out of reach the ability to listen to the broadcast rhythms and sounds of the Cold War. Nevertheless, the BBC's Written Archive Centre, housed alongside the BBC Monitoring Service at Caversham in Berkshire, is a wonderful and incomparable source of information about life in Britain since the 1920s and the United Kingdom's engagement with the rest of the world since 1932. Embodying in every one of its files principles of public value, it lacks the capacity and resources necessary to satisfy the increasing and important research demands made on it. Meanwhile, at The Public Record Office, part of The National Archives of the United Kingdom, successive initiatives in the last twenty years have precipitated the declassification of previously restricted files, resulting in a steady stream of releases that illuminate the political economy of overseas broadcasting.[19] What emerges is a more accurate reading of the ways in which the World Service 'co-habits', as Anthony Adamthwaite put it, with its funding stakeholders in Whitehall and makes accommodation with their strategic interests.[20]

This has been an important development in understanding the role of international broadcasting in the conduct of British public diplomacy: the assumed dividend that has until now underwritten government funding of the World Service. A euphemism for 'propaganda'[21] – a term that two world wars had done much to discredit – 'public diplomacy' was coined in its modern-day form in 1965 by former American diplomat Edmund Gullion as 'the cultivation by governments of public opinion in other countries'.[22] It is easy to see how those wishing to make full use of the levers of diplomatic power might look to broadcasting to fulfil such an aim. Indeed, the projection of carefully selected versions of British identity had been at the core of the Corporation's mission overseas since the first broadcasts of the Empire Service. Yet, as becomes quickly apparent from the archives, any suggestion of a link between the BBC and government strategies of influence poses the dilemma of how to accommodate the often competing aims of the broadcast professional and the Foreign Office official. At the heart of this debate is the issue of credibility with audiences over the long term: in the provision of truthful news and associated analysis and the creative and cultural capital exercised in engaging listeners. In the context of the emerging Cold War, this was a domestic challenge that would have profound implications for the style, tone and ambition of British overseas broadcasting for generations to come.

The episodic institutional history of overseas broadcasting contained in Asa Brigg's five-volume *History of Broadcasting in the United Kingdom*, originally published between 1961 and 1979, is an invaluable resource, which indicates both its genuine importance as the first official draft of the BBC's history and the relative paucity of subsequent studies that have attempted to engage in a debate about overseas broadcasting from Britain. More often than not, it has been practitioner-based exposition and memoir that has lifted the curtain on broadcasting to foreign countries. From Tangye Lean's 1943 *Voices in the Darkness* to John Tusa's 1992 *A World in Your Ear*, broadcasters have been alive to the opportunity to explain the development, purpose and techniques of international broadcasting in their own terms.[23] Likewise, those involved in managing overseas communication strategy in Whitehall have helped flesh-out what has been a relatively unheralded part of the government machine from policy-making, in the case of Charles Hill's *Both Sides of the Hill*, to practise, as laid out in Robert Marett's *Through the Back Door*.[24] The BBC has itself provided regular, if rather self-promotional, accounts of the means and impact of overseas broadcasting in various publications, broadcasts and lectures.[25] Until recently there have, however, been relatively few attempts to shed a genuinely historical light on the World Service. The clearest exception to this is the book by a former Managing Director of External Broadcasting, Gerard Mansell, *Let Truth be Told*, which, despite the obvious sympathies indicated in the title, successfully combines the sensitivities and intuition of the insider with evidence-based research.[26]

More recently, a revitalized appetite for researching the BBC World Service, directly linked to the increasing quantity and quality of primary source material available, has been evident. This can be seen in the study of the government's overseas information services where it is now possible to examine in some considerable detail what John Black described as Britain's 'propaganda instrument', the Whitehall machinery supporting it and the place it occupied in wider government policy.[27] An example of this is the declassification of files relating to the Foreign Office's infamous covert propaganda unit, the

Information Research Department (IRD).[28] Early accounts of its work were severely hampered by the lack of access to the official record,[29] but releases in chronological tranches since 1995 have generated a new round of analysis as demonstrated in Hugh Wilford's 1998 article, which sought to reveal 'Britain's secret Cold War weapon'.[30] Combined with the Foreign Office's less notorious, but just as illuminating, Information Policy Department (IPD), there now exists an archival spinal column which reveals the wider architecture of Whitehall's anti-communist and propaganda activities.[31] The result is an emerging literature on Britain's machinery of persuasion, propaganda and political warfare after the Second World War as these sources are digested and processed into scholarly output. Important contributions in this field include, Andrew Defty's detailed examination of IRD's early years, James Vaughan's excellent analysis of the failure of UK and US post-war strategic communications in the Middle East, John Jenks' take on British propaganda in the Cold War and Lowell Schwartz's valuable comparative study of the formation and application of US and UK propaganda policy.[32]

Only a few studies, however, have attempted to fully synthesize analyses of overseas broadcasting with government policy during the Cold War. As with Tony Shaw's history of broadcasting at the time of the Suez crisis (ostensibly in relation to domestic coverage), and the recent *Cold War History* special journal issue on 'Radio Wars', they are required reading for anyone attempting to understand the intricacies of the relationship between the government and the BBC.[33] Likewise, Gary Rawnsley's comparative case studies of overseas broadcasting by the BBC and Voice of America (VOA) are well-judged assessments of the realities of Cold War broadcasting.[34] What these otherwise excellent studies lack, however, is a sense of the wider context of the World Service's editorial and institutional response to the Cold War, its translation into practice and the concurrent development of post-war relations with the government in general and the Foreign Office (FO) in particular. In this regard, Michael Nelson's insightful *War of the Black Heavens*, a comparative history of the Western broadcasters (BBC, VOA, Radio Free Europe and Radio Liberty), is better at highlighting the signifying moments and trends in the Cold War history of the BBC than providing a detailed examination of how they were negotiated. The story of how the BBC's External Services came to terms with the Cold War and the tone, over time, of its fundamental relationship with Whitehall and the government is one that has, so far, only been partially told.

Covering the first decade in which the BBC once again took editorial control of all its overseas services, in English and other languages, this book examines how the External Services responded to the Cold War in its broadcasts over the Iron Curtain and elsewhere, revealing a missing dimension of Britain's frontline engagement with international communism. This is done by exploring the evolution of the BBC's post-war relationship with the British government which funded overseas broadcasting through a grant-in-aid, the geopolitical and diplomatic contexts in which the BBC broadcast, and the ways in which the BBC sought to engage strategically important audiences around the world, particularly in Central and Eastern Europe and in the Middle East. Incorporating analyses of policy, production and reception, this approach aims at illuminating the life cycle of British international broadcasting as well as understanding how editorial ethics, key personalities and audience assessment moulded a narrative of the Cold War that was to influence output for decades to come. The way in which the BBC subsequently set about translating the Cold War experience for audiences abroad, at the behest of Whitehall, quickly became a core element of its broadcast remit. As such, the tone of its broadcasts across the Iron Curtain was the outcome of continuous, complex and often difficult negotiations with the British government set against the broadcast experience and in-house editorial assessments of the Corporation, all played out in a highly charged and volatile international environment.

The need to rethink the purpose of overseas broadcasting forms the focus of the first part of the book. The Second World War had demonstrated the influence and importance of broadcasting abroad, both in its own right and as an adjunct to wider government strategies. It had also shown, in contrast with the German propaganda instrument, the value of building credibility with audiences through, as far as circumstances allowed, objective and truthful reporting. It had, however, become a very large and expensive operation which posed tricky questions about its ongoing financial and editorial management. Indeed, such was its perceived importance to Britain's post-war diplomatic effort it was not immediately certain that an independently minded BBC was the right home for these services. These considerations found expression in the process of planning that started in 1944 and which led, three years later, to a new Royal Charter for the BBC. The settlement was intended to mark out a new era in British broadcasting: a return to normality for the domestic services and the institution of a permanent peacetime arrangement for overseas broadcasting. However, little time would be found for equilibrium as a new threat emerged on the international horizon and the world steered away from the devastation of hot war into the icy, and no less dangerous, waters of the Cold War.

This is followed by an examination of institutional and editorial responses, at the BBC and within government, to these new strategic conditions. The Cold War was not the only issue that concerned the External Services as they broadcast across the globe, but it did provide a uniquely common theme against which they would have to define themselves. And as it became clear to all but the most optimistic that the Cold War would be a protracted battle, the gearing of sensibilities as well as of practice towards it that took place within the External Services from the beginning of 1948 were to have an enduring effect on output until the collapse of communism in Europe 40 years later. Broadcasting was a 'long-term weapon' ideally matched for such an arms-length conflict, but defining the voice of Britain and establishing its multifaceted tone for the politically as well as culturally varied ears of the BBC's many audiences around the world made for, as will be seen, a very considerable challenge. This was particularly so in the case of Europe, the first frontline of the Cold War, which the BBC considered 'as the most important target' and to whom nearly half its foreign-language services were beamed.[35]

What ensued was an acute phase of re-engineering of External Services output in response to prevailing geopolitical conditions which brought into sharp focus the essential principles of Cold War broadcasting. It also highlighted the varied geography of the External Services' relationship with Whitehall: those terrains on which there was consensus and those where conflict and disagreement would mark and scar the landscape. This was a creative tension which required delicate negotiation if the constitutional equilibrium, as set out in the BBC's Charter Licence and Agreement, was to be maintained. Surveying the global remit of its overseas services, the book will explore the wider context in which the BBC's Cold War activities were framed as a geographic 'world service'. It will also examine the strategic orientation of its services in the context of the post-war economic environment and the government's willingness to pay for them. In this period of austerity, it is difficult to fully appreciate the challenges faced by the External Services without coming to terms with the political and budgetary pressures also bearing down on them.

The unresolved and fractious economic arguments which ran through the 1950s posed a genuine challenge to the BBC's strategic autonomy and were subsequently to play their part in what would become a period of intense activity for the External Services as they came to terms not only with major international developments, but conflict on the home front with the British government. Events in Central and Eastern Europe in the middle of the decade also raised concerns about the efficacy of international broadcasting and the lengths to which outside broadcasters should and could interfere with the internal affairs of other countries. Meanwhile, in the Middle East the BBC's credibility with audiences was stretched to near breaking point as it sought to reconcile political and public division at home with the projection of Britain abroad. The British government's threat to seize control of the External Services at the height of the Suez crisis and the BBC's determination to resist resulted in a new appreciation of the balance of forces between Whitehall and the BBC, which has remained the basis of the relationship to this day and continues to inform editorial policy at the BBC World Service.

It will be argued that the tone of the relationship between Whitehall and the BBC's External Services, how they learnt to speak to each other after the Second World War, was instrumental in defining the task of overseas broadcasting from Britain during the Cold War. In conjunction with the journalistic abilities and cosmopolitan sensitivities of the staff engaged in making programmes, it was essential in establishing the voices with which the BBC spoke to its many audiences around the world. This ongoing, critical and often unobserved discourse between broadcaster, funder and audiences accompanied the regular diet of broadcast output whose tone was continually modulated to reflect the political, cultural, economic and practical imperatives bearing down on it. Examining the ecology of this relationship, from its post-war planning stages to its nadir during the Suez crisis, it is intended to provide an assessment of the BBC External Services through a cycle of experience that fundamentally shaped the principles and practice of overseas broadcasting and which continues to inform and frame the international output of the BBC into the twenty-first century.

Part One

From Total War to Cold War

1

Planning for Peace

The Second World War was the making of the multilingual 'world service' we recognize today. Expanding from one English-language service at the beginning of 1938 to well over forty by the middle of the war, it not only recast the scale and organization of BBC overseas broadcasting, but gave the Corporation a new strategic significance in the conduct of British military and foreign policy. This explosion in foreign-language broadcasting was consequently imprinted with wartime contingencies and exigencies, as was evident in the varying degrees of government oversight applied to programme output, for example by the Ministry of Information (MOI). The controlling impulse was strongest and most apparent in the case of Europe, to which BBC broadcasts, from September 1941, came under the supervision of the newly formed Political Warfare Executive (PWE).[1] Established to direct, co-ordinate and control political warfare and propaganda activities, such was the significance of BBC programmes to occupied Europe that PWE's London headquarters were moved to the home of the European Services, Bush House, in March 1942.[2]

This intimate, though sometimes strained, relationship, which included the issuing of weekly directives by PWE Regional Directors to their broadcast counterparts, puts into perspective the extent to which the European Services had, for operational reasons, come under government control during the war. It also helps to explain some important conditioning factors when considering how the BBC transformed itself from an international broadcaster at war to one reorganized for peace. When considering its future role, the wartime BBC had expected that it would be necessary to maintain two separate overseas services 'until the time comes when what we know as our European Division becomes an integral part of the BBC, free from the direct control of the PWE'.[3] The segregation of these services from the rest of the BBC's activities reveals the corporate mentality towards a branch of the organization that since its foundation (a definable European Service having emerged only in August 1939)[4] had never been able to establish itself independent of the wartime context. Moreover, apart from the English-language services that had effectively avoided such oversight arrangements, the degrees of control hitherto exercised over foreign broadcasts posed a series of important questions for policy-makers in terms of prescribing the appropriate balance between editorial independence and government direction in the future. The wartime Chairman of the BBC Board of Governors, Sir Allan Powell, had been keenly aware of this delicate balancing act when he noted the 'silken cords' that linked the Corporation with the government could sometimes become 'chains of iron' when the controlling impulse was flexed.[5] Resolving this dilemma took some time to work out.

In the autumn of 1943, nearly a year after Allied offensives at El Alamein and Stalingrad began to turn the tide of war against the Axis powers and publication of the Beveridge Report in the United Kingdom pointed towards a future free from the 'five giants on the road of reconstruction' – Want, Disease, Ignorance, Squalor, Idleness[6] – the BBC's Director-General Robert Foot informed the Corporation's Governors that he was 'now engaged in clearing my own mind . . . with regard to the problems which will face us in the future'.[7] After consulting senior executives and programme Controllers, he proposed a comprehensive review of the Corporation, its purpose and the activities of all its services in the post-war world. Foot's review, co-written with William Haley who had been appointed to the new post of Editor-in-Chief from the *Manchester Evening News* in August 1943, defined in broad terms the reorganization of the BBC's output. It envisaged that after the war there would be 'five programmes, three in this country . . ., one European, and one Overseas Group comprising all the rest of the world excluding Europe'.[8] Crucially, it was argued that the collective broadcast offer should be paid for out of the licence fee, as had been the case before the war, thereby insulating the Corporation from the kind of external governmental interference it had encountered since 1939, albeit in the pursuit of British war aims. It would take until April 2014, a further 71 years, before this particular ambition was achieved.[9]

Then, as now, the fate and future of the BBC were not entirely in its own hands. Both its constitution, under the rubric of its Royal Charter, and the nature of wartime practice required the intimate involvement of the government of the day. Accordingly, while senior management at Broadcasting House in London's Fitzrovia began the process of reconceptualizing the radio world around them, policy-makers and officials in Whitehall and Westminster turned their attention to restructuring the government's strategic communication operations. Responding to the request of the Prime Minister, Winston Churchill, to supply policy recommendations for a post-war transition period of up to two years,

Brendan Bracken, Minister of Information, suggested a small committee to advise the government on 'its attitude towards the future of radio broadcasting in this country'. Meanwhile, the Deputy Prime Minister, Clement Attlee, thought the BBC should be looked at in a wider context that examined 'international as well as domestic issues'.[10] Consequently, on 27 January 1944, the War Cabinet established a Ministerial Committee chaired by the newly appointed Minister of Reconstruction, Lord Woolton, to 'enquire into future broadcasting policy'.[11] Here, the value of broadcasting across the world in English, a job the BBC had been doing since 1932, 'for all those who think of the United Kingdom as home, wherever they may be'[12] was affirmed by the committee. And with six years' worth of experience as to the value derived from foreign-language broadcasting behind them, there was little dissent among Ministers from Bracken's view that the 'broadcast voice of Britain has become a great influence in Europe' and that 'the Government will wish to have the BBC's services to foreign countries continued after the war'.[13] It was, nonetheless, taken as axiomatic that 'the Government would have to exercise a much greater degree of control over overseas broadcasting than over home broadcasting'.[14]

With more than half of the BBC's foreign-language services beamed across the channel, Europe, both strategically and in terms of the critical mass of effort the BBC had put into engaging overseas audiences, would prove to be the key to the wider shape and overall future design of the External Services. Haley, who by then had succeeded Foot as Director-General, met with the Broadcasting Committee in October 1944 along with Sir Allan Powell, the Chairman of the Board of Governors, and was invited to submit a paper on Broadcasting to Europe. Mirroring the government's own provisional timetable to peace, the 'first transitional period', Haley reported, 'will come to an end with final defeat of Germany'. The second, 'when BBC broadcasting to a Europe nominally at peace would serve the ends of SHAEF [Supreme Headquarters Allied Expeditionary Force] and of the British Government', would last for one year. After this the third period would see 'the Government . . . divest themselves of their present control over [the] European Division and return all responsibility for its activities to the BBC'.[15] In thinking his paper through with the assistance of 'a small divisional committee', Haley tried to imagine what the post-war requirements of a liberated Europe would be. In terms of content, and unhampered by the editorial needs of war, 'The most we should seek to do is to make available British news, British culture, and a projection of life to those who wish to make acquaintance with them', a view which accorded with that of the Broadcasting Committee.[16] But what of the make-up of the BBC's continental audiences? Following the end of hostilities, Haley felt the profile of the BBC's listenership would change radically: 'Once the dark silence of Hitler's five year blackout of news has been lifted there will not be the same overwhelming need for the clerk and the peasant in Europe to listen to the BBC.'[17] This expectation ran in the face of the BBC's wartime experience of broadcasting for mass consumption but Haley believed that with the inevitable redevelopment of indigenous broadcast networks, the Corporation could not expect to maintain such a numerically large and demographically wide audience. Therefore, it was argued that BBC broadcasts should be aimed at 'a much more restricted circle; newspapers, publicists, [and] men . . . who take an interest in international politics': in effect, the decision-makers, opinion-formers and male educated classes of liberated Europe.[18] In pursuit of this, it was proposed that the number of services should be reduced to the 'great European languages' of French, German, Spanish, or Swedish, at least one of which this elite target audience could be expected to speak.[19] When ministers met on 24 April 1945, just two weeks before Victory in Europe Day, to discuss 'broadcasting to foreign countries', it was generally agreed that they indeed should be reduced to a 'comparatively small scale'.[20]

Figure 1 William Haley, BBC Director-General, February 1952

Managing Editor at the *Manchester Evening News* from 1930 and then Managing Director of Manchester Guardian and Evening News Ltd., Haley joined the BBC as Editor-in-Chief in 1943 before becoming its Director-General the following year. After overseeing a fundamental reorganisation of the Corporation he left the BBC in 1952 to return to newspapers as Editor of *The Times*.

This, then, was the initial broad-brush strategy for post-war overseas broadcasting allying the removal of direct government intrusion into programming with a reduction in scale to reflect a peacetime remit of projecting Britain abroad. In practice, governing mindsets were to change significantly with the end of the war as an evolving global communications landscape revealed new challenges and opportunities. The BBC had originally envisaged a European Service, reduced from a wartime peak of 50 broadcasting hours a day (across all languages) to a peacetime level of 9 hours, within an overseas framework that encompassed broadcasting in English overseas, a Latin-American Service and an Arabic Service.[21] Yet, within a very short space of time, not only had the locus and make-up of government decision-making changed but so too had some of the underlying assumptions about the role of international broadcasting in the future. The dissolution of the Coalition government in May meant that the Broadcasting Committee was unable to complete its deliberations. It was left to the new Labour Government and the Lord President of the Council, Herbert Morrison, to finish the job under the auspices of a Cabinet Committee (GEN 81).[22] As this committee worked its way towards a finished report, a rather different vision of BBC foreign services reorganization began to emerge. Speaking off the record in November at the BBC's annual General Liaison Meeting, Haley, who had met with Morrison's committee in October, revealed

> he had come to the conclusion, and the Government had agreed with him, that it would be far more sensible to build the Overseas Division service by service, from the bottom up; instead of making a global picture first and fitting in the services, as a result of which the Division would probably be either over-sized or inadequate.[23]

This was a far more pragmatic and piecemeal approach to the future of overseas broadcasting than originally planned and a world away from the handful of languages recently proposed by Haley. It reflected a more flexible approach which was in keeping with conditions on the ground where there was 'strong evidence that the European Service retains a surprisingly large audience and that our friends on the Continent are most anxious that it should continue'. Therefore, while there was an overall reduction in output after the war, the change was to be found in the volume of transmissions and not in the number of languages broadcast.

It was on this revised basis that GEN 81 presented its *Report on Broadcasting Policy* to the Cabinet, which was discussed and approved on 17 and 20 December 1945.[24] With the BBC's current Charter, Licence and Agreement due to run out on 31 December 1946 after a period of ten years, debate about the future of British broadcasting moved to Parliament where a White Paper on *Broadcasting Policy* was duly considered in July 1946.[25] The constitutional settlement was finally enacted when the new Charter came into force on 1 January 1947, the first ever to deal with foreign language, as well as domestic, programming. However, it was only one element of the post-war reorganization of the BBC: the legislative framework within which the detail would be worked out.

Meanwhile, as the Corporation peered over the precipice of Charter renewal and imagined its role abroad in the future, senior management set about organizing its own thoughts in a paper on 'The Principles and Purpose of the BBC's External Services'.[26] As this important document acknowledges, the heart of its activities was news – 'the kernel of all overseas broadcasting'[27] – about which the White Paper had laid down that the 'treatment of an item in an Overseas news bulletin must not differ in any material respect from its treatment in a current news bulletin for domestic listeners'.[28] Reflecting this and outlining arguments that remained germane to its overseas task over the long term, the BBC argued the 'purpose of such a news services is threefold':

1. It acts as a prime source of fact and information for anyone who cares to take it, either professionally as journalists, publicists, politicians, or as private citizens.
2. It makes the truth available in places where it might not otherwise be known. By its presence, it forces newspapers and broadcasting in authoritarian countries themselves to approximate closer and closer to the truth.
3. Within the Commonwealth, where it is often rebroadcast on Dominion internal services, it has a different purpose. Here it provides both a wider coverage of subject than those local broadcasting services would otherwise enjoy and also a link between parts of the Commonwealth.[29]

In addition, the paper gave voice to an article of faith for the Corporation that had been learnt through the tough experience of the war years: 'it is not a function of the BBC's external services to interfere in the domestic affairs of any other nation. The services do not exist to throw out Governments or to change regimes.'[30] Instead, overseas broadcasting, and Talks programmes in particular, should 'provide a means of displaying the British way of life' and 'British democracy at work and leisure'.[31] As will be seen, there were times when such principles were somewhat challenged by broadcast practice.

Working out the formal institutional relationship between the government and the BBC was another area that occupied a considerable amount of time in advance of the new Charter. During the war, this had been the business of the Postmaster-General, the Minister of Information and the PWE covering technical, policy and operational issues. With the dissolution of PWE and MOI by March 1946,[32] it was nonetheless thought 'essential to retain some effective central organisation to handle Government publicity'. The result was the establishment of a new organizational structure, the Government Information Services (GIS) to co-ordinate the activities of the newly minted Central Office of Information (COI), the British Council, the Information Departments of concerned ministries, such as the Foreign and Colonial Offices, Information Officers at overseas Embassies, other official and non-official bodies, and the BBC.[33] This would then define the 'broad outlines to be followed by official publicity [that] will in future be agreed interdepartmentally through the Ministerial and Official Committees'.[34] While the Postmaster-General was to remain responsible for technical issues, in terms of wider policy it was decided, after some initial hesitation, that the Lord President (who was responsible for the COI and oversaw the GIS) would act as 'the Minister who will answer Questions on major broadcasting policy save where they fall clearly within the province of one of his colleagues'.[35] The government's reluctance for any one minister to be formally associated with responsibility for the BBC,[36] an independent legal entity, was matched by the very strong desire of the Foreign Office (FO) to take the lead on matters of overseas broadcasting. In September 1945, the Foreign Secretary, Ernest Bevin, had asked his Cabinet colleagues for a 'decision in principle that foreign publicity is an instrument for foreign policy, and that the Secretary of State for Foreign Affairs must be responsible for it'.[37] This was supported three months later by the Official Committee on GIS and subsequently by the Cabinet where 'in so far as the Government may accept responsibility for the policy behind overseas broadcasting services, the responsibility should lie with the overseas Ministers, each in his own sphere'.[38] As a consequence, the FO took control of the day-to-day relationship between the government and the External Services of the BBC.

British governments have repeatedly emphasized the editorial independence of the BBC and programming content was publicly upheld, along with technical know-how, as within the Corporation's sphere of influence. Nevertheless, successive BBC Licences had included two powers which offered ministers the opportunity to apply political pressure and the 1947 Licence was no different. The first stated that the 'Corporation shall whenever so requested by any

Department of His Majesty's Government . . . send . . . any announcement or other matter which such Department may require to be broadcast' while the second gave the Postmaster-General the ability to 'require the Corporation to refrain from sending any broadcast matter (either particular or general)'.[39] This provided the government the right to either force or prevent broadcasting by the BBC of certain material or particular programmes. But it was the influence derived from these powers, rather than their actual use, which was key as indicated by the wartime experience of the Postmaster-General, Harry Crookshank: 'the existence of the right has on occasion facilitated agreement concerning the withdrawal of items to which serious exception may be taken without formal exercise of the veto'.[40] As Lord Asa Briggs, the first official historian of the BBC, has persuasively noted, government 'could always influence what might be called "the temperature"' of the BBC's broadcasts'.[41]

Far more specific to the External Services, and far more pervasive, was the stipulation in the White Paper and then the Charter that the BBC would 'remain independent in the preparation of programmes for overseas audiences, though it should obtain from Government Departments concerned such information about conditions in these countries and the policies of His Majesty's Government towards them as will permit it to plan its programmes in the national interest'.[42] This was the outcome of the Broadcasting Committee's problem of how to exert a greater degree of control over overseas broadcasting. Through this guidance mechanism, the FO and other departments received their right of access to the External Services and the direction and preparation of programme output. The fact that this was accepted by the BBC also indicates the value it perceived to be getting by adhering to such a consultative relationship not the least of which was the genuine desire, with limited resources, to be apprised of conditions in reception territories and the wish not to misrepresent the 'national interest' by being unaware of British strategic priorities – something broadcasters would have been particularly sensitive to from their recent wartime experience. Understanding this balance was central to the first directive issued by Sir Ian Jacob when he joined the BBC as the new Controller of European Services in July 1946. When visiting the FO, Service Directors should 'seek to learn all they can, they should listen to the views expressed, but they should not act on guidance received directly from the Foreign Office departmental officials without testing it by our long-term standards, referring as may be to me'.[43] This was a point clearly understood by Haley who wrote in October 1946, 'The desire to distort information is, in this country, rarely in evidence. The desire to suppress information, particularly news whose publication may be inconvenient from a short-term point of view, is more apparent.' However, it was

> precisely this kind of news to which the overseas listener is inclined to attach great value, and by which the independence and integrity of the BBC's news services are judged. This, quite frankly, is not always understood in official circles but by now the BBC has had long experience in maintaining its point of view and persuading others of the strength of its case.[44]

Although increasingly well versed in defending itself against direct political pressure, there was another crucial element of the relationship between the BBC and the government that had very important implications for the independence of the External Services – finance. From the start of the Broadcasting Committee's deliberations, the Postmaster-General had correctly linked the BBC's disposition towards an increased licence fee after the war, from which all broadcasting activities could be funded, with the Corporation's attempts to divest itself from financial dependence on the state.[45] Until 1 September 1939, the BBC's activities were funded out of a licence fee, but since then all costs had been covered by a Treasury Grant-in-Aid.[46] When planning the Corporation's post-war financial arrangements and the reinstatement of a licence fee, Haley originally estimated the cost of the European Services at £500,000 a year with the total per annum cost of overseas broadcasting loosely estimated at £900,000.[47] Reflecting his vision at the time of a reduced overseas operation, he calculated that with an increased licence fee of £1 (up from 10/–) providing around £10 million in revenue it could be possible for this to cover the entirety of the BBC's output.[48]

Such a significant organizational leap into the unknown, especially in the context of the variable broadcast demands of the post-war world, induced a sense of caution on the part of the BBC,

> While stating the complete financing of the BBC's sound broadcasting activities out of its revenues as a proper objective, therefore, I suggest we would have to seek some half-way house to begin with so that we could see how we went on. The presence of a provisional Treasury guarantee in the background need not deter us from reaching our goal.[49]

But as the real cost of maintaining many, if not all of the language services in Europe, the Middle East, Far East and South-East Asia, North and Latin America became apparent through 1945, it was agreed by the Cabinet in December that 'the cost of overseas broadcasting should be borne by the

Exchequer independently of any licence fee revenue'.[50] A revised estimate for the BBC's External Services of £3,150,000 ultimately secured the argument, turning a transitional funding expedient into lasting financial control for the government.[51]

Haley and the Board of Governors had been aware from an early stage of what the consequences of such an arrangement might be. It was recognized, for example, that 'Subsidisation inevitably involves some degree of control'.[52] This was also understood by the Official Committee on GIS at the beginning of 1946 where it 'was pointed out that there was a close link between control of expenditure and control of policy'.[53] While acknowledging that 'the content of the [overseas] service should be the responsibility of the BBC', Ivone Kirkpatrick, a member of the committee who was instrumental in defining the post-war relationship between the Foreign Office and the Corporation, explained that 'the scope and character of overseas broadcasting should be ultimately fixed by the Foreign Secretary or other responsible Minister'. He then went on to lay out before the committee his view of the relationship between the BBC's foreign services and the government in a clinical analysis:

> This ultimate Government responsibility was inherent in the Government's control over the grant-in-aid for overseas broadcasting. It was not intended that the Government should accept any formal responsibility for the conduct of the overseas services, but finance would be provided on the basis of an approved programme, and the Government would be fully entitled to bring pressure to bear on the BBC in order that the service should accord with the aims of Government policy. The ultimate sanction would be a financial one.[54]

Not only was this unnervingly prophetic of the approach he was to take with the BBC ten years later during the Suez crisis, but it clearly exposed, as the new Charter was being prepared, a disposition within Whitehall towards the kind of leverage the government might seek for its funding of the External Services.

The spectre of Parliamentary scrutiny over these funding arrangements was also perceived by the BBC as a potential challenge to its autonomy. The June 1946 Report of the House of Commons Select Committee on Estimates proposed an official audit arguing the Grant-in-Aid required 'the same close financial scrutiny as is normally applied to the direct functions of Government'.[55] This was despite the 1936 Ullswater Committee concluding that to criticize the BBC's accounts 'by comparison with the detailed Estimates presented to Parliament for Government services would be to overlook the constitutional difference between the two cases'.[56] For Haley, who perceived the Select Committee's recommendations as the thin edge of the wedge leading to the future scrutiny of all the BBC's accounts, this raised 'the one main issue – that of the BBC's independence'.[57] The result was a settlement brokered by the Treasury whereby the government's Comptroller and Auditor General would 'inspect and vouch' a total figure rather than examine a detailed estimate.[58]

The Grant-in-Aid now tied the BBC to the machinery of government and the political and administrative currents that flowed through it. Meanwhile, back at Broadcasting House in the autumn of 1946 the Board of Governors congratulated Haley 'on the amount of independence he had managed to secure for the Corporation' on the question of funding.[59] This may seem at odds with the original aim of BBC management to cut the fiscal link with Whitehall, but it indicates both how far the ground had shifted since negotiations on the post-war shape and purpose of broadcasting began, and the limited extent to which the BBC was able to dictate the terms of the new constitutional settlement. It had to be increasingly careful and tactical about how and when it exercised its influence. An example of this was the secret agreement Haley negotiated with the Treasury that went beyond the terms of the financial provisions of the Charter. As he informed colleagues, he had extracted a

> written assurance from the Treasury that they would resist any encroachment on the BBC's independence in respect of its Home services as a result of the agreement to afford the Comptroller and Auditor-General access to the accounts of the Grant in Aid Services . . . [which] . . . could be produced in the future for the Treasury or Cabinet, but was not for publication in Parliament or elsewhere.[60]

The fact remained, however, that along with the assistance in funding, the government had acquired an unprecedented level of peace-time control over the BBC and with it greater influence over its activities.

Speaking in the July 1946 Parliamentary Charter Debate the Lord President, Herbert Morrison, who with the Postmaster-General had presented the White Paper on *Broadcasting Policy*, publicly laid out his understanding of the relationship between the government and the BBC:

> Clearly, it would be unthinkable for Broadcasting House to be broadcasting to Europe, at the taxpayer's expense, doctrines hopelessly at variance with the foreign policy of His Majesty's Government; but for reasons which I hope will commend themselves . . . it appeared to the Government to be equally undesirable that the Foreign Office should themselves become responsible for the foreign services. In the first place, the conduct of a broadcasting service requires a different sort

> of experience and imagination from the conduct of diplomacy. . . . Secondly, broadcasting is a fulltime job. Thirdly, and most important of all, we believe that the foreign services will better retain the respect of listeners abroad and of the public at home if, like the Home Services, they are removed as far as possible from the danger of being used to push the interests of political parties instead of the nation as a whole.[61]

Morrison then went on to explain how this balance between government control and editorial independence would be achieved,

> The Corporation will accept the guidance of the Foreign Office on the nature and scope of its foreign language services, and there will be a very close liaison between the two of them. . . . But once the general character and scope of a service has been laid down, the BBC will have complete discretion as to the content of the programmes themselves.[62]

Determining what was precisely meant by Morrison's term 'character and scope', echoing the phrase used by the Official Committee on GIS five months earlier, was a problem exercising minds at the BBC. Haley understood its meaning to relate to 'the time and money devoted to the different language transmissions' but was unsure whether 'it will extend to actual content of a service'. It was possible, he thought, that the 'Government might take a view it had a right to order what it was paying for' – the *quid pro quo* of funding.[63] That being said, there was at the same time in many parts of the government an understanding of, and genuine interest in, the value to be had from an avowedly independent BBC that could use its wartime reputation for credibility to represent British news, views and way of life to a world audience. To diminish this would be to erode the effectiveness of British overseas publicity policy.

The main conditions of the five-year Charter were clear. Overseas broadcasting would continue with a global remit and the External Services would accept guidance and funding from the government. Editorial independence of foreign broadcasting was affirmed, although due consideration would have to be given to the policies of His Majesty's Government. It gave the government the right to prescribe to whom, for how long and in what languages the External Services broadcast, which was an extension of its willingness to fund these activities. Yet, at the same time, the Charter was a document of intent and did not offer a detailed set of instructions for the management and conduct of the External Services. Key government and BBC figures would be just as important as the institutional and constitutional architecture surrounding them, if not sometimes more so, in determining the temperature and tone of day-to-day relations. Rather, it provided a space in which an evolving appreciation of the post-war requirements of overseas broadcasting could be allowed to develop. In this respect, the commission to broadcast in the 'national interest' represented a conceptual frame as much as a practical demand around which political, strategic and editorial interests could be aligned without being explicitly linked. The lack of a detailed prescription for overseas broadcasting and reliance on broad policy strokes helped construct a constitutional distance between the broadcaster and Whitehall. It was, nonetheless, a fiction of a distance which concealed an ongoing negotiation concerning the ever-present competition that existed between notions of editorial integrity and independence, on the one hand, and the desire to exert influence over programme-making to bring it in line with British geopolitical interests, on the other. As such, in respect of its overseas services, the new Charter was an act of pragmatic politics between the BBC and the government.

2

The Home Front

With the dissolution of the MOI at the end of March 1946, the government's new communications infrastructure set about defining 'the picture of Britain which it should be the aim to put over'.[1] The resulting paper by the Ministerial Committee on Overseas Information Services on the 'Projection of Britain Overseas'[2] identified publicity themes that were intended to guide the activities of overseas departments. It also offers a revealing snapshot of what might be considered, in modern terms, the public diplomacy agenda of the day. 'Britain as a Political and Social Democracy' emphasized freedoms of speech and political choice, a comprehensive system of social services and industrial welfare and the 'greatest experiment in a planned economy in a free society that the world has ever known'. 'Britain as a World Power' placed the country at the centre of a worldwide association of peoples through which British systems of social and political democracy should be spread abroad. 'Britain and World Trade' espoused the idea of expansionist and multilateral policy-making to develop the world's economic resources, because 'the rest of the world cannot be prosperous unless we are prosperous'. Lastly, the theme of 'British Commonwealth and Empire' advertised a non-exploitational vision of community as both liberal and dynamic.[3] It was on this last point that the Ministerial Committee brought about the end of Empire – in publicity terms, at least – well before the wind of change swept through Harold Macmillan's government over a decade later. The post-war momentum of independence movements, the pejorative connotations associated with empire-building and growing international criticism of unethical systems of governance, especially from Russia and America, made this a particularly sensitive issue for the British government, so recently the liberators of Europe. Accordingly, in May 1947, three months before the independence and partition of India, ministers agreed that the word 'Empire' should be dropped in favour of 'British Commonwealth'.[4]

Although tasked with constructing and co-ordinating the grand narratives of the government's overseas publicity, resulting in an inevitable turf war with the Foreign Office (FO), the Overseas Information Services committees, official and ministerial, were at arm's length from the day-to-day business of the BBC's External Services. Where the two did come together, as with the allocation of wavelengths and broadcast infrastructure, it was generally in terms of technical or logistical problems that required an interdepartmental perspective. Rather, it was with the overseas government departments and the FO in particular – those working at the coalface of foreign policy analysis and implementation – that the BBC necessarily established a pattern of close liaison. The move away from wartime practices and the construction of a constitutional divide between officials and broadcasters meant that as institutional practices changed during this period of transition, much depended on key individuals to negotiate and interpret the road ahead. Leading the way in this respect and fundamental to establishing the early post-war tone of relations were Ian Jacob and Ivone Kirkpatrick. This duo not only patrolled the boundary between the two institutions in this formative phase, but effectively defined where that boundary lay and in doing so, left a deep imprint on how the relationship was to be negotiated in coming years.

Figure 2 Ian Jacob, Controller, BBC European Services, July 1946

Military Assistant Secretary to the War Cabinet 1939–45, Jacob was appointed Controller European Services in 1946. Promoted the following year to take charge of all overseas broadcasting, he briefly returned to government service in 1952, at the request of Churchill, as Chief Staff Officer at the Ministry of Defence and deputy military secretary to the Cabinet, before returning to the BBC as its Director-General, 1952–60.

On 21 March 1946, the BBC's Board of Governors authorized the Director-General to secure the services of Major-General Edward Ian Jacob as Controller of the European Services; his appointment was confirmed two weeks later.[5] In doing so, the Board assigned one of the most diplomatically sensitive jobs in the BBC to a man who, during the war, had played a vital role right at the centre of government. Since 1939 he had been Military Assistant Secretary to the War Cabinet and in this capacity had been at the very nexus of international policy development and the prosecution of the war. He had a close working relationship with Churchill, accompanying the Prime Minister to Allied summits and getting to know, at close quarters, American and Russian representatives, including Presidents Roosevelt, Truman and Marshal Stalin.[6] According to Churchill's wartime Private Secretary, John Colville, Jacob was a 'man of tireless industry . . . far above the average in both intelligence and commonsense'.[7] He also had an up-to-date appreciation of Britain's post-war European interests, not least from his position on the Labour government's ministerial European Control Committee from July 1945, which was tasked with handling 'the day-to-day problems arising in connection with the control or administration of ex-enemy territories in Europe'.[8] In addition to being specifically assigned the duty of keeping Clement Attlee informed of the Committee's work, he was also appointed Secretary to the Defence Committee.[9] Moreover, in the period between accepting the job at the BBC and leaving government service, Jacob was the military representative of the unsuccessful mission led by Lord Stansgate to negotiate a new treaty with the Egyptian Government.[10] He, therefore, had a breadth of experience and field of knowledge well suited to his job as Controller of European programmes and then as Director of all overseas services. He was in the inner circle of the military, diplomatic, political and intelligence spheres of British government by the end of the war and these were associations and links that were to provide him with a subtle appreciation of international developments and governmental attitudes.

Kirkpatrick, on the other hand, was a government official and diplomat who moved to the BBC before returning to the FO. With a keen interest in the uses of propaganda, from his service in the First World War, he became Foreign Adviser to the BBC in February 1941 under the auspices of the MOI. After the creation of the PWE in October, he took on the role of Controller of European Services (as the PWE manager in the BBC) with a seat on the BBC's Control Board.[11] The dual nature of his role – as the senior link with the government's machinery of propaganda and as the executive overseeing broadcasts to the continent – was at first both confusing and controversial. It nevertheless reflected the operational and strategic importance of the European Services during the war and as the initial inconsistencies were worked out and the arrangement became accepted, there was an increasing appreciation of the additional benefits that this new Controller's links with Whitehall could effect. As Briggs has pointed out, 'With Kirkpatrick in Bush House, the BBC was sure of something more than mere protection.'[12] Kirkpatrick understood the importance of broadcasting overseas and its value and potential as an aid to government objectives. This philosophy and the means by which the European Services and the government produced and directed broadcast output worked well at a time when everything was directed to the war effort and there was a synergy of aims. Yet, as has been shown, after the war and as a member of the GIS Committee, Kirkpatrick was clear in his mind that in peacetime 'the Government would be fully entitled to bring pressure to bear on the BBC in order that the [overseas] service should accord with the aims of Government policy'.[13]

In March 1944, Kirkpatrick returned to the PWE as Deputy Director-General (Political)[14] and then, six months later, to the FO, working on the Allied Control Commission for Germany. After a period as British political adviser to General Eisenhower, he was subsequently appointed Assistant Under-Secretary responsible for organizing the FO's information work, and superintending its Information Departments, which included responsibility for liaising with the BBC.[15] It was Kirkpatrick who put Jacob's name forward for the job of Controller of European Services: handing on the baton, as it were.[16] Today, the appointment of a military administrator with no experience of broadcasting to take charge of the BBC's output to the continent and then all overseas services might appear highly suspect, if not incredible. However, by the particular circumstances of the day it was less controversial than at first might appear. The precedent set by Kirkpatrick and followed by Jacob reflected the strategic significance of European transmissions, and overseas broadcasting more generally, as well as the dual responsibilities of a national broadcaster during war and in its immediate aftermath. The 'chains of iron' which bound broadcasting to government had yet to be formally severed by the time Jacob joined the Corporation. It also reflects a recurrent theme as the amphibian nature of post-war public service saw a number of senior government officials join the upper echelons of the BBC in the ensuing years.

Jacob was regarded by Haley as 'the ideal man' to manage overseas broadcasting.[17] He understood the development of policy and the practices of government while his appreciation of international developments was a great advantage to Haley whose main preoccupation was domestic broadcasting. He was plugged-in on both sides of the institutional divide, but this being the case where did he draw the line between the two? At the beginning of his tenure at Bush House, Sir Ian Jacob established rules governing his staff's relationship with the government's overseas departments.[18] While Service Directors should project British 'activities and the British way of life', they should not be swayed by 'day to day fluctuations in political policy'.[19] Neither should they bend to pressure not to broadcast material uncomfortable for the government. For Jacob there were three reasons to 'cause the rejection of a news item': if it jeopardized military security; if serious damage to British foreign policy would result (and any such rejection should be made on his authority); if the report was 'both mischievous and unsubstantiated'.[20] The first and last of these appear relatively clear-cut but the second exception, the most opaque but also the most important, is open to a far greater degree of interpretation and questioned assumptions about what it meant to broadcast in the 'national interest'. Philosophically, Jacob saw the Corporation as representative of the society it served:

> One often hears the phrase: "The BBC says . . ." But the BBC has no entity in the sense of having views and opinions of its own. It seeks to hold a mirror to British opinion, and to reflect what the ordinary man and woman in Britain feels. British public opinion finds its expression in the Press, in speeches and writings, in books and periodicals. By quoting this material, and by bringing a great variety of people to the microphone, the BBC tries to show to its listeners the different currents of thought, the full and democratic flow of ideas, and the diverse opinions, that go to make up the voice of the British people.[21]

In this analysis, the BBC was a morally neutral organization that performed the function of a national weathervane, signalling the prevailing trends of culture and thought in society along with the dissemination of impartial news – a zeitgeist broadcaster transmitting messages of British identity around the world. But how did Jacob determine the principles he thought should be used to govern the editorial policy and output of the European, and then External, Services?

Ideally, the 'spread of truth and the full ventilation of facts are highly desirable in themselves', Jacob announced in his July 1946 directive for the European Services.[22] However, the continued turbulence experienced in post-war Europe, amplified by the worsening relations between the Soviet Union and her wartime allies, forged a belief that Britain must nevertheless continue 'to struggle against calumny and insidious propaganda of a different way of thinking. Our part in counteracting this is not by refuting it, but by seizing and retaining the initiative.'[23] Passive objectivity alone would not be enough and the BBC would once again have to take on a proactive role in confronting those forces which threatened the stability of Europe and beyond. Jacob was clear that this did not mean the BBC conducting a campaign of political warfare, but his sense of purpose must be put in the context of having just lived and worked through the Second World War and it is perhaps not surprising that 'alignment' with the government's foreign policy was, for him, a necessary element of the 'national interest':

> When, as now, the British people are engaged in a struggle to maintain their existence and way of life in the face of a campaign of propaganda and subversive activity, openly designed to overthrow them, we must not in any way shrink from giving full expression to the British view, and to assist by all means in our power the national effort. Only in this way shall we be framing our programmes in the national interest.[24]

It was in the actual making and content of the programmes that government involvement was to be avoided and where the editorial independence of the BBC had to be maintained.

Jacob and Kirkpatrick were instrumental characters that mobilized considerable authority within the BBC and FO, but institutional liaison required more than just leadership. Orchestrating effective and efficient linkages in this period of overseas broadcasting repatriation was both an organic process, inheriting wartime customs, and one designed to eliminate undue external influence. William Haley emphasized this asymmetry as a virtue when he noted in his paper on the 'Principles and Purpose of the BBC's External Services' that the 'methods of liaison to reach the understanding adumbrated by the Lord President vary from service to service. It is – to my mind rightly – not formalised throughout the Corporation.'[25] By the time of the new Charter, the result was a conglomerate of interactions that collectively formed the relationship between the External Services and government.

On issues of outstanding importance, the Director-General would be consulted; otherwise matters of policy would be handled between Kirkpatrick and the two overseas Controllers, Jacob and John Beresford Clark (who was in charge of all broadcasting outside of Europe until Jacob was made Director of Overseas Services, supervising both divisions). Meanwhile, regionally grouped language services maintained their own channels of communication. The Latin-American Services were in touch with the Head of the Latin-American Department in the FO and took it upon themselves to be proactive in consulting the Board of Trade, the Ministry of Civil Aviation and the Admiralty on related matters of guidance.[26] The Director of Eastern Services (DES) attended weekly meetings at the Eastern (Political) Department of the Foreign Office in addition to going to monthly meetings of the Middle East Information Department (MEID) in the same Ministry.[27] By March 1947, the Far Eastern Services had likewise arranged to attend the FO's Far Eastern Information Department Weekly Directive Meeting along with the British Council.[28] There were also regular meetings with the Colonial Office about Palestine and telephone contact with the Foreign Office over Persia and Egypt.[29]

Supplementing guidance by phone on day-to-day questions, the Board of Trade established regular conferences at its Overseas Information Division, where between 12 and 14 BBC representatives would mix with Information Officers of the Foreign Office and representatives of the COI to discuss economic and industrial subjects.[30] In a similar, but reversed, manner, the India Office briefed the DES as a channel to all BBC departments, while in the European Services there were 'individual contacts between the various service directors and their regional opposite numbers in the Foreign Office'.[31] It was within this network of institutional and personal interfaces that the material nature of the relationship was revealed and the line between government influence and the Corporation's independence drawn in detail.

Managing the change from wartime to peacetime relations did not, however, always run smoothly. As Haley acknowledged in the autumn of 1946, there 'have been occasions when it has been necessary for the BBC to take a firm line to distinguish "information" or "guidance" from "directives"'.[32] Neither did the emerging machinery of liaison always engender better relations. Commenting on the MEID, the BBC's DES, Donald Stephenson, described its staff as 'an uninspiring collection of dug-outs and second grade women', while he thought the Chairman of the Middle East Publicity Committee 'not only knows nothing about publicity but knows still less about the Middle East'.[33] What particularly concerned Stephenson, however, was the 'failure on the part of the FO to distinguish between control of Foreign Office publicity (i.e., absorption of the old MOI) and control of external publicity media – the BBC, the Press etc.' He felt there was a deliberate willingness to exploit what he called 'extra-constitutional practices', 'if ever weakness on the part of the BBC or of a newspaper provides opportunity'.[34] Haley agreed, noting that 'We must take a firm line against any nonsense' and that 'the position must remain that we are not prepared to accept their directives or to operate outside the terms of the White Paper.'[35]

Nevertheless, it would seem that some parts of Whitehall were slower at adapting to these post-war working conditions than the BBC would have liked. In his own region, Stephenson was concerned that the continuing wartime impulse to interfere in the BBC's output was 'harmful to the more lasting interests of this country, since much of the energy which we might devote to constructive broadcast planning is dissipated in countering ill-conceived and positively dangerous representation from the FO'.[36] An example of this was the problem of 'inspired' news items originating from the FO. In the spring of 1947, a bulletin on the BBC's Arabic Service had reported the content of a letter to the *Egyptian Gazette* from 'An English Friend of Egypt' – a typical 'anonymous harangue' as Stephenson characterized it. The Near East News Editor, Mackenzie, was concerned that there was no definite policy to deal with such items and set about trying to define one based 'on a proper understanding . . . of the relations between the Foreign Office and the BBC'.[37]

Mackenzie believed that 'the duty of the BBC is to follow in its broadcasts the general policy of HMG, but it is allowed the widest freedom in the selection, editing and presentation of day-to-day broadcast material'.[38] Stephenson concurred, adding that on issues where 'the Foreign Office want us to implement or support some point of policy, either by our own origination of broadcast material or by carrying the material originated at other sources, this must always be a matter of mutual agreement'. However in order to maintain 'a proper atmosphere of cooperation and assistance', Stephenson continued,

> where the FO particularly press us, in circumstances of urgency, to carry an item of the kind on which your memo is based; and when we are satisfied that the item is at least quite harmless, however, ineffective we may consider it to be; then in such cases I think we are usually well advised to accede to such a request.[39]

This, he argued, would then 'strengthen our arm in those other and more frequent cases where we feel that a request item is so inept or indeed harmful that we rightly refuse to have anything to do with it'.[40] Three months after the new Charter came into effect, this example from the Eastern Services points towards a heavily qualified concept of independence that relied on a system of trades between broadcasters and their counterparts in Whitehall to establish an editorial line that could, if required, be defended. It also reflected a lack of clarity about how relations on the broadcast Home Front should be conducted now that the emergency of war was over.

The new Charter and the debates leading up to it had mapped out a static set of intentions within which the purpose of broadcasting overseas had been declared. It also laid out the duties levied on the Corporation as the price paid for its independence from direct government control, albeit under Grant-in-Aid funding. These were, however, constitutional arrangements that required practical interpretation. The relationship between the government's overseas departments, in particular the Foreign Office, and the Corporation's External Services was fundamental to this as was their experience of each other under war conditions. Key personnel interpreted the relationship in the light of their own understanding of the aims and objectives of overseas broadcasting, which set the tone for the departments under their control. The architecture of liaison, asymmetric, permissive and often ad hoc, likewise reflected the sense of uncertainty and change experienced by the External Services as they made the transition from war to peacetime activities. This was as much a psychological shift, especially in the case of broadcasts to Europe, as it was a constitutional one for both the BBC and Whitehall. And it was not yet complete when the British government and the BBC were faced with a new strategic challenge which would define, perhaps more than the Charter ever could, the practical relationship between the two and what it meant to broadcast in the 'national interest' in the decades to come.

3

The Cold War Challenge

The introduction of a new Royal Charter at the beginning of 1947 signalled the end of wartime controls and explicitly confirmed the Corporation's constitutional authority and responsibility for all its overseas broadcasts. Yet, while the BBC was re-engineered for a world at peace, the British government was simultaneously coming to terms with the growing threat perceived to be posed by the Soviet Union. A year earlier, the Foreign Secretary had suggested that in the case of Poland and Czechoslovakia 'the provision of information about British life and culture', an essential element of the BBC's broadcast remit, 'is probably our most effective single means of preventing them from being absorbed into a closed and exclusive Soviet sphere of influence and of keeping open the doors between Eastern and Western Europe'.[1] However, the failure to arrest further Soviet consolidation by the end of 1947 led Bevin to confront his Cabinet colleagues with the problem of Eastern Europe, where 'Totalitarian régimes now rule':

> In Yugoslavia, we have a pure and fully-fledged Communist régime on the Soviet model. . . . In Roumania, all legal opposition has now been eliminated, the Government has recently been purged of all but Communists. . . . In Bulgaria the only legal Opposition party and the Opposition press have now been suppressed. . . . In Hungary matters have not got so far, but the Communists, by their control of the Ministry of the Interior and its machinery and police, can terrorise all important opponents into submission, or flight.[2]

The 'rapid extinction of human rights and the fundamental freedoms' he outlined recalled an assessment made by the Corporation's Overseas Intelligence Department in July 1940, after the Wehrmacht had chased the British Expeditionary Force from Dunkirk.[3] 'Broadcasting', they said, 'is now our only means of addressing a great part of Europe'.[4] Less than a decade later, this was again true. Confirmation of this came in February 1948 when communist forces in Czechoslovakia, concerned about their possible failure at elections due in May, took advantage of a disagreement over communists in the police force to repudiate their commitment to the Coalition government, of which they were a part, and the notion of power-sharing. With Soviet backing, they took control of the country and ushered in a new and particularly belligerent phase in the developing Cold War.[5]

Before the coup, it was estimated by the Czechoslovak Ministry of Information that one in five people listened to the BBC. After the overthrow of Dr Edouard Benes' government, the United States Social Services Research Council calculated that one out of every two owners of radios listened to the BBC, a number that increased to three out of every four when the highly popular Sir Robert Bruce Lockhart was broadcasting.[6] Indeed, the BBC's audience in Czechoslovakia was considered to be 'far greater than that of the Czechoslovakian Broadcasting System'.[7] During the coup, listeners were able to receive gripping first-hand accounts of the communist takeover from the BBC's recently appointed Prague correspondent, Patrick Smith, as well as international reaction and western condemnation.[8] As the *BBC Yearbook* noted, 'it is no exaggeration to say that in Czechoslovakia in February and March almost every set capable of receiving London was doing so day by day'.[9] The Czechoslovak coup and the subsequent dramatic events of 1948, particularly the Soviet blockade of the western zones of Berlin in June, provided a practical example of how broadcasting overseas, though not capable of effecting dramatic or immediate change, was an essential and sometimes the only means of maintaining a tangible link with countries and their people behind the descending Iron Curtain or in particularly sensitive parts of the world such as Iran, the greater Middle East and South East Asia, where the strategic battle of the early Cold War was being played out.

1948 would prove to be a pivotal year in the Cold War and, by extension, for the BBC, which reported its emerging realities and implications. How it did so was as much conditioned by events overseas as it was by deliberations at home, both of which had been evolving for some time. In the Spring of 1946, the Joint Intelligence Committee (JIC), the co-ordinating and analytical nexus of British intelligence, attempted to assess 'Russia's Strategic Interests and Intentions', which in turn revealed the early development of a core British planning assumption. Reporting to the British Chiefs of Staff, it reasoned:

> The long-term aim of the Russian leaders is to build up the Soviet Union into a position of strength and greatness fully commensurate with her vast size and resources. They are convinced of the greatness of Russia's future under the Soviet system. We believe it to be their firm conviction that, within the next fifty years

> or perhaps a hundred years (unlike Hitler, they are not pressed for time), the Soviet Union will inevitably become the most powerful, the richest and the best ordered country in the world.[10]

Part of the Soviet Union's strategy, the JIC argued, would be to use 'all weapons, short of major war . . . to weaken foreign countries', key among which was the 'full use of propaganda', including radio broadcasts.[11] As frictions between the USSR and her wartime allies worsened, the value of overseas broadcasting by the BBC consequently increased as a means of projecting the British counterpoint.

It was frustration at just such a tide of Soviet propaganda targeted at Britain and the West that prompted the Permanent Secretary at the Foreign Office (FO), Sir Orme Sargent, to request in March 1946 a paper on how to counter these attacks. Written by Christopher Warner, Under Secretary responsible for Soviet affairs, it was one of the first papers considered by the FO's newly established Committee on Russian Policy (Russia Committee), set up to 'study Soviet activities and co-ordinate counter-action'.[12] The paper, 'The Soviet campaign against this country and our response to it', argued in favour of publicity denouncing communism as a form of totalitarianism although not directly attacking the Soviet Union.[13] The subsequent plan for a long-term propaganda campaign against communism, devised by a working party led by Ivone Kirkpatrick, envisaged a collective effort involving British Missions overseas, the COI and the BBC as part of the government's information services machinery.[14] Initially approved by Prime Minister Clement Attlee, the Foreign Secretary considered the plan too negative and while still pursuing a settlement with the Soviet Union was unwilling to see it implemented. Therefore, when it came before the Russia Committee it was decided that nothing should be done before the next meeting of the Council of Foreign Ministers.[15]

The failure of this attempt at a co-ordinated response to Soviet propaganda was nonetheless important for bringing together key officials at the FO in agreement on the principles of how a counteroffensive should be conducted and in offering an institutional forum within which these ideas could be maintained and fostered: the new and increasingly significant Russia Committee which effectively set the background tone of the government's policy towards the Soviet Union. The significance of this would be fully realized over a year later when the issue was once again on the government's mind. The Soviet withdrawal from Marshall Aid talks in July 1947, the creation at the end of September of the Communist Information Bureau (Cominform) to co-ordinate the actions of Communist parties in Europe, and the failure of the Council of Foreign Ministers in December to resolve treaty negotiations on Germany and Austria all sounded the end for hopes of a constructive settlement.[16] Bevin reported to his Cabinet colleagues,

> It must be recognised that the Soviet Government has formed a solid political and economic block behind a line running from the Baltic along the Oder, through Trieste to the Black Sea. There is no prospect in the immediate future that we shall be able to re-establish normal relations with European countries behind that line.[17]

Up to this point, he explained, overseas publicity had been 'confined to supporting and explaining the current policy of His Majesty's Government in foreign affairs and at home, to advocating our way of life, and publicising our social-democratic programme and achievements'. Where the Soviet Union and communism were concerned, British information services had been 'non-provocative, and we have not attempted systematically to expose the myths of the Soviet paradise'.[18] Now, different tactics were needed and in anticipation of the final diplomatic failure, on 23 October 1947 Bevin requested that plans be drawn up for a new and more aggressive propaganda offensive.[19]

Christopher Mayhew, Parliamentary Under-Secretary of State for Foreign Affairs and Chair of the Official Committee on Overseas Information Services, had likewise been frustrated by the West's disinclination to respond to Russia's 'worldwide campaign of subversion and propaganda'[20] and had written to Bevin arguing that 'if the Council of Foreign Ministers failed, we should launch a sustained worldwide anti-communist propaganda offensive'.[21] At the behest of Bevin, Mayhew was instructed to consult with senior officials and after a meeting with the architects of the earlier proposal, presented to the Foreign Secretary a paper on 'Third Force Propaganda'.[22] A subsequent meeting with the Prime Minister at Chequers on 27 December 1947 resulted in the drafting[23] of a Cabinet paper with the help of Warner, who in April 1948 took over responsibility for the FO's IPD and the six regional Information Departments from Kirkpatrick.[24]

Matters were brought to a head on 8 January 1948 at a crucial discussion by the Cabinet on 'Foreign Policy in Europe', which co-ordinated several key policy strands. Ministers were presented with four memoranda that reviewed Soviet policy, evaluated recent events in Eastern Europe, advanced the idea of a union of Western European countries and laid out plans for overseas communication strategies.[25] The last of these, entitled 'Future Foreign Publicity Policy', explained that 'we must be prepared to pass over to the offensive and not leave the initiative to the enemy, but make them defend themselves'. In order to do this, 'We should adopt a new line in our foreign publicity designed to oppose the inroads of Communism, by taking the offensive against it.'[26] Ministers expressed concern that 'too much emphasis' was being laid on the 'anti-Soviet aspect' and that this would 'fail to rally the Socialist forces in Western Europe and would make it more difficult to foster cultural relations with Eastern European countries'.[27] Nevertheless, the Cabinet endorsed the Foreign Secretary's recommendations for the future direction of Britain's overseas publicity which, in effect, gave executive authority to embark on a non-shooting war against the Soviet Union and communist forces throughout the world in a 'vigorous systematic attack' as Sir Ian Jacob, now Director of BBC External Services, later described it.[28]

Figure 3 Ralph Murray, BBC Governor, July 1968

Murray joined BBC News in 1934 before becoming the BBC's foreign correspondent at the League of Nations from 1936. During the war he worked in covert propaganda operations before relocating to Bush House in 1942 as Regional Director (Balkans) for the Political Warfare Executive. After the war he was appointed the first Head of the Information Research Department. After retiring as Ambassador to Greece in 1967 he joined the BBC Board of Governors, 1967–73.

In Cabinet, Ernest Bevin argued the 'most effective method of countering Soviet propaganda was to provide specific information refuting the misrepresentation made by the Soviet Government'.[29] Answering back in this way would, however, require some adjustments to the machinery of government, necessitating the creation of 'a small Section in the Foreign Office to collect information concerning Communist policy, tactics and propaganda and to provide material for our anti-Communist publicity through our Missions and Information Services abroad'.[30]

This resulted in the Information Research Department (IRD) with Ralph Murray, a former PWE Regional Director for the Balkans at Bush House and future BBC Governor, as its first head. During January and February 1948, Kirkpatrick and others set about its rapid establishment with particular emphasis laid on the recruitment of journalists and writers from Iron Curtain countries and by 25 February Sir Orme Sargent was able to inform departments at home and missions overseas in Circular No.21 of the operational status and purpose of IRD.[31] Funded initially by a budget of £150,000, and supplemented by an additional £100,000 from the Secret Vote, care was taken not to advertise the arrival of IRD.[32] While the existence of the department was not concealed, it was felt that 'to avoid creating embarrassment for the Foreign Secretary in his dealings with foreign Governments through diplomatic channels', its output should be non-attributable and its specific anti-communist function should be kept a secret.[33]

The re-conceptualization of Britain's overseas information policy and the institutional adjustments that followed in its wake had inevitable and deep implications for the BBC, as will be seen. On this point, the Cabinet paper had been observant of the constitutional niceties between the government and the Corporation when it stated that the 'fullest co-operation of the BBC Overseas Services would be desirable'.[34] In fact, Bush House had been keeping a keen eye on the development of these proposals for some time, but from a rather unusual perspective. In the late summer of 1946, as Ivone Kirkpatrick was preparing his proposals on anti-communist propaganda, Ian Jacob was engaged in discussing with the FO the nature of the BBC's new Russian language service and advocating the use of anti-communist material, and calling for more ministerial speeches critical of communism that could be reported across the world by BBC.[35] By October, Jacob had been invited to join the Foreign Office's Russia Committee and as such, with Sargent, Warner, Kirkpatrick and Mayhew, was intimately involved in the very creation of the new publicity policy and Whitehall's plans for a propaganda campaign. Indeed, it was the Russia Committee that was given initial responsibility for instructing the activities of IRD and to whom the department reported. It seems Jacob considered the best place to maintain the delicate balance between the two institutions was, at times, inside both of them. It remained to be seen whether under these new conditions the ties that bound the External Services of the BBC to Whitehall would turn out to be silken cords or chains of iron.

The Soviet Union's tightening grip over vast areas of Europe from 1945 and its ideological and military dominance over territories so recently liberated from war made it clear to both the British government and the BBC that broadcasts to these countries would have a special role to play in 'letting in daylight from the whole of the outside world' and the beaming-in of the Western, and particularly British, world view.[36] As Ann Applebaum notes, the notion of an Iron Curtain appeared far more tangible in these early transformative years of the Cold War where it really 'did seem as if the USSR would succeed in turning the widely varying nations of Eastern Europe into an ideologically and politically homogeneous region'.[37] Once again, a 'dark silence' had descended on the eastern half of the continent and the BBC began receiving reports of people tuning to its broadcasts 'in the same spirit as they were listened to by inhabitants of occupied Europe during the war'.[38] Following the Cabinet's decision on foreign publicity, Bevin requested from Jacob information on whether the BBC was 'reflecting in their overseas broadcasts the changed international situation resulting from recent events on both sides of the Iron Curtain'.[39] Jacob considered that this was indeed what the BBC was doing as 'listeners to the European Services are now hearing from Britain first a great and encouraging story of Western resurgence, and secondly an ever sharper criticism of Communist actions and Russian policy'.[40] The view at the FO was rather different. It had detected from the results of a review of BBC services to Central and Eastern Europe what it considered to be 'an over-developed sense of objectivity' that resulted 'not so much in a reputation for fairness . . . but in pulled punches & obscured viewpoints'.[41] What was needed, argued officials, was for the BBC 'to adopt a more aggressive attitude'.[42]

The pattern of broadcasting overseas was one of concentrated short bursts made up of news, associated comment and the projection of British political, cultural, scientific, economic and industrial life.[43] In Europe, and more particularly its eastern half, this was typically done in either 15- or 30-minute broadcasts. For example, the daily programmes to Hungary, Czechoslovakia, Rumania, Bulgaria and in Serbo-Croat at the beginning of 1948 consisted of two 15-minute transmissions of news and press review and a half-hour programme of news followed by comment, features and talks produced either centrally by the European Talks and Productions Departments or generated within each service depending on its resources. Broadcasts to Albania (where US and UK intelligence services were at the time engaging in covert operations to detach the regime from the Soviet sphere)[44] and in Slovene had even fewer programme options available to them, having a transmission time of just 15 minutes a day while Poland had an extra 30 minutes over the average and broadcasts in English to Europe covered nine transmissions totalling two and three-quarter hours a day.[45]

The government review commissioned in November 1947 asked His Majesty Representatives to comment on what they thought the BBC should broadcast to the countries to which they were accredited and within Bush House there was 'general agreement' among the relevant Programme Organizers (heads of the language services) with the comments made by the British Missions concerning objectivity and passivity.[46] Nevertheless, Jacob claimed that since the review, European Services output was indeed now being 'planned in line with the Government's publicity policy' as the Foreign Secretary informed ministerial colleagues at the end of April 1948.[47] This assertion was immediately put to the test with a second review, commissioned on 17 April, in which Missions were asked whether 'the new publicity policy . . . and change in public opinion here regarding [the] Communist threat are now automatically reflected in their output to Eastern Europe'.[48] This generated four further areas of criticisms and gave the FO an agenda for change in the BBC's broadcasts to the Soviet satellite states.

As before, the first two themes dealt with what was perceived to be the 'false objectivity' of transmissions.[49] When reporting on life in Britain, the European Services adhered to the principle of representing a range of domestic views on the issues of the day, mainly from newspaper reports that covered the political spectrum. However, it was felt that this genuine attempt at an unbiased projection of Britain gave listeners without an inner knowledge of British society and its psyche an impression 'of complete bewilderment at the apparent conflict of opinion which conveys an atmosphere of indecision and confusion'.[50] By contrast, news of events behind the Iron Curtain (which were to an increasing extent unverifiable) and on international developments from Soviet sources were considered to be presented in too straight a way and consequently bore the imprint of Soviet propaganda without corrective comment. In the eyes of the FO, the 'Soviet point of view is presented in clear-cut positive form, whereas the British view emerges as muddled and indecisive'.[51] The third theme suggested that more time in these short broadcasts should be devoted to politically oriented material while the fourth consistent theme suggested 'more attention should be paid in the selection of news items to the particular interests of listeners' and that content as a whole should be tailored more towards local tastes in order to attract and keep the audience.[52] With recommendations in hand, the key question for the FO was how it would approach the BBC to effect the change it wanted.

Jacob's successor as Controller of European Services, Tangye Lean, brother of the film director David Lean, felt the criticisms were strikingly unreasonable 'to anyone actually engaged in the broadcasts' and he was 'satisfied that a very high proportion of it is unfair and that the impression of an overwhelming indictment which steadily builds up is grossly misleading'.[53] Nevertheless, he did consider that there 'are various points . . . which we find helpful' such as the need for 'more news items concerning the particular audience addressed', more 're-writing of news items . . . which are misleading or even incomprehensible unless put into the appropriate perspective' and the need for 'consideration of the special regional attitude of mind in comment and programme material in general'.[54] Likewise, in the FO there was a sense that 'the chief defects of the services concerned could probably be remedied without any radical alteration of existing practice'.[55]

Christopher Warner, now in charge of the IPD, invested a great deal of energy in cementing a relationship of mutual trust between himself and Jacob. As noted, the two knew each other from their attendance of the Russia Committee as well as the Committee on Colonial Information Policy, a suitably anodyne and opaque title for a group that was highly influential in developing and co-ordinating the government's Cold War propaganda themes.[56] Jacob likewise valued a shared appreciation of the challenges facing the External Services and in April 1948 renewed his suggestion that Lean be put in touch with the head of the IRD, Ralph Murray, so that 'projects could be talked over and . . . suggestions could be made by us'.[57] This initiative resulted in their meeting for the first of many times along with the Controller of Overseas Services, Robert McCall, for lunch on Wednesday, 9 June at the Café Royal, Piccadilly. However, it was the IPD and not the infamous IRD that was to have a more influential and important role at this formative stage in reorienting the BBC's overseas services and in continuing to advise the Corporation of Foreign Office and government opinion. IRD, by contrast, was at this point a generator of material to be used under the rubric of anti-communist publicity rather than the architect of that policy.

Having prepared much of the ground over the preceding months, by the beginning of September 1948 Warner at last felt in a position to discuss with Jacob 'the views that we have formed as a result of the reports received from our overseas posts'.[58] At a meeting between Mayhew and Warner, Jacob and Lean, it was hoped to extract from the BBC executives a commitment to harden the Corporation's broadcasts to those countries under the shadow of communism through a sharper critique of communist doctrine and practice and a more unequivocal representation of the British case and attitude towards international developments. Afterwards, Missions in Central and Eastern Europe were informed that Jacob had accepted that at times 'the BBC broadcasts suffer from what has been called "false objectivity"' and that a contextual balance needed to be found 'to avoid giving too much weight to minority views as regards the Soviet orbit and Communism'.[59] There was, however, a reticence to embark on a full-scale programme of refuting Soviet misrepresentations not least, as Jacob argued, because the Corporation's emphasis on the truth already did 'broadly counter misrepresentations' and occasionally steps were taken to refute specific Soviet 'lies'.[60] He also felt, and for this there was some measure of sympathy in the FO, that a policy of answering back would hand the initiative to the Soviet propagandists – a position that had been assiduously avoided when dealing with Goebbels' political warfare machine during the Second World War.

The other major issue on which the FO wished to see change (and for which there was already a constituency of support within the European Services) was the selection of broadcast items relevant to particular audiences. This had constitutional as well as practical implications for the BBC when it came to the central component of its overseas broadcasts – news. The government's July 1946 White Paper on *Broadcasting Policy* had stated that the 'treatment of an item in an Overseas news bulletin must not differ in any material respect from its treatment in a current news bulletin for domestic listeners'.[61] This central tenet had subsequently come under reconsideration when His Majesty Representatives were asked 'whether you consider these regulations should be varied'.[62] The response was mixed, but in general it was concluded that while there was no need for a specific change, 'more attention should be paid in the *selection* of news items to the particular interests of listeners'.[63] Back at the BBC, this particular suggestion sparked a major row between Jacob and the Director of the Spoken Word George Barnes, who was responsible to the Board of Management for the Corporation's News Division. Barnes thought it axiomatic that there was at least 'one service which is unaffected by considerations of home or overseas policy'.[64] News, he argued, should be 'determined by what happens and not by what anyone wants to happen or the effect anyone wishes to make'.[65] For Jacob, the Cold War had made this approach, even from a broadcasting point of view, anachronistic: 'The truth of the matter seems to me to be that broadcasting to one's own people is quite a different professional job from broadcasting to foreign countries, and efforts to try and escape from this difference are efforts to put one's head in the sand.'[66]

Adjudicating in the dispute, the BBC's Director-General, William Haley, also appreciated the need for news bulletins to have relevance for audiences, but was deeply conscious of finding the right balance between editorial flexibility and the BBC's historic and constitutional duty.[67] While observing the overriding principle that the treatment of overseas news would not differ from that of domestic news, he nonetheless acknowledged that 'treatment' was not synonymous with 'selection' and saw no 'objections to providing, within the framework of its requirements, regional news bulletins assessed with an eye to the audiences' particular interests'.[68] The quality and integrity of the news would continue to be judged by the same professional standards across the Corporation, but its balance and selection would be devolved. Although nuanced, the extra degree of latitude this afforded the External Services altered the established editorial calculus within the BBC, resulting in the beginning of a divergence in news production outlook between the domestic and overseas services. Unlocking this sensitive issue, alongside the BBC's discussions with Whitehall, was the precursor to the internal publication of a very important paper by Jacob in October 1948 that marks a fundamental stage in the post-war development of the External Services. As he informed senior staff, the role of the BBC 'has been defined very broadly by Parliament in a White Paper on broadcasting, and again in the Charter and Licence'.[69] In the light of the significant changes in internal reorganization and external contexts, both national and international, it was necessary to issue 'further interpretation . . . for the guidance of those concerned in our output' and 'to establish basic principles and methods' that could be employed in order to meet an up-to-date understanding of what it meant for the External Services to 'frame their programmes in the national interest'.[70] Entitled 'The Task of the Overseas Services of the BBC', it might be considered the first Cold War directive issued by the BBC for broadcasts abroad.

Months of research, analysis and discussion within and between the BBC and Whitehall had led to this revised statement of editorial principles for overseas broadcasting. The triumvirate of broadcasting aims remained: presentation of objective news, reflection of British views on current affairs and the projection of British life. But while the object continued to be the presentation of a world picture, 'each bulletin should be built specifically for the audience to be addressed. The bulletin when heard by that audience must not only sound objective, but must be highly relevant and of close interest.' It was also necessary to impart a contextualized appreciation where 'statements, speeches, etc. . ., which we quote and which may contain inaccuracies, or which are misleading, should be placed in their true setting by reminding the listener of the facts'. Accordingly, although the 'BBC has no view of its own', in 'matters of international controversy a fair statement of the issues involved must always be given, though the audience must be left in no doubt what the British view is'. But where the FO had argued that clarity demanded the elimination of confusion among the competing voices of Britain, Jacob was adamant that 'conflicting opinions which have serious backing in this country should be allowed expression in proportion to the weight of this backing. Apparent contradictions that may arise from presenting these views helps to demonstrate the tolerance which is a cardinal feature of British democracy.'[71] It was the application of this principle concerning balance that would ultimately send the relationship with government fissile in 1956.

Weighing these ingredients was a major preoccupation for the BBC. The defining criterion was relevance: 'first to the general world situation, and secondly and more particularly to the situation in which our listeners find themselves'. This was fundamental and anchored the output of the External Services to its geopolitical context while at the same time bringing the audience's needs into the editorial process in a way that had not been explicitly prescribed like this before. The particular demands of broadcasting to Central and Eastern Europe meant that 'nothing should figure in our output which is not consciously planned as being there for an object'. As a consequence, the 'exposition of British life and achievement in its main social, economic, scientific and cultural aspects' was to have an increasingly diminished role: 'When we are speaking to people under great political stress, we may have to confine our output almost entirely to news and current affairs, as anything less relevant to their situation would prove exasperating.'[72]

A year on, almost to the day, from the Cabinet's decision to adopt an anti-communist publicity policy, Warner felt confident that the strategic realignment of BBC services had in large measure been achieved. At the beginning of 1949, he wrote to Mayhew,

> the BBC have moved a long way in the direction of gearing their transmissions to Eastern Europe to the Cabinet's publicity directive. My impression is that General Jacob has completely accepted the principle that the programmes to Eastern Europe should be almost entirely political, hard hitting and designed to enlighten the BBC's listeners on the matters which their Communist masters

> conceal from them or distort and that the necessary reorganisation of the transmissions to Eastern Europe is now bearing fruit and they will continue to get better.[73]

This positive review was based on a report prepared by Barbara Ruthven-Murray of the East European Information Department who, as Warner noted, 'has always been one of the BBC's severest critics'.[74] Ruthven-Murray had observed,

> a radical improvement in the BBC Services to the Soviet Satellite countries over the past few months so that the services as a whole are adequately reflecting our publicity policy in: (a) attacking the principles and practices of Communism, representing it as a threat to Western Civilisation, and describing in some detail the Communists' control and exploitation of the Eastern European countries; (b) stressing the high standard of living, the civil liberties, social progress, and cultural development enjoyed in this and other western countries; and (c) supporting the development of Western Union in all its manifestations.[75]

These changes accorded with the BBC's own assessment of its output at the beginning of 1949. Reviewing the Central European Services for the BBC Board of Governors, Patrick Ransome of the External Services' Research Unit found that 'during the past year certain very marked changes have occurred in the output'.[76] In particular, he noticed several altered characteristics such as a much greater emphasis on news of world affairs at the expense of the projection of Britain and a heavy reliance on press reviews as a vehicle for this. As he wryly noted, 'time is certainly not wasted on descriptions of camping in Cornwall or recordings of noises at a wildfowl exhibition!'[77]

BBC External Services were experiencing an ever-increasing engagement with the Cold War, driven by events overseas as well as editorial changes at home. The voice of Britain, particularly in broadcasts to Central and Eastern Europe, was beginning to speak in the context of a new idiom that reflected contrasts between Britain and countries behind the Iron Curtain (and by extension between ideas of East and West) while emphasizing a communality of mind between the people of Britain and those listening under communist domination. The argot of political and ideological differentness was employed to shine a light on oppressive methods of internal governance and the part these states played in the strategic interests of the Soviet Union. At the same time, a direct appeal was made to listeners in a vernacular that spoke of universal principles of justice and freedom denied to them, but demonstrably in evidence in Britain. Inherent in much of this was the message that the plight of listeners had not been forgotten by the people of Britain.

Did these changes undermine the Corporation's independence from government? In terms of specific content and the reliance of programme-makers on the FO, the answer was no. The agent of the government's anti-communist publicity policy, IRD, had limited success in getting its product directly used by the European Services at this stage. Its 'Digest' of activities in communist countries and special papers on related issues such as 'Forced Labour in Russia' and 'Trades Unions in Russia' were used by many services as valuable background information, but very little direct use was made of it in broadcasts.[78] It was in the overarching administration of editorial policy that the influence of the FO, supported by the ears of the Diplomatic Service, was much greater. This was demonstrated by the success with which Warner had argued for changes in the style and tone of BBC output. However, the very nature of the method used by Warner revealed the acceptable limits of the FO's power in this respect. Consensus and negotiation were the watchwords of the relationship at this formative stage and the FO's success in shaping the nature of the BBC's broadcasts to Europe, and by extension to the rest of the world, depended on its powers of persuasion and a subsequent acceptance within the BBC of its arguments. This is not to say that relations were not often difficult and combative; they were, but this was closely and consciously managed by senior staff on both sides. What was significant, however, was the extent and manner in which the FO and its relevant constituent parts, IPD, IRD and Diplomatic Service, had become fixed points in the ecosystem of Cold War overseas broadcasting. The BBC was wired-up to the development of policy in Whitehall, in terms of both relations between key individuals and the institutional architecture of liaison. While this was not hard-wiring, when strategic changes did occur in the direction and administration of foreign policy, vibrations in the constitutional as well as the extra-constitutional ties that bound them together were most definitely felt in Bush and Broadcasting House.

Ian Jacob liked to emphasize the reflective nature of broadcasting in the 'national interest': the BBC as a 'mirror held to reflect the views and activities of the British people'.[79] In his directive to the European Services at the beginning of 1948, he had argued that 'opinion in Britain . . . does not believe there is a fatality in events which cannot be modified, and it is our task to reflect this impression'.[80] As the currents of the Cold War flowed ever stronger in the coming months, the British public awoke to the growing international crisis. By November, remarking on the 'striking intensification of the antagonism between the East and West', Jacob acknowledged that

> the "cold war" is now spoken of quite openly by responsible people. The British Delegation at the United Nations has been making a succession of attacking speeches, the battle against Communism in the Trade Unions has been joined, and the press is full of articles on the Communist menace in all forms.[81]

Accordingly, by the point at which the Cold War became an issue of widespread domestic concern and debate in Britain, a point clearly reached by the end of 1948, it was perceived to be in the 'national interest' that the External Services take up an essentially anti-communist stance, in line with the direction of public opinion. This was a position with which Jacob was not entirely comfortable preferring, as he told his colleagues on the Russia Committee, 'to emphasize the advantage of living under a democratic regime than to try and explode the "myth" of the Soviet Union'.[82] He nonetheless understood that the 'positive projection of Britain in the long term sense tends to get crowded out by the mass of important current events revolving round the great world struggle which has developed'.[83]

Despite his reservations, and those of others in the BBC that 'we are tending to become too preoccupied with Russia and with events taking place in Eastern Europe, at the expense of the more positive exposition of Western civilisation', he could see that the 'kind of readjustment that I think we shall have to consider is doing rather more in Eastern Europe at the expense of Western Europe or elsewhere'.[84] Just a few months after joining the BBC, Jacob had set out his conception of where the BBC External Services fitted into the gamut of broadcasters around the world:

> Many nations broadcast to their neighbours. Some use their opportunity to indulge in undisguised political warfare; others seek to amuse; others combine information with interest, in a synthesis of friendship. It is among the latter that the BBC places itself, in the confident hope that by straightforward, friendly, and impartial speaking it is contributing to the future peace of the world.[85]

As the Cold War assumed ever greater significance in the politics and practice of overseas broadcasting, a critical question for the External Services, as it framed its output on the basis of government advice balanced by public opinion and its own professional experience, was the extent to which its own editorial outlook would come to be defined by the radio war in which it was now engaged.

Part Two

Through the Iron Curtain

4

The Imagined Audience

Reorganization of the BBC's overseas operation after the Second World War was as much a conceptual challenge as it was a practical one and the consequent shift in broadcast tone reflected an intellectual engagement with the editorial problems presented by the Cold War. This was true of establishing a new peacetime relationship not only with the British government, but just as importantly with the BBC's audiences around the world. However, on this last point there was a considerable gap in the BBC's knowledge which would impact heavily on the Corporation's ability to meet the needs of audiences behind the Iron Curtain. Although a significant part of the domestic BBC's work since 1936, it was not until 1947 that a dedicated audience research department was established for overseas services with a complement of just five staff under the leadership of Asher Lee.[1] Until this point, assessment of audience tastes, tolerances and expectations had been a co-operative endeavour with information about listeners and reception conditions scavenged from as wide a range of civil and military sources as possible. This precedent of multi-agency input and the practice of government in debating with broadcasters about how to approach audiences and to what ends had become part of the background to overseas broadcasting.

Out of an estimated 175 million adult radio listeners in Europe after the war, twenty million were thought to listen to the BBC in the course of a week or a fortnight.[2] Soon after the introduction of the Royal Charter in 1947, Ian Jacob, then Director of European Services, laid out the 'intelligence' needs of services to the continent:

(a) Knowledge of what is going on in the country concerned – political, social and cultural developments.
(b) Knowledge of the distribution of receiving sets, their nature and type, and of the listening habits of the different sections of the people.
(c) Assessment of the size, type and distribution of our audience, and of their programme preferences.
(d) Knowledge of what is being read or heard by our listeners from other sources.

(e) Collection of systematic and widespread reaction to our programmes.
(f) Study of and reply to mail received from listeners.
(g) Advice, based on all the information gathered, to those directing output and those directing publicity.[3]

In pursuing these requirements a distinction was quickly established between East and West in terms of access to information. In Western Europe it was possible to employ a wide range of research tools: structured surveys, listener competitions that offered prizes in return for critiques of BBC output, general correspondence, listening panels, questionnaires, staff visits, Foreign Office reports and interviews with overseas visitors and refugees.[4] For those engaged in broadcasts to Central and Eastern Europe many of these analytical resources were not available in any systematic sense. And as the authorities in Central and Eastern Europe sought to tighten their grip on communication with the outside world, the once numerous letters from listeners began to dry up. With the implementation of Defence of the Peace Acts in satellite countries from 1950, which made it a crime to pass on information received from western broadcasters, the BBC's listeners were understandably wary of being identified, let alone of revealing their programme preferences.[5] Increasingly, the BBC had to balance its own limited appreciation of life behind the Iron Curtain with the intelligence it received from the Foreign Office (FO).

Figure 4 Listener Research, BBC European Service, Bush House, April 1948

Audience research behind the Iron Curtain presented considerable challenges to the BBC's overseas broadcasters. Listener Research staff examine every letter sent to the BBC for useful information.

After his arrival at the BBC in the summer of 1946 as Controller of European Services, Jacob set up a Political Information Section as part of his office to act as the processing centre through which information from the FO would pass. Here documents supplied by the FO and other government departments would be kept in safe custody and used to draft 'background notes and guidance directives' as well as to produce summaries in order to provide, first the European and then the whole External Services, a 'complete picture of the international scene'.[6] The staff employed in the Section also served the News Division as Diplomatic Correspondents, which in effect made them the appointed agents of liaison between Whitehall and the BBC to 'supplement by personal contact the information received in documents'.[7] Under this arrangement the BBC routinely received telegrams from the FO. Until November 1949 these came under headings such as 'Political Distribution', 'German No.1 Distribution' and 'European Reconstruction Distribution'.[8] Following a reclassification of the Foreign Office system, the BBC received a reduced service under the heading of 'Foreign Office and Whitehall' supplemented by 'Economic and Social', 'Weekly Political Summary from Berlin to Wahnerhide' and until June 1951 the 'FRAME' series on European Reconstruction.[9] In addition, at the beginning of 1948 the British Ambassador in Belgrade, Charles Peake, had wondered whether it would be useful to 'institute a system whereby all events which require mention or comment in the BBC's Yugoslav service shall at once be reported to you in separate telegrams'.[10] A few days later John Sterndale-Bennett in Sofia told colleagues in London that he would 'try to keep you constantly advised by telegram of items of news which could with advantage be emphasised here'.[11] By the summer of 1948, a separate system of telegrams from Eastern and then also Central Europe was established under the prefix 'ASIDE', which specifically contained 'information which has been ignored or wrongly reported in those countries, and guidance on the treatment of such material' for the BBC.[12] As such, British Missions behind the Iron Curtain became a critical ear with an important part to play in advising both the FO and the BBC on the requirements of broadcasting to these territories.[13]

Foreign Office telegrams of 'general importance or exceptional interest' were passed by the Political Information Section to Tangye Lean, in his capacity as Editor of the European Services, in time for his daily meetings with senior service chiefs at 10.30 a.m. It was then up to Lean to decide what elements of these documents would be passed on. In addition, heads of services would be given a number of less sensitive telegrams to look at after the meeting. The sometimes highly classified nature of this information led to a concern that there was 'a real danger of small, single pieces of paper getting mislaid'.[14] At the end of November

1948 it was decided that 'sight of the FO telegrams must be greatly restricted', resulting in an overhaul of handling arrangements.[15] More was to be put in Lean's morning file with a clearer guide to the contents that could be passed on, but no one outside the Political Information Section, other than the Editor of the European Services, would have access to original documents. Instead, telegrams received by the Political Information Section

> will in future be summarised in this office and sent to the interested individuals under some such title as "Regional Gleanings". There will be no mention in these Gleanings that they are based on FO telegrams, but the source will, of course, be understood . . . and we shall feel able to write somewhat more freely if Service Heads are not permitted to retain them.[16]

In this way the Political Information Section acted as an important filter in the flow of information from the FO and other departments to the inner reaches of the External Services. Meanwhile, Warner proposed an arrangement whereby His Majesty Representatives in Central and Eastern Europe and the BBC 'should keep up a two-way correspondence, our Missions sending material which they would like to see used by the BBC (separate from short-term material included in ASIDE telegrams), and criticisms of the BBC broadcasts'. This was welcomed by Jacob and instructions to Information Officers were sent out by the FO in October.[17] Consequently, Asher Lee was put in touch with British Missions for the purpose of 'technical reports' on BBC output.[18]

Broadcasting in Russian

1948 had proved to be a very important year of transition for the BBC, setting in motion many trends in output that were to mature in the coming years of the Cold War. More attention was paid to disputes between the Soviet Union and the West as the political content of European broadcasts was increased and greater emphasis put on local and regional news agendas. In stark contrast the BBC's broadcasts to Russia remained, as one Foreign Office official noted towards the end of the year, 'almost entirely non-political', consciously avoiding the kind of critical engagement that had become such a marked characteristic of its regional counterparts.[19] This reflected an editorial belief that the Russian listener had been 'so oversupplied with Soviet political propaganda that he required enticing to listen to the BBC with a good deal of culture and entertainment'.[20] The initial result was a curiously asymmetrical approach to broadcasting over the Iron Curtain, one that was defined by BBC and government expectations of audience needs.

Broadcasts by the BBC in Russian to the USSR began on 24 March 1946, just one month after the FO had submitted a request that it should do so. That evening, listeners were given a talk on what to expect from the European Services of the BBC.[21] That they did not already know was the consequence of a number of factors which had prevented regular broadcasting in Russian during the Second World War while the BBC spoke to the rest of Europe in its various native tongues.[22] Assumptions about the lack of demand in the USSR for news from Britain, in addition to the relatively small number of privately owned radio sets (as opposed to the highly controlled wired–wireless and cabled speaker networks) played an important, though contingent, part in decision-making.[23] More significant were diplomatic and political sensitivities which prevented setting up a service, as Julian Hale has noted, for 'fear of upsetting the delicate relations between Britain and her essential but difficult ally'.[24] At the beginning of 1946, as it became increasingly important to the government to construct a counteroffensive against Soviet propaganda aimed at the West, such nervousness was swept aside.[25]

Once up and running, broadcasts in Russian assiduously avoided taking a combative approach. The purpose of these programmes, as the BBC's Board of Governor's noted, was 'to build up a large and friendly audience,[26] and to

> present listeners in the Soviet Union a straightforward, honest News Bulletin, a comprehensive review of Britain, Parliament, and other British institutions, scientific and cultural achievements and sporting events (particularly football and chess) which we know to be of interest; and to elucidate in a varied manner and from as many fields as possible the British way of life.[27]

It was certainly not the intention to 'indulge in polemics'.[28] Accordingly, the visit of the Delegation of the Supreme Soviet of the USSR to the BBC on the first anniversary of the Russian Service provided an 'admirable opportunity for the projection of Anglo-Russian friendship'.[29] Although members of the delegation declined the offer to speak on the Russian Service, Colonel-General Gromov expressed the hope, in a speech at Bush House, that these broadcasts would help to create an understanding between the British and Soviet peoples.[30] This was certainly the intention behind the sympathetic broadcast description of the Delegation's visit to the Marx House library, which 'reflected the emotion felt by the Russians on seeing the room where Lenin edited his newspaper'.[31]

Soon after broadcasts began, the British Charge d'Affaires in Moscow estimated that there were two million receiving sets in Russia.[32] Using projections contained in the Soviet Union's own five-year post-war reconstruction plan, the

BBC believed that in addition to the 6 million wired–wireless radio points, by 1947 five and a half million radio sets capable of picking up shortwave frequencies (those able to travel vast distances) had been manufactured in the USSR.[33] Starved of anything other than these official figures, British assessments rose to between 6 and 7 million sets by the end of 1949 and 8 million by 1951.[34] These increases provided a substantial enough reason to make broadcasts by the BBC an essential element of Britain's communication strategy to the Soviet Union, with a pattern of three daily transmissions of 'news and programme' (04.30, 16.45 and 19.45 GMT). Beyond the news bulletins, 'controversial topics were usually not handled directly', resulting in a predominance of projection-of-Britain material 'carefully angled for an audience largely ignorant of many of the assumptions of West European life and long subjected to a thorough process of conditioning by Soviet propaganda'.[35] Discussion of world affairs was restricted to a weekly talk by the regional commentator, Anatol Goldberg, the twice weekly selection of press comment and other very occasional talks.

The British Embassy in Moscow (and the Diplomatic Service more widely) quickly became an extremely valuable source of intelligence concerning audibility and assessments of the tone, as Jacob informed his colleagues on the Russia Committee, where he stressed 'the urgency of making available to the BBC background material'.[36] In 1946–47, 130 letters were received from listeners across the USSR, but this figure dramatically ebbed in the following years. Interviews with visitors to Russia provided an important source of information as did talks with members of the Soviet Armed Forces stationed in Europe, which revealed listening by some Red Army units despite strictures against this. Refugees also helped provide the semblance of a profile of the Russian listener.[37] All available evidence received careful attention as in the case of Mrs Watts, a British resident in Moscow for 11 years, who reported the 'English and White Russian intonation' of BBC announcers that gave an 'old world' atmosphere to the broadcasts.[38] These comments were supported by a Listening Panel at the British Embassy in Moscow, leading the Press Attaché there to describe the broadcast tone as 'exaggerated Oxford' – most unpopular with the Russian listener.[39] As a consequence, a great deal of reorganizing effort was put into developing contemporary accents and improving translations of centrally produced material with, for example, the recruitment of staff from Displaced Person Camps in Germany and others from the émigré, dissident and migratory Russian-speaking post-war diaspora.[40]

The Russian Service lagged behind other BBC programmes to Eastern Europe, which had become progressively tougher in their criticism of communism and

Soviet policy. Over time, however, its light-touch approach and the audience tastes this assumed began to be seriously questioned. By July 1948 the British Embassy in Moscow was arguing that the 'BBC's programmes would probably be more attractive if they contained more politics' and in November the Russian Service introduced a new series of weekly political talks titled *The International Scene as I see it from Britain,* in which well-known commentators gave their interpretation of current affairs.[41] An early set of these, four critical talks by the editor of the *New Statesman*, Kingsley Martin, very quickly became the subject of attack in Soviet publicity. This delighted staff at the FO's IPD as evidence that broadcasts 'are really getting under the skin of the Soviet authorities and if the BBC material is having this effect then we can be sure that the broadcasts are exercising an influence on the minds of ordinary listeners'.[42] This shift in emphasis at the BBC could also be seen in Goldberg's regular Sunday commentaries, *Notes By Our Observer*, which now dealt more directly with the clash between Russia and the West, although his 'approach was always a friendly one, the note being one of regret at the strained relations between East and West rather than of reproach for Russian behaviour'. Likewise, press reviews 'showed no tendency either to avoid controversial topics or to conceal the gravity of the situation as seen through the eyes of responsible British journalists'.[43]

In line with these changes an interesting new development at the beginning of 1949 was the transmission of a series of talks on the Russian Service by Grigori Tokaev, a Colonel in the Red Army and specialist in long-range rocketry, who had defected to Britain at the end of 1947.[44] This was the first time the BBC had put a Soviet defector on air and in doing so broke what until then had been somewhat of a taboo in the External Services over the ethical value of such a move. In a House of Lords debate at the beginning of March, the former Permanent Under-Secretary at the Foreign Office, Lord Vansittart, criticized the poor use of refugees and émigrés by the BBC.[45] Meanwhile, the JIC was making great efforts to encourage deserters to the West and in co-operation with IRD hoped to make use of the BBC's German and Russian Services for this purpose.[46] To this end, the FO asked the BBC 'to be as free as they can in getting émigrés to broadcast'.[47] Considerable care had to be taken with such an approach, however, as was demonstrated when the British Embassy in Moscow challenged the BBC over a possible interpretation of incitement following broadcasts by the former Prime Minister of the Russia Provisional Government, Alexander Kerensky.[48]

By the spring of 1949 there was an emerging consensus in the FO and at the BBC that Russian output should better reflect Cold War concerns. Staff at the Moscow Embassy believed that 'news and politics build up an audience for the "entertainment" rather than the other way round',[49] while the Parliamentary Under-Secretary of State for Foreign Affairs, Christopher Mayhew, questioned the effect of Soviet indoctrination on the BBC's audience in Russia:

> If it means that they are so indoctrinated that they have strong moral inhibitions against listening, I should have thought that this would deter them from listening to our broadcasts whether or not entertainment was mixed in with them. If, however, it merely means that they utterly disbelieve our propaganda, it is surely a reason for changing the nature of our political broadcasts, rather than for cutting them down in favour of entertainment.[50]

The newly appointed Head of East European Services at the BBC, Hugh Carleton Greene, formerly in charge of its wartime German Service and just returned after two years leading the British-controlled Nordwestdeutscher Rundfunk radio station in Hamburg, agreed that 'it is the political items which attract the average listener'.[51] But by 1949, who was the average listener to the Russian Service and how did this affect assessments of their broadcast needs?

Believing the BBC's audience in the USSR to be largely composed of the intelligentsia, the FO suggested seizing the 'opportunity of increasing the doubts they already feel about the correctness of the Party line as well as the reliability of Soviet propaganda'.[52] In doing so, Warner pointed out to Jacob,

> attacks on the Russians as a people would obviously be absurd; but we agree that even attacks on Stalin, and to some extent on the Soviet Government, would be likely to defeat our object. But Soviet publicity is evidently the Achilles heel of the regime, and as such is an obvious target.[53]

This accorded with the outlook of the British Ambassador in Moscow, Sir Maurice Peterson, who thought 'the main attack should not be on the Soviet Government, leaders, policy, or outlook – the defences around these are too strong – but on Soviet sources of information'.[54] While not discounting the value of this, at the BBC a slightly different analysis was being developed:

> It seems, however, unnecessarily pessimistic to assume that our audience stands solidly behind the regime and resents any criticism of its present Government. I am speaking of *our audience* (which, it should not be forgotten, includes the armies of occupation outside Russia: the morale of the army is inclined to be rather shaky) and not the Russian people as a whole.[55]

Moreover, reports of Communist Party members being expelled for tuning into western radio broadcasts were, Greene suggested, proof that 'listening is by itself evidence of doubt and becomes more and more the first faint sign of opposition'.[56]

In concluding that the process of subversion had already started by the time listeners sought out BBC's transmissions, Greene argued for a broadening of the broadcast palette rather than focusing on the 'weak spot' that was the Soviet information services and running the risk 'of thinking too exclusively in terms of counter-propaganda.' Instead, the BBC should be engaged in 'attacking the Marxist-Leninist ideology and the whole basis of the Soviet regime'.[57] As was subsequently noted by the FO in March 1949, 'during the last few months the Russian Service has taken on a completely new complexion'.[58] And when Patrick Ransome reviewed Russian output that summer he perceived a complete change in policy: 'Cautious methods . . . have been abandoned, and have, it would seem, given place to undisguised political warfare.' By this time, however, another change had taken place that was to epitomize the broadcast effort to the Soviet Union just as much as the content of the programmes. On 25 April 1949, the Russians started jamming BBC broadcasts on a systematic basis. As Ransome noted, 'the gloves are off'.[59]

Figure 5 Hugh Carleton Greene, BBC German Service Director, January 1946

The Daily Telegraph chief correspondent in Berlin from 1938, Greene joined the BBC German Service in 1940 which he subsequently led. Seconded in 1946 to oversee the reconstruction of broadcasting in the British Zone of Germany, Greene returned to the BBC in 1948 in charge of its East European Services. After a further secondment to the Colonial Office to run psychological warfare operations against communist insurgents in Malaya, he was made Assistant Controller (1952) and then Controller (1955) of BBC Overseas Services, eventually becoming Director-General of the BBC in 1960.

Hugh Carleton Greene, now with regional responsibility for Russian programming, was later to write that 'even in the coldest of Cold War conditions the objective of propaganda to Soviet Russia was rather different from what our hot war objective had been in the case of Germany'. The BBC's main aim, he noted, was 'to get our audience to accept our view of events . . . and a subsidiary aim was to shake the faith in Stalin'. However, unlike transmissions to the satellite countries where 'Russian rule might be shaken off', Greene recalled that 'no one in his senses could believe that it should be any part of our objective to contribute to the overthrow of the Soviet regime or to "liberate" the Soviet people, who had probably no desire to be liberated anyway, at least from the outside'.[60] Jacob likewise believed that there were greater 'divergencies of view and cleavages of opinion' in Russian society (and the BBC's audience in particular) than the British Embassy in Moscow and the FO had hitherto given credit for.[61] With a much heavier emphasis on world affairs, broadcasts to Russia 'now openly criticise the Soviet regime, correct its anti-Western propaganda, and inform listeners of facts and ideas which their own authorities withhold [sic] from them'. Goldberg 'preserved the fundamentally friendly tone which has always characterised his broadcasts to Russia', though he was increasingly resolute in his criticism, while fellow regional commentator David Graham (who spoke as an 'indignant outsider' rather than a 'disillusioned friend') was far more denunciatory.[62]

These variations in the pitch of the Russian Service were not purely tonal, but also extended to programme content. Analysis of Soviet propaganda techniques, which the FO had considered so important, became a regular feature as did, following Greene's proposal, a wider critique of the Soviet regime and its ideological underpinning. Merely stating the Western case was no longer the editorial objective of a service which now 'sought to expose both the duplicity and expansionist purpose of the foreign policy of the USSR and also the ruthless and despotic nature of the Soviet regime itself'. But there was some concern at the BBC about whether 'these distinctly diverse elements combine to form a comprehensive and coherent propaganda campaign, or whether listeners conditioned to expect the expression of one single and clear-cut point of view only might convey an impression of uncertainty and even dishonesty'. Might these broadcasts 'suggest a willingness by the BBC to use any convenient weapons'?[63] However, a more pressing concern for broadcasters and officials after the advent of jamming was whether the Russian Service had any listeners left at all.

By the end of May 1949 the Cabinet's Colonial Information Policy Committee (CIPC) summed up the position as being one where 'a listener in Russia who really wanted to do so *could* hear the BBC and the Voice of the USA, but it would not be at all easy'.[64] Reporting to the Board of Governors, Jacob thought that while the 'less keen' listener might have been discouraged from tuning in by the jamming, 'it was equally probable . . . that those who are really keen will have been spurred to greater efforts to hear our Services'.[65] Nevertheless, the question of whether to continue Russian broadcasts was exercising minds in Whitehall. A quick review revealed that they should be maintained, not least because the gain from redistributing the money and transmitter time saved ('about an hour's broadcasting a day in one other language which we are using already') was negligible.[66] In addition, experience had shown that it was precisely in those 'countries deprived of freedom of information by their own governments' that the BBC was most listened to and that, in the long run, 'results might be achieved'. Certainly, it was felt that if the transmissions were stopped, 'minds which are being kept just open would be completely closed and cut off from the West'.[67] Just as important, though with little connection with programmes or their audiences, was the desire to tie-up Soviet resources:

> The Soviet jamming operation, which in practice is likely always to be incomplete, is estimated to be (at its present level) ten or twenty times as expensive, especially in skilled manpower of which they are believed to be short, as our counter-operation. If our broadcasts were stopped, most of these Soviet resources might not be immediately employable in increasing their output of propaganda, since the equipment required for jamming is not as a rule useful for broadcasting; but they would of course be most valuable to the Soviet authorities for other purposes.[68]

Despite the implementation of 'crash starts' to reduce the ability of jammers to fix on a transmission before broadcast, the increasing effectiveness of the Soviet operation, combined with worsening atmospheric conditions which limited the short-wave range available, precipitated a re-evaluation of the BBC's audience at the beginning of the 1950s. With reports from Moscow (confirmed by the BBC's listening station at Tatsfield) that 'all wavebands in all three BBC transmissions have been completely obliterated',[69] Greene set about establishing a credible rationale for the service's continuation which had at its core a profile of the BBC's audience. His report identified four categories of listeners: officers in the Army; small numbers of intellectuals, high officials and managers with good sets and homes away from centres of population; a few enterprising political prisoners in remote parts of Russia; the official monitor and a restricted number of high officials who receive the monitoring reports.[70]

An alternative view, put by the Controller of European Services, Tangye Lean, raised the question that 'if we are only going to broadcast to a tiny minority, and accept that limitation so completely, then I doubt whether it is worth the tremendous effort we are making'.[71] Greene saw it differently, arguing the BBC should not worry about 'offending, and losing, listeners who are loyal to the regime as distinct from the country'. After all, the peculiar status of Army Officers – in direct contact with the West and less affected by jamming when posted outside of Russia – gave them either greater opportunity for desertion, or when they returned from duty, more cause to become agents of disaffection.[72] The British Embassy in Moscow had also come to the conclusion that 'the BBC are now broadcasting to a mere handful of people in the Soviet Union' and that 'the effective audience is confined to members of the Soviet armed forces outside the Soviet Union'.[73]

Beyond the effect of atmospheric conditions on short-wave propagation, good in summer and bad in winter, and interference as a result of the sunspot cycle, particularly bad in this period, listening conditions continued to be better outside the major centres of population where it was possible to hear entire BBC programmes.[74] Nevertheless, direct testimony of listening was very hard to come by. In 1948, first-hand intelligence of listening was based on a British Information Officer from Moscow asking questions of people he met while on holiday on the Volga. The following year eight members of the Soviet Occupation Force in Germany were questioned about listening habits, while in 1950 the only real indication of listening was a conversation between a member of the British Embassy in Moscow and a young Russian who, when asked whether broadcasts could be heard since the start of jamming, replied, 'Oh, yes! They come through occasionally.' 1951 was even less auspicious with 'no hard evidence of continued listening' reaching the BBC. Instead the Corporation relied on indirect reports and attacks on the BBC in the Soviet press and radio, to infer the impact of its broadcasts. By 1954 the pattern of active Russian audience research was aptly characterized in a BBC review: 'Sources', it wearily noted, 'have been rather sparse'.[75]

There was one initiative taken by the BBC, however, that had a very clear outcome. This was the establishment on 12 February 1950 of a weekly religious programme for the Slavonic Orthodox Church, following a successful experimental broadcast on the Orthodox New Year in January. With announcements made in Russian, Bulgarian and Serbo-Croat, the services in Church Slavonic included readings from the liturgy of the Orthodox Church and recordings of Orthodox choirs.[76] The intention of these programmes was to allow an expression of religious freedom to contrast with the anti-theological doctrine of communism while complementing the message of political and cultural freedom carried in other broadcasts to Europe. While these programmes were obliterated in Moscow, to begin with good reception was reported in Belgrade and Sofia.[77] After just over six months, though, increased jamming and poor propagation conditions in the target areas led Jacob to inform the Governors that 'it is of no value to continue the experiment' and the programmes were dropped – perhaps the first such cancellation by the BBC as a result of jamming.[78]

What, though, would the determined listener have been able to hear on the few frequencies that got through? The pattern of all three of the BBC's broadcasts was a nine to twelve minute news bulletin followed by two talks. As a necessary concession to jamming, the morning and afternoon programmes were usually repeats of the transmission from the previous evening. The main emphasis remained on world affairs and even the few remaining projection-of-Britain programmes were 'designed to counter communist misrepresentations, to demonstrate the inferiority of Soviet Russia in material resources and to illustrate the advantages of living in a democracy where state planning was not synonymous with absence of individual freedoms'.[79] This led Patrick Ransome to question whether such a programme diet would have any effect on 'those who have scarcely begun the adventure of independent thought'.[80] The Assistant Head of East European Services, David Graham, demurred and wondered if they would be

> listening to a foreign radio station at all if they had not begun this adventure rather seriously? Both jamming and frequent articles in the press make it clear that no good Soviet citizen listens to a foreign radio. It is a wicked and rather dangerous thing to do, and must, I think, imply some degree of disillusionment with Soviet doctrine and practice.[81]

As such, programmes like Walter Kolarz's *Public Opinion in Soviet Russia* in which he detailed the Party's system of internal propaganda continued, as did series' on Soviet defectors and weekly eyewitness accounts of life in forced labour camps for 'detained counter-revolutionaries' in *The Land of the DC's*.[82]

The continued vulnerability into the 1950s of the Russian Service, in the face of serious challenges to audibility and editorial focus, was never far from the minds of broadcasters and officials. With the BBC predicting that broadcast penetration through the Iron Curtain was unlikely to get any better for the time being, matters were once again brought to a head by the Foreign

Office as it sought a 'means of increasing the political dividend that can be got from broadcasting to the Soviet Orbit', where attacks on Soviet communism were more likely to have an impact, at the expense, if necessary, of the Russian Service.[83] The view from the BBC was that the abandonment of Russian broadcasts in favour of services to the satellites was simply not practicable.[84] The Head of European Programme Operations, H. G. Venables, pointed out that the very small savings made by a reduction in the Russian Service would not be enough to increase broadcasts to the Soviet satellites and that other services to Western Europe, Scandinavia, Iberia, Germany, Italy, the Middle Eastern, as well as the General Overseas Services would have to be reduced for this to be achieved.[85] Besides, as Graham noted, if 'the Soviet Government wants to jam our broadcasts to satellite countries, its jammers at Minsk, Lvov and Simferopol are well placed for the job. . . . If we cut down our Russian output we will ourselves provide the means for jamming our satellite output.' For the External Services the result would be 'profoundly discouraging, and would weaken morale and lower professional standards, with effects which could not be made good "quickly in the event of an emergency" '.[86] In response to an alternative Foreign Office proposal to use 'slow morse', as had been done during the Second World War, to at least supply the needs of the Russian monitors and the officials who read their reports, the fact that no more than 600 words an hour could be transmitted made it quite unsuitable to the task of replacing the spoken word.[87] Jacob's considered response was that 'we should leave the Russian operation as it is', and the FO subsequently dropped its proposals, though not its ambition to influence the tone of Russian Service output.[88]

Broadcasting to Central and Eastern Europe

In May 1950 the Defence Committee of the Cabinet considered a report by the British Chiefs of Staff entitled 'The Need for an Increasingly Offensive Cold War Strategy'. In it they argued that Britain should 'give the Russians no ground for a degree of apprehension that might drive them to a preventative war'. The 'moral victory' of the Berlin airlift showed 'their historic tendency to hold back in the face of determined opposition still holds good'. As a consequence, Britain and her allies 'could afford to adopt a more forward strategy in the Cold War' without being 'unduly anxious about provoking the Russians'.[89] Building on this analysis a year later, the reinvigorated Overseas Information Services Ministerial Committee defined the aim of overseas publicity as,

> To further our ends in the "Cold War" by exposing Soviet and Communist ideas, regimes, ends, policies and manoeuvres, by encouraging resistance to them everywhere in the free world and, behind the Iron Curtain, by enlightening the ignorance imposed upon the peoples of the Soviet Union, China and the satellite countries . . .[90]

The challenge for the BBC, considered by the FO as 'by far the most important propaganda weapon we have in the "orbit" countries', was how to respond to this strategic context.[91] The independent control exercised by the Corporation had prevented overseas broadcasting from becoming a mere tool of British foreign policy, but what were the limits to which the BBC was prepared to go in the robustness of these transmissions?

In his paper on the 'Task of the Overseas Services of the BBC' Jacob had meditated on whether the rise of negative broadcasting 'implies that we are to conduct political warfare'.[92] His answer appeared to be an emphatic no, 'the BBC itself is not conducting anything',[93] but his explanation was somewhat equivocal:

> When as now the British people are engaged in a struggle to maintain their existence and way of life in the face of a campaign of propaganda and subversive activity openly designed to overthrow them, we must not in any way shrink from giving full expression to the British view and to assist by all means in our power the national effort. Only in this way shall we be framing our programmes in the national interest.[94]

The view of Patrick Ransome, in his regular monthly summaries of output for the BBC Board of Governors, was that services to Eastern Europe were indeed 'engaged in open political warfare' with a much greater degree of 'special angling' and comment on internal affairs by individual services.[95] The FO, for its part, found it equally hard to define 'what it is legitimate for the BBC to do in this respect', but on one key issue there was an accord of outlook which effectively put a ceiling on the extent of BBC activities: the External Services would 'stop short, in their broadcasts to the Orbit, of inciting listeners to subversive action vis-à-vis their governments'.[96] Missions in Eastern Europe were subsequently informed that,

> we have to guard against arousing false hopes that our strength will be used within a foreseeable term for the liberation of the peoples now suffering under

> the Communist yoke; and, indeed, there is some evidence that the peoples of Eastern Europe in their despair are likely to be too easily encouraged to hope that the forces of the West are about to march.[97]

There was, however, one communist country in respect of which the BBC took a rather different approach.

The expulsion of the Yugoslav delegates from the Cominform in June 1948 and the subsequent Soviet denunciation of Tito had shown, as Tangye Lean noted, 'more vividly than anything else that has happened the extent of subservience Russia demands from her satellites'.[98] Accordingly, he told staff 'We must prolong this sudden flash of light so that glimmers of it penetrate into the most rigidly Communist minds.'[99] The FO had been seeking to secure a post-war 'working relationship' with Belgrade for some time, building on the wartime assistance given by Britain to the Partisans.[100] The peculiar position of Yugoslavia – a communist European country, but no longer part of the Soviet 'belt' – also led to a rather different approach being taken in BBC services. As broadcasts to other countries in Central and Eastern Europe became markedly more anti-communist in tone, criticism of communist Yugoslavia itself was, as far as possible, avoided. This challenged assumptions in the FO about publicity in Iron Curtain countries with the British Ambassador in Belgrade, Sir Charles Peake, arguing that the BBC's broadcasts were not making 'an adequate contribution to the projection of the Government's anti-Communist policy'.[101] At the same time it was considered desirable to 'widen the gulf that now separates the Yugoslav leaders from their former allies . . . to the point when it becomes unbridgeable, so long as that does not entail the fall of the Tito faction to their Cominform enemies'.[102] This was a contradiction in terms for the European Services broadcast remit, resulting in BBC broadcasts in Serbo-Croat and Slovene containing very little political programming or comment beyond press reviews. This led some in the Foreign Office to suspect that the substantial effort the BBC had put into cultivating links with the communist Yugoslav partisans during the war now made them 'loath to put out anything more than they were absolutely obliged to which might be unwelcome hearing to the same audience now'.[103] Either way, the resolution of this dilemma was to have a significant impact on services to Iron Curtain countries over the coming years.

The essential difference between Yugoslavia and the Soviet satellites for the purposes of broadcasting, according to the FO, was the public 'pride in their leaders who were the heroes of the Yugoslav resistance during the war and, unlike Communist leaders in the other Eastern European countries, were not appointed by Moscow'.[104] The FO estimated that 80 per cent of the population in Iron Curtain countries at the beginning of 1949 were 'anti-regime'.[105] The same could not be said about Yugoslavia. In addition, the Tito/Cominform split had established an undeniable differentiation between the oppressive and exploitative style of communism imposed by the Soviet Union on her satellites and a model more akin to national self-determination. The difficulty was to avoid offending these national sensibilities, while giving time to themes that were critical of communism but which did not, as Warner explained to Jacob, 'militate against our desire to attract Tito away from the Soviet orbit and towards co-operation on practical grounds with the West'.[106] Warner's remedy was to

> avoid attacking Tito's regime and the Communist ideology on which it is based and . . . concentrate entirely upon differences between the Cominform and the Soviet Union on the one hand, and Tito on the other, and on factual information about the factors which might constitute common ground between Tito and the West, without of course drawing the moral.[107]

By the beginning of February 1949 a new line in publicity to Yugoslavia was agreed to by Jacob, Warner and Mayhew.[108] No opportunity should be neglected 'of reminding the Yugoslav listeners of the implacable hostility of the Soviet Union and its satellites . . . to Tito and his Government.' Time should also be given to 'positive publicity for Western democracies, using every possible opportunity of contrasting the freedom which their inhabitants enjoy with the servitude of the subjects of the Kremlin'.[109] And any criticism 'should be subject to overriding proviso that such attacks should not be such as might tend to weaken Tito's authority & regime'.[110] This was the application of what Mark Selverstone describes as the 'wedge strategy', which was a long-term attempt to cleave a space between indigenous national communist aspirations and the sovietization of Yugoslav society.[111] In the coming years broadcasts to Yugoslavia retained an air of peculiarity with programmes, as Ransome described it, having 'more in common with our broadcasts to democratic countries than with those designed for other communist regimes in East Europe'.[112] The effect of this was to open up a critical discourse within and between the BBC and the government on different genres of communism and how to respond to them, which until then had not been systematically explored by British publicity to Central and Eastern Europe. When the Russia Committee had questioned whether all manifestations of communism should be treated as Soviet-inspired Jacob noted 'that the present British propaganda line was that communism meant subservience to the Kremlin'.[113] The example of Yugoslavia offered an alternative and contextualized

Figure 6 Christopher Cviic of the BBC's Yugoslav Section, September 1955
Listeners in Yugoslavia get the opportunity to sample the sounds of rural Britain.

interpretation which acknowledged the importance of indigenous communist movements and their association with expressions of national identity and patriotism.

Reflecting this new sensibility, the notion of the 'sovietisation' of the satellites (as opposed to their 'communisation') led the British Ambassador in Budapest, Geoffrey Wallinger, to argue that the 'underlying aims of our publicity on this theme should be to nourish and sustain the traditional and deep-rooted pride of the Hungarians in their own history and culture and their resistance to the imposition of an alien culture'.[114] Based on similar analyses, the idea that 'our publicity should be aimed at detaching the Communists in the satellite countries from their allegiance to Stalinism, using the Tito deviation as an example', gained considerable ground among Mission staff as well as Foreign Office officials in London.[115] So much so that by the time Warner came to discuss this with Jacob in May 1950 the government's publicity policy had, in practical terms, already changed. So too had the BBC's editorial approach to Central and Eastern Europe where the 'primary and undisguised purpose is to expose the imperialist character of Soviet foreign policy and to discredit Stalinism as a corruption of the original ideas of the Russian Revolution'.[116] This had been skilfully done in David Graham's serialization of Isaac Deutscher's *Stalin: a Political Biography*, and in his scripts on banned sources for a history of the October Revolution.[117] In talks widely used by both the Central and East European Services, Kolarz examined speeches made by members of the Politburo 'to illustrate the remarkable and unscrupulous changes in Soviet policy' in his series *Ten Years Ago*.[118] Meanwhile, in November 1949 the Bulgarian Service's weekly *Dobson's Political Chronicle* (written by the broadcaster, civil servant and historian Malcolm Mackintosh) attacked the recently introduced system of 'communist justice' asking, 'Is there anything Bulgarian left in Bulgarian public life?'[119] The general picture that emerged from European Service output by the 1950s 'was one of economic strain, political terror and administrative oppression . . . threatening the national life of the satellites should they ultimately be incorporated into the Soviet system'.[120]

This shift in the BBC's approach to Iron Curtain audiences, both conceptually and in practical broadcasting terms, evinced a number of initiatives examined by the BBC and FO at this time. One was the request from Hugh Carleton Greene for the provision of 'current political jokes' from British Embassies and Legations in Eastern Europe for inclusion in programmes.[121] Another, more substantial, proposal was intended as a set-piece response to a new approach being taken by Russia in its strategic communications with the satellites and the rest of the world. Its 'Peace Campaign' was designed to engender a benign interpretation of the Soviet Union's foreign policy objectives at a time when the West's growing unity could be portrayed as a prelude to aggression against communism, particularly in the light of the European Recovery Programme (Marshall Plan) from April 1948 and the signing of the North Atlantic Treaty in April 1949, establishing NATO. The campaign argued that rather than being a source of menace, 'Soviet might', as Wallinger characterized the Russian position, was 'by its very mightiness, a factor for peace'.[122] To counter these assertions Wallinger suggested that 'we might ourselves develop a slogan of our own in the word "Truth"'.[123] By September, the Russia Committee (on which Ian Jacob sat) considered 'the publication of a steady flow of facts to prove Russian insincerity' as the best antidote, concluding that 'the most successful method was likely to be some positive campaign with a simple slogan'.[124] However, when the Foreign Office proposal that 'our publicity services should run a "truth" campaign to counter the Communist "peace" campaign, using some slogan or refrain similar to the wartime device of the "V" sign' reached Jacob in his capacity as Director of External Services, it was met with a stern refusal. Instead of slogans, he preferred that such themes should manifest themselves 'as a natural part of the output, and should not appear to the listener as being a special stunt or an obvious line of propaganda'.[125] For example, the rule of law and the contrasts between the British and Soviet judicial systems had for a long time been the subject of regular programming in such series as *Freedom Under the Law* by Lord Justice

Denning and *The Law at Work* which presented trials in Britain 'as illustrations of the application of fundamental legal principles'.[126] This style of broadcasting subsequently drew its dividend by putting into sharp contrast judicial abuses within the Soviet sphere such as the trial of the Hungarian Foreign Minister, Laszlo Rajk, on the politically motivated charges of conspiracy to overthrow his own government and his subsequent execution in October 1949. As Warner informed Missions in Eastern Europe, the 'BBC's reputation for presenting the truth is already an accepted fact, and it would not be likely to be further enhanced by . . . constantly proclaiming it'.[127]

Discussions such as these over the approach to be taken in broadcasts to Europe were enhanced by further liaison between officials at the FO and the BBC. Greene's request for an increase in information received from the Diplomatic Service revealed the extent to which programmes over the Iron Curtain had become reliant on these sources for guidance, reports on propaganda trends and items of internal news.[128] Writing to Information Officers across the region, the Foreign Office's Eastern European Information Department remarked that,

> in some respects our activities now almost resemble those of the war-time PID [Political Information Department] in the way that we not only give the BBC guidance on and the background to current political events, but also bring to their attention items from Orbit propaganda, domestic and external, which they can turn to account.[129]

By the summer of 1950 an arrangement was worked out between Tangye Lean and Ralph Murray to consult on issues of long-term planning. For some time the BBC European Service's Walter Kolarz had been in very close touch with IRD and, as Murray noted, 'has had the run of the department to a large extent'.[130] For example, when preparing an important new series for the European Services entitled *Communism in Practice* he had consulted with IRD 'in conformity with his usual habit of discussing the most useful themes for broadcasts and the material which can be made available to illustrate them'.[131] News of this venture led Murray to suggest that there may be 'advantage in our forming some sort of a joint body' in which to discuss 'forwardly planned output on Communism'.[132] As a result, it was arranged for Gordon Mosley (Overseas Talks Manager) and Donald Hodson (Head of European Talks) to meet on a quarterly basis with Murray at the FO to keep each other 'informed of the trends . . . and also to discuss any forthcoming points of foreseeable importance'.[133] The first of these meetings was held in November 1950.

As Cold War broadcasting and the BBC's relationship with the British government settled into an established pattern in the 1950s, a further challenge to engaging audiences over the Iron Curtain emerged. From 1950 the BBC's receiving station at Tatsfield, Surrey, started reporting intermittent jamming of BBC and VOA bulletins to Cominform countries.[134] This was a major concern, as Jacob informed the CIPC, because if 'the Russians were likely to extend their jamming to our programmes for the satellite countries. . . . Apart from any questions of expense (which might be got over) it would not be possible to concentrate enough transmitters on the services to all the satellite countries without entirely disrupting our programmes elsewhere.'[135] As it turned out, it was VOA broadcasts that attracted the attention of Soviet jammers from May 1950, but this scare prompted the BBC to prepare contingency measures. Between 21 and 23 July the BBC began to prime audiences in Central and Eastern Europe for the possibility of jamming:

> Listeners may have noticed from time to time sporadic interference to our broadcasts in the form of intentional jamming from stations in the USSR. We want to assure you that if this jamming intensifies to the point at which you are regularly unable to listen at the usual times, we shall make efforts to maintain our service to you by every means at our disposal. To do this will almost certainly mean a change of broadcasting time and of wavelengths and listeners will have to search for the new broadcasting periods.[136]

The threat of interference subsequently hung over the BBC's European operation until Saturday, 1 December 1951 when the Soviet Union introduced systematic jamming of the Polish Service. Over the following six months this was rolled out to cover other services to Central and Eastern Europe. The Finnish Service was jammed from January 1952, followed by broadcasts in Czechoslovakian from February, Hungarian in March, Bulgarian and Rumanian in April, and Albanian in May 1952.[137] BBC and British government fears about jamming had now been realized, resulting in a new phase in Cold War broadcasting and epitomizing the emergence of a 'radio arms race' on either side of the Iron Curtain.

The fear of offending and switching off listeners had guided the mind's eye picture of audience needs until the British Cabinet decision on publicity policy in January 1948. By the early 1950s, the editorial shifts of the previous few years meant that BBC services to Central and Eastern Europe were primarily intended for audiences 'already overwhelmingly hostile to communism',[138] and specifically designed to undermine the Soviet propaganda machine and target Russian oppression in the satellite states. The projection of Britain as a broadcasting creed fell victim to editorial requirements that increasingly devoted the major share of transmission time, beyond the news bulletins, to political comment. The loss of civil liberties, the sovietization of the satellites and Russian exploitation became regular themes in output.[139] And as the Cold War intensified, the BBC's European Services found themselves on the auditory and psychological frontline of the Cold War.

In managing these changes, Jacob relied on three orientating factors to guide his leadership of BBC overseas broadcasting. The ideas and opinions of the people of Britain combined with the advice and guidance offered by the government gave the raw material for the third, the corporate mind of the External Services heavy in experience of broadcasting in war conditions, to assemble an editorial line based on the Corporation's interpretation of the national interest. Meanwhile, the Cold War architecture of audience research – diffuse, discursive, political and speculative – required not just a leap of imagination, but a leap of faith in arriving at editorial conclusions that could only be judged in hindsight. Traditional methods were substituted by a process of intuitive engagement, which combined broadcast professionalism, a negotiated and ongoing dialogue with the FO, and a tacit knowledge of audience tastes and expectation. The advent of jamming, and with it a new radio war, not only underlined the fragility and vulnerability attending the job of broadcasting, but made it a political and cultural emblem of the Cold War contest.

Although there may have been little change in the basic format of transmissions to Central and Eastern Europe from the late 1940s into the 1950s – relatively short broadcast periods with news at the centre supported by press reviews, comment, talks and features – the tone of these programmes radically altered. A means of broadcasting for the Cold War was forged, one that continued to depend on the objectivity of the news output, but which had gained an editorial selectivity used to criticize the oppressive methods of communism and advertise the freedoms of British and Western democracy. What was established in this period was metabolized by the External Services so that the very nature of broadcasting overseas by the BBC was, henceforth, infused with Cold War purpose.

5

The Radio Arms Race

In the United Kingdom, the BBC had been a monopoly broadcaster from the 1920s up to the mid-1950s, responsible to the British people through a Royal Charter and the payment of a Licence Fee. Since December 1932, its overseas operation, first in English only and then in over 40 languages, had to survive in a far more dynamic and competitive environment in which broadcasters, governments and publics, at home and abroad, made a range of political, diplomatic, military and cultural demands of its output. Since the introduction of foreign-language services from 1938, itself a response to the activities of Italian and German broadcasters in North Africa, the Middle East and Europe, the BBC has to varying degrees always been engaged in an international radio war. The apogee of this was reached during the Second World War, when programmes were explicitly committed to the defeat of Germany and the Axis powers. By way of contrast, BBC services in the Cold War, as has been noted, relied on an implicit adherence to the demise of Soviet communism. Broadcasting to Europe and the rest of the world in the late 1940s and 1950s nevertheless continued to be a battle for the hearts and minds of listeners in a world of competing ideological and geopolitical interests. The ability of radio to transcend the internal controls of the state consequently made it a key weapon in a vicarious conflict increasingly being fought on the cultural battlefield. This was reflected in the major scaling-up of overseas output by the Soviet Union and America to a level that by the turn of the decade surpassed the BBC's, until then the world's largest foreign broadcasting operation.[1] It also revealed the emergence of a Cold War radio arms race where competing states expended considerable energy and resources in getting their broadcast messages heard in the face of determined opposition.

Jamming and counter-jamming

From Monday, 25 April 1949, BBC services to Russia were jammed for the first time on all short-wave frequencies.[2] The Corporation's receiving station at Tatsfield initially identified over 60 separate Russian transmitters jamming BBC broadcasts from the United Kingdom in addition to VOA programmes to Russia from New York and Munich, which were also being jammed. This figure soon rose to between 200 and 300 and reports from Moscow and Turkey indicated that 'broadcasts in Russian were completely obliterated'.[3] The BBC had previous experience of being jammed during the Second World War, but it was immediately realized on both sides of the Atlantic that the sophistication, scale and potential longevity of this new attack required a co-ordinated response from Britain and America. This was despite the British Foreign Secretary, Ernest Bevin, just a year earlier arguing against 'any system of collaboration which would commit us to following a common Anglo-American policy in anti-Communist propaganda'.[4] As the Russia Committee noted at the time, following a meeting between Warner and his new opposite number at the US State Department, George Allen, it had been agreed that in British and American foreign publicity 'there would be advantage in aiming at the same targets from somewhat different angles'.[5] However, the imposition of an editorial veto did not preclude technical collaboration or the sharing of resources in pursuit of a common aim and jamming provided just such a focus.

The immediate response by the State Department was to suggest that the BBC and VOA should broadcast continuously for 24 hours a day on two transmitters carrying repeats of their Russian language programmes. The BBC, with a close eye on the expense of these counter-jamming measures, thought differently. Already fighting to stave off cuts in the External Services budget, the Deputy Director of External Services, John Beresford (J.B.) Clark informed Jacob that a cheaper alternative was an 'increase in the frequencies employed for any of the existing UK or USA bulletins'.[6] This was subsequently translated by Jacob for consumption by the Board of Governors: 'Experience has taught us that the only way to defeat jamming is to increase the number of frequencies on our transmissions in the hope that there will not be enough jamming transmitters at work to blot them all out everywhere.' It was also important, Clark thought, 'not to take panic measures without careful thought', as 'any change which did not affect the Jamming and which was, therefore, abandoned would constitute a minor Russian victory'.[7] Accordingly, on 7 May 1949, in addition to the regular half hour BBC broadcasts in Russian at 04.30, 16.45 and 19.45 GMT, two new simultaneous BBC and VOA transmissions were introduced at 03.15 and 14.15 GMT (06.15 and 17.15 Moscow time) for an experimental period of one month.[8] At these times, the maximum number of transmitters were available to the BBC and VOA, with additional stations in Honolulu and Manila used by the United States and Singapore by the BBC. On average, over the first two weeks of this experimental period it was estimated that between 12 and 25 per cent of BBC and VOA broadcasts got through the jamming, between 17 and 32 per cent were partially jammed and between 50 and 60 per cent were completely jammed.[9]

Collaboration was quickly seen to be the key to any possible success in breaching an aerial Iron Curtain. In a telegram from the US Embassy in Moscow to the State Department it was proposed that 'long-range research' into counter measures should be given due priority as 'our relative superiority over Sovs is greater'. In a compelling reference to the most spectacular US/UK joint research project of the Second World War, it also suggested that 'time on our side if best US and Brit brains resources pooled as in development of A-bomb'.[10] The Foreign Office (FO) agreed that particular stress should be laid on planning ahead and close co-operation, though they remained somewhat sceptical of the assertion by their US colleagues that the 'drive for air mastery is a vital part of drive for world mastery'.[11] Nevertheless, in coming to terms and engaging with the Cold War 'radio race' that was emerging, it was important

> to realise that we are up against a determined attempt, planned well in advance and likely, so far as can be foreseen, to continue for years, to stop up a channel through which Western ideas were reaching the Soviet public. Indeed, the jamming is likely not only to continue but, if necessary, to be intensified.[12]

And just as in other vital collaborative spheres of the post-war special relationship between Britain and America, the broadcast effort, if only in terms of resources, would have to be highly integrated.

In the years after the Second World War, the BBC had considered a number of proposals for the use of its transmitters for relaying broadcasts of the VOA.[13] The BBC took the position, albeit contingent on the views of the FO and the rulings of the General Post Office, that although airtime could be provided when the Corporation itself was not broadcasting, no frequencies used by the BBC should be made exclusively available.[14] In addition, the Americans should not be allowed to run, using their own personnel, a radio station in the United Kingdom. It was, nonetheless, suggested at the beginning of 1948 that they might like to use, at their expense, the Woofferton broadcasting station near Ludlow on the Shropshire and Herefordshire border, which had been scheduled for closure in April 1948.[15] Accordingly, on 18 July the first of two regular daily transmissions of VOA were broadcast from Woofferton.[16]

In the time between the invitation to use this transmitter and the offer being taken up, American broadcasts to the Soviet Union were jammed first in the Far East and then from April in Europe. Three months later, jamming of Vatican Radio broadcasts to the Soviet Union also started, as well as of the VOA transmissions relayed by the BBC.[17] The occasional interference of BBC Russian Service programmes led Ernest Bevin in May 1948 to declare that if BBC broadcasts were being jammed 'it would be to their credit'.[18] It was not until nearly a year later, however, that the BBC received the full attention of the Russian jammers. That it happened – a response to the increasing tension between East and West and the desire of the Soviet authorities to eradicate external voices that sought to undermine internal support for the state – was perhaps easier to understand than why, after three years of the BBC broadcasting to the Soviet Union, it had taken so long.

Jacob thought previous reports of interference could be ascribed to the Russians 'preparing an organisation for jamming and . . . trying out parts of it, rather as a battery of artillery registers on the target before opening fire for effect'. He speculated that soon after the BBC started broadcasting in Russian, 'the Soviet authorities must have come to the conclusion that the only hole in the Iron Curtain would become dangerous and must be stopped up', suggesting 'it had probably taken them a year or two to perfect their system and organisation for jamming'.[19] In a cold conflict dependent on vicarious displays of strength, it perhaps took this period of time before a comprehensive jamming campaign against UK and US radio could be mounted. The considerable success of that offensive, regardless of its timing, now required a co-ordinated and well-considered response. This came on 9 July 1949 after further consultation between the State Department, the BBC and the FO. The result was the abandonment of the experimental transmission schedule and the institution, despite the US desire for consecutive broadcasting periods, of three half-hour BBC broadcasts a day to Russia, synchronized with transmissions of VOA at 03.15, 14.15 and 21.15 GMT.[20] In addition, a new scheme was introduced to make it 'more difficult for Russian jamming stations to operate with complete efficiency'. For example, the 21.15 broadcast was carried on 23 transmitters, but from a larger pool of frequencies. Accordingly, the BBC was 'able to vary each time to a small extent the actual frequencies used', which meant any jamming operation had to anticipate that all of the available frequencies would be used, thereby dissipating their grouped coverage of the ones that were in use.[21] Initial reports from Moscow indicated that the new schedule was relatively successful with 95 per cent audibility of BBC broadcasts being claimed soon after the change.[22] Hard evidence was difficult to come by, but reports from cities around the Soviet Union such as Helsinki, Warsaw, Istanbul, Tokyo and Tehran suggested 'that the present large scale effort provides possibilities of listening over large areas of the USSR'.[23] There were, however, other reports in July which pointed towards heavy local jamming of broadcasts in the large centres of population, with reception there increasingly problematic.[24]

In the autumn of 1949, as the BBC was dealing with the consequences of sterling devaluation and facing the prospect of a massive cut in the government's overseas information services budget, the US Congress granted a non-recurrent appropriation of $11,000,000 for use in improving facilities for international broadcasting.[25] This was very nearly the entirety of the External Services budget for 1949/50 and puts into sharp contrast the relative means at the disposal of these two broadcasting operations and their outlook when it came to new collaborative projects.[26] The disparity was reflected in discussions between Jacob and, first, Charles Thayler, and then his successor in the State Department in charge of VOA, Foy David Kohler, which looked at 'the possibilities in various parts of the world for the establishment of new broadcasting facilities' either by the United States alone or jointly with the United Kingdom.[27] The American proposals included improvements to existing facilities, extensions to their short-wave operations, and the erection of two powerful medium-wave transmitters in the Western Pacific and the Middle East to broadcast primarily to the Soviet Union and the countries bordering it as well as to China and Japan. In pursuit of this they asked for assistance and expertise and even suggested that the BBC install and run the Middle East station.[28] Financial constraints alone meant that the Corporation was unable to commit to anything more than assisting with technical surveys, but there were also other concerns with these plans for expansion. It was felt that America should be discouraged from establishing any more broadcasting stations in Europe.[29] In addition, as Jacob pointed out to senior colleagues, the BBC should not

> take part in the erection or operation of broadcasting stations in order to save the Americans the trouble of doing the job themselves. Any new stations that were brought into operation would be carrying American programmes only because we should not have the money to make use of any time on the air which might be available.[30]

Meanwhile, there was no objection to the extension to the type of scheme that had been employed at Woofferton, although there were potential difficulties over origin, ownership and operation of transmitting equipment in these circumstances.[31] Consequently, while a high degree of technical co-operation and sharing of information was maintained between the BBC, the US State Department and VOA, another great collaborative leap forward at that time was to prove too costly for the BBC.

While Britain was examining the parameters of the broadcasting special relationship in 1949, the United States Information Service (USIS) of the State Department was also eager to explore ideas of co-operation with as many partners as it could find. Following the advent of blanket jamming in April it was the view of the American Embassy in Moscow that a counteroffensive should be worked out not just with Britain, but with 'other like-minded countries' as an essential part of any plans.[32] Tapping into the opportunities offered by new post-war international organizations, Jacob was informed in October of their 'idea of approaching the other Atlantic Treaty [NATO] powers with a request that they should help strengthen our Russian broadcasts' either by broadcasting simultaneous Russian programmes of their own or by relaying VOA and BBC programmes. The FO saw no diplomatic objection to this and agreed to joint US/UK approaches to a number of countries as well as the Brussels Treaty Powers.[33] A year later, however, these parallel advances had achieved relatively little, with only Italy responding positively to the suggestions.[34] Indeed, when the question was raised at The Hague and at the Permanent Commission of the Brussels Treaty in London 'considerable resistance was shown on all sides to the idea that countries should relay Voice of America'.[35] While the FO informed the BBC of this reaction, it conveyed to the Americans the more diplomatically framed suggestion that more support might be raised through NATO.[36] This route, though, proved equally unsuccessful as many of those approached declined to assist, either through a lack of broadcasting capability, disinclination to transmit another country's programmes, or fear of inviting the attention of Soviet jammers and the opprobrium of the Soviet Union – a particular concern for Scandinavian broadcasters.

Jamming had certainly quickened the pace of US and UK co-operation in the field of broadcasting but, according to a BBC paper on jamming in May 1951, not quick enough. The Russians had 'kept pace with, and possibly gained on, the combined and extended UK and USA broadcasts to the USSR and satellite countries'. Nevertheless, it was thought that 'on average three or four or sometimes more frequencies are clear of interference out of the fifty or more frequencies' by then being used. As has been seen, the relative success of jamming called into question the value of maintaining BBC broadcasts in Russian. The continuation of these programmes, almost irrespective of whether they could be heard, was a public statement of intent by the BBC and the British government of their ongoing engagement with (and status within) the radio race between the power *blocs* of East and West. It also implied the extent to which, in the face of Soviet jamming, the BBC had established an interdependent relationship with the American government in beaming its services over the Iron Curtain, something that only intensified with the introduction of a more widespread jamming campaign from the end of 1951. This was not, however, the only field in which these transatlantic partners pursued their own rather special relationship.

BBC Monitoring Service

While BBC and American co-operation on counter-jamming measures became an essential ingredient of the wider strategy of broadcasting over the Iron Curtain into the 1950s, such collaboration was not unique. Since the early 1940s a valuable relationship had been established between the United States government and the Corporation for the interception and analysis of broadcasts, transmissions, telephony and telegraphy by foreign countries or organizations. Such work, with its obvious connections to the world of intelligence gathering, does not at first seem to be the most likely task of an organization dedicated to the output of broadcast material and independent, by Charter, from government instruction. The story of the BBC Monitoring Service, however, has from its beginnings mapped a curious path between the duties of public and national service.

Monitoring of English news broadcasts by foreign stations began in the FO during the Italo-Abyssinian war of 1935.[37] By the late summer of 1937 this enterprise was extended to cover Italian broadcasts in Arabic from Bari Broadcasting Station to the Near and Middle East and Sigmar Hillelson, an Arabic scholar from the Sudan Civil Service, was employed to monitor and report on these broadcasts.[38] When transmissions in Arabic by the BBC began a few months later in January 1938, informed by material monitored from both Italy and Germany, Hillelson was relocated within the Corporation's structure, bringing together in a loose arrangement the combined needs of the FO and the BBC.[39] But it was not until over a year and a half later, on the eve of the outbreak of the Second World War, by which time the BBC was broadcasting in the vernacular to the Middle East, Latin America and Europe, that a comprehensive Monitoring Service of a stand-alone and recognizable form was fully established.

In March 1938 the BBC began broadcasting in Spanish and Portuguese to Latin America and staff undertook occasional monitoring of other country's broadcasts in these languages via a line feed from the Tatsfield receiving station through the Control Room at Broadcasting House.[40] Used for internal editorial purposes, the transcripts they produced were also distributed to interested Government departments.[41] This *ad hoc* arrangement regarding monitoring in the BBC's increasing number of language services (broadcasting in French, German and Italian began on 27 September 1938) and the interchange of material between the Corporation and Whitehall characterized the early stages of the monitoring effort. On the eve of war, preparations were made for 'an enlarged scheme of monitoring' on a 24-hour basis outside of London.[42] On Friday, 25 August 1939, the day before a state of emergency was declared in Britain and a week before the declaration of war with Germany, the decision was taken to mobilize and move the BBC's unit to Wood Norton near Evesham in Worcestershire, which the BBC had just acquired as part of its evacuation and dispersal plans in the event of war.[43]

Once at Wood Norton, as Asa Briggs notes, 'the basic principles of professional monitoring' were very quickly established.[44] Composed of three main operational departments – Reception, Information and Editorial – the organization quickly grew in size and stature.[45] The work of the Reception Unit soon became a task of immense proportions and by August 1944 monitors roved across wavebands, 'patrolling the ether' and listening to around 1½ million words a day in 32 languages.[46] The Information Bureau, also working on a 24 hour basis, 'received the monitors' reports and determined the distribution of the material'.[47] In addition to the Corporation's own use, by May 1940 a teleprinter service had been established to the Admiralty, Air Ministry, the War Office, the FO, the MOI, Electra House and the Home Office.[48] The number of government departments directly connected to Wood Norton, in addition to the BBC's Home, Overseas and European News Departments, was to increase further and by the end of the war teleprinter links were also in use to Supreme Headquarters Allied Expeditionary Force (SHAEF), Ministry of Home Security, 10 Downing Street, Political Intelligence Department (Foreign Office), Ministry of Economic Warfare, Federal Communications Department (USA) and the Office of War Information (USA).[49] At its wartime peak in July 1942, 30,000 words in 'flash messages' were being sent daily to government departments.[50] Meanwhile, by April 1940 the Editorial Unit was producing a *Daily Digest of World Broadcasts*, the forerunner of the standard post-war *Summary of World Broadcasts*, of between 100,000 and 150,000 words and a more concise *Daily Monitoring Report* of around 4,000 words.[51] These reports were then distributed to between 600 and 650 departmental and other recipients.[52] The Unit also separately published an *Index to the Daily Digest* and a special 'one-page document . . . prepared daily for the War Cabinet'.[53] From this vast reservoir of information the Editorial Unit also produced 'a daily statement on trends in enemy propaganda'.[54] This analytical capacity was to have continued significance after the war when utilized by the Foreign Office's Russia Committee as the foundation for its 'Trends in Communist Propaganda' publication, which informed the government's anti-communism strategy and was presented on a regular basis to the CIPC.[55] The scale of the task undertaken by the Monitoring Service during the war and the speed with which it functionally and organizationally addressed the technological, editorial and logistical challenges it faced were remarkable.

This explosion in activities led to growing concern that Wood Norton, designated as the BBC's transmission centre in the event of evacuation from London, had become overcommitted, in terms of people and machinery, to the monitoring effort.[56] In April 1943 the Service moved operations to a new site, formerly the old Oratory School, in Caversham in Berkshire, with reception facilities cabled in by land lines from nearby Crowsley.[57] It was from this new home that staff contemplated the task of monitoring after the war. Immediately after the cessation of hostilities in Europe, the Treasury was keen to make reductions in the size and cost of the Monitoring Service which, in common with the BBC's other overseas services, was paid for out of a Grant-in-Aid. This approach fitted with Haley's opinion of February 1945 that 'a smaller and less elaborate organisation' was anticipated.[58] However, and in keeping with the trajectory of post-war planning experienced across the External Services, it soon became apparent, as the Board of Governors noted, that 'After the liberation of a large part of Europe the amount of material to be covered actually increased, owing to the removal of the former central direction of propaganda from Berlin and the consequent diversification of broadcasting in Europe.'[59] By the beginning of 1947, Monitoring output was organized on the basis of extensive summaries arranged in three parts each week with the *Monitoring Report*, including 'all important comments on world affairs and events', still published each week day.[60] Part I, covering Russia and Eastern Europe, came out three times a week while Part II, Germany and Austria, was published once a week as was Part III, covering the remaining countries of the world whose broadcasts were monitored by the BBC.[61] As a result, despite major reductions in staff numbers and a consequent increase in the volume of material to be monitored, the Monitoring Service was maintained as a large-scale operation.[62]

Monitoring Service output continued to be circulated 'throughout the BBC and in various departments of His Majesty's Government', but questions were raised about whether passing these documents 'to foreign Governments, various public bodies, and the Press',[63] as had been done for allied countries during the war, should be stopped. There was particular concern that such a wide distribution would reveal Whitehall's internal thought processes: '. . . it is inevitable that selection of material will be made in light of the special interests of Government departments and it might be embarrassing if these special interests were detected by foreign governments'.[64] This was not entirely the case, however, in regard to the United States monitoring effort, which has maintained an intimate relationship with the BBC Monitoring Service, involving the sharing of open-source intelligence, up to the present day. A week after the Japanese attack on Pearl Harbor, the BBC's Frank Benton, Senior Supervisor of the Information Bureau, had noted in his logbook for 15 December 1941: 'Four Americans, members of the American Monitoring service, are coming to Wood Norton some time this week to start a sort of European outpost for their service. They propose to send home by transatlantic telephone, three times every 24 hours, a précis of material put out by European stations which are normally inaudible in the United States.'[65] Staff of the Federal Communications Commission's Foreign Broadcast Intelligence Service were soon joined by personnel from the US Office of War Information (OWI) and collectively they heralded the start of a still-active co-operative monitoring endeavour between the BBC and the US intelligence services.

American wartime monitoring had been split between the OWI and the Foreign Broadcast Intelligence Service, but at the end of hostilities the monitoring work of OWI was absorbed by the latter.[66] This was not a lasting settlement and the 'functions, equipment and personnel of the monitoring service operated by the Federal Communications Commission were ultimately transferred to a new post-war body, the Central Intelligence Agency'.[67] In this new structure a Foreign Broadcasts Information Service (FBIS) was established to conduct the US monitoring effort within that part of the Central Intelligence Agency (CIA) 'responsible for the collection of material from overt sources',[68] maintaining 'a large editorial staff' at Caversham and supplying 'up to 20,000 words of BBC material by telegraph to Washington every day'.[69]

The sharing of monitored material between the BBC and the United States had been expedited by the needs of war, but in 1947 further steps were taken to enhance this relationship when a reciprocal arrangement was made with the FBIS whereby the Corporation would receive 'a service of about 20,000 words a day from the Far East and Latin America'.[70] At the same time, the British Government gave permission to the Americans for the erection of a monitoring station on the island of Cyprus, then under British administration: 'an unsinkable aircraft carrier' in the eastern Mediterranean, as Richard Aldrich has described it, 'of growing importance to both Britain and the United States'.[71] The increasing interdependency of the UK and US monitoring effort was underlined the following year with the signing in the spring of 1948 of an agreement 'for the dove-tailing of the monitoring operations of the two countries so as to avoid duplication as far as possible, and for the complete pooling of the intercepted material'.[72] The negotiations, led by the Head of FBIS, Colonel Whyte, and the Head of the Monitoring Service, Malcolm Frost, took place during a particularly interesting period of time in the wider story of US-UK post-war co-operation. Just two years earlier British and American intelligence services had divided the world between them in terms of signals intelligence (Sigint). The UKUSA Security Agreement of 5 March 1946 – only recently avowed – linked the British Government's Communication Headquarters (GCHQ) with its American counterparts in a global network of listening stations which forms one of the unseen, yet founding, building blocks of the transatlantic intelligence relationship.[73] The 1948 agreement, formalizing relations between the BBC and the CIA in the field of Communications Intelligence (Comint), considered synonymous with Sigint under the terms of the UKUSA agreement, established the monitoring of foreign broadcast transmissions as well as intercepting telephony and telegraphy as an embedded part of the Cold War special relationship between Britain and America.

By the time of the 1948 agreement the FBIS liaison section at Caversham was well established and formed an analytical and production cell that selected 'from the raw material provided by the BBC monitors items of likely interest to the American Government, which are transmitted by high-speed radio-telegraphy circuits direct to Washington'.[74] The pooling of intercepted material was augmented by the planning of coverage in order to make the best use of resources between the two monitoring organizations.[75] The BBC monitoring station at Caversham focused primarily on European broadcasts, the Moscow domestic service and foreign-language broadcasts from the Russian capital. The FBIS station in Cairo, a UK MOI monitoring operation transferred to the FBIS in 1946, had special responsibility for the Middle East with its output having been 'the major interest of the BBC' beyond the Corporation's own operations. An American monitoring station in California listened to Latin America while one in Maryland near Washington received shortwave transmissions from around the world. There were also stations in Hawaii and Tokyo that tuned into Russian regional stations in the Far East as well as other Far Eastern broadcasters.[76] The output of these US stations fell into three categories. The first were summaries of all transmissions intercepted and these were distributed to American government departments, members of the press in Washington, including radio representatives, and the Library of Congress. The second type of document produced were those classified as 'Restricted' and available to government departments only, such as summaries of transmissions in Morse code or by mechanical systems of transmission, including the world press services. The third, classified as 'Secret' and only available within the US government on a very limited distribution, were 'special reports prepared to the demand of the State Department or US intelligence departments'. Out of these, the BBC received reports from the first two categories as part of its collaborative agreement with the Americans.[77]

The division of responsibilities and flow of monitored information across the Atlantic by direct teletype circuits between FBIS headquarters in Washington and the BBC in Caversham was further enhanced, on the American side, by a considerable investment in capacity. However, the construction of new monitoring facilities at Okinawa, to supersede Hawaii and Tokyo, and in Cyprus, to replace the Cairo station, in addition to the new stations already built in California and Maryland stood in stark contrast with the development of UK monitoring in a period of austerity.[78] The desire to amalgamate on one site the receiving, listening and production parts of the Monitoring Service had been evident even before the move to Caversham and the perennial problems with reception and accommodation that came with it. At the beginning of 1948 Jacob had recommended the purchase of Crowsley Park, the receiving station at that time being leased, in preparation for an eventual move of the whole operation.[79] By the end of the year 'the modernisation of our Monitoring installation' was considered the 'main task' facing the service with Jacob acknowledging that the 'equipment at Caversham Park is obsolete and uneconomical both in quantity and arrangement'.[80] These problems, he thought, 'will be remedied when we concentrate the Service at Crowsley in a new properly designed building with modern equipment'.[81] This view was echoed by Malcolm Frost who suggested that the contrast between the new generation of US monitoring stations and operations at Caversham 'provides much food for thought when planning our new station at Crowsley'.[82] It soon became apparent, in the light of the climate of austerity in Britain and the economic challenges facing the government (not least with the country still reeling from the shock of devaluation the previous year), that any move to Crowsley was unlikely 'in a period of less than three years'.[83] As the fiscal screw was further turned at the end of the decade, with the government taking much tighter control of capital investment programmes such as these, alongside Treasury pressure for cuts in the External Services' budget, plans for Crowsley never got beyond the drawing board and the process of piecemeal modernization at what is still the home to the BBC Monitoring Service at Caversham, began.

The significant investment made by America in its global network of listening stations was a vital part of what J.B. Clark characterized as the 'harmonious interests' of US and BBC monitoring operations. Likewise, the vast experience of BBC monitors, in what was still a relatively young intelligence discipline, had a valuable role to play in guiding and assisting the professional development of their American counterparts. A very special monitoring relationship consequently ran alongside close co-operation in the field of counter-jamming. The value of this to the BBC and, by extension, the British government who paid for both its broadcasting and monitoring activities, was considerable. The global nature and significance of BBC overseas services was both emblematic of Britain's stature and influence on the international stage, and a serious concern for the Exchequer at a time of extreme financial uncertainty. The challenge posed by Soviet jamming, first to Russian broadcasts and then to other services across the Iron Curtain, intensified the dilemma between managing limited resources and projecting the voice of Britain abroad. The opportunity to share some of this burden with America was consequently welcomed, reflecting a complimentary communications strategy, as long as it did not interfere with the editorial independence of either party. In the case of the Monitoring Service this is a continuing co-operative endeavour. That these initiatives were undertaken at all after the Second World War was a response to the ideological, diplomatic, technological and economic demands of a radio arms race which placed the BBC firmly on the frontline of the Cold War.

Part Three

Global Reach

6

A World Service

After the Second World War the BBC was in charge of the largest and most comprehensive international broadcasting station in the world. For the Corporation and the government this was emblematic of Britain's post-war status as a victorious power, as well as indicating the significance of broadcasting in extending the reach of British influence at a time of depleted national resources. Over the next decade the BBC would continue, in English and other languages, to present Britain to the world alongside its core journalistic function of delivering accurate and timely news broadcasts. However, this brief period in which Britannia ruled the airwaves saw international competitors gain on and then pass the BBC in terms of scale. In 1947, the year of the BBC's new Royal Charter, its European Service was broadcasting 272¾ 'programme hours' a week while the Overseas Service transmitted 479½ programme hours.[1] A decade later the respective figures were 245¾ hours in the European Service and 356 hours for the Overseas Service.[2] These totals represented a relative decline in the External Services output while its direct competitors, VOA, Radio Moscow and Soviet satellite stations, passed these levels of output by the start of the 1950s.[3] Nevertheless, the reach and extent of the BBC's overseas services was still hugely impressive, outstripping its domestic operation, and allowing the BBC to speak directly and daily to many millions of people around the world.

Publicly, the aims of BBC overseas broadcasting remained the same regardless of the audience being addressed. As the 1953 *Annual Report and Accounts* put it, programmes were intended 'to form friendly links through information, culture and entertainment; to give news of world-wide importance as it is known in Britain; to show what the British nation as a whole was thinking about the news; and to reflect the British way of life'.[4]

Figure 7 Bush House canteen, November 1960

Resembling a cosmopolitan 'united nations', the Bush House canteen was the venue for cultural, political, intellectual and journalistic engagements of all kinds: perhaps the most important 'office' in the building.

While this was a central tenet of the Corporation's broadcasting brief abroad, it was not evenly applied throughout. There remained a variety of approaches used by the BBC which reflected the political and strategic significance of particular reception territories as well as the cultural expectations and tastes of the audiences addressed.

Broadcasts in English had after the war become the largest single overseas service transmitting virtually around the clock, across multiple time zones and with a range of listener profiles in mind.[5] At its core was the General Overseas Service which most closely resembled BBC domestic broadcasting and which offered 'a comprehensive programme for British listeners in all parts of the world'.[6] Intended to 'reflect every aspect of life in the United Kingdom, and to play its part as a carrier of information to and from the members of the Commonwealth and Empire', it also incorporated programmes for British Forces stationed overseas.[7] Meanwhile, the BBC's North America Service to the United States and Canada relied almost entirely on rebroadcasting by local stations and the BBC Transcription Service (producing hardcopy recording) in order to compete in this highly developed broadcast marketplace. In the United States, rebroadcasting of BBC programmes in December 1955 alone reached approximately 4,200 programme hours, reflecting American interests in, and cultural sympathy with, their cousins across the Atlantic.[8]

With 183 local stations rebroadcasting 1,800 hours of programmes and a further 328 stations transmitting 56,000 hours of transcription material in 1950, the Latin American Service also made good use of these alternatives to direct broadcasting from Britain. However, the cutting of shortwave services in Spanish by half and those in Portuguese by two-thirds in 1952 sparked a severe dwindling of source material and output was 'reduced to a trickle', leaving the projection of Britain in Latin America seriously weakened.[9] In contrast, the importance of Arabic broadcasts, the nucleus of the BBC's Eastern Service (including Persian and Hebrew), was never really under threat from cuts in the government Grant-in-Aid as regional tensions repeatedly underscored its significance. Listeners, according to the BBC's Research Unit, were 'provided with programmes which in their diversity amount to what is in effect a "Home Service"', with 'as much attention devoted to Islamic history and culture as to life in Britain or to world affairs'.[10] Also part of the Eastern Service, programmes for India and Pakistan (English, Hindi, Tamil, Marathi, Bengali, Sinhalese and Urdu) blended a majority English-language listenership with a still considerable vernacular one in the decade after independence and partition.

Responding to the pace and importance of developments in the region, the BBC's Far Eastern Service in English, Cantonese, Kuoyu, Burmese, Malay, Thai, Japanese, Indonesian and Vietnamese had to adapt quickly to major changes, albeit within relatively short broadcast periods (15–30 minutes). Reviewing output in 1949, the BBC's Patrick Ransome wondered whether improvements could be made by engaging more directly with these events:

> I realise, of course, that it would be dangerous to give colour to charges of interference in the purely internal affairs of highly nationalistic states, but the fact remains that our Far Eastern Service itself says nothing to Malaya about her Communist warfare, to Burma about her minority troubles, to Japan about her reparations or to China about her civil war. . . . Is not this pushing caution to the point of evasion?[11]

By degrees, however, this reticence was lessened and with a new high-powered transmitter at Tebrau in Singapore coming on-line in May 1951, the BBC spoke with a renewed confidence about the conflict in Korea, the rise of Maoist China and on other regional challenges in Indochina, Malaya and Formosa (Taiwan).

The predominantly English voice of the BBC's Colonial Service (Hausa was introduced in 1957) complemented the General Overseas Service by providing programmes of special interest to West Africa and the West Indies, East Africa, the Falklands and Malta by direct broadcasting and rebroadcasting through local services. Throughout, associations with the United Kingdom were reinforced in, for example, cultural, educational and sports programming as part of a shared commonwealth of interests at a time when the prospect of independence was beginning to be made real in countries such as Sudan and Ghana (Gold Coast). In line with this development the Colonial Service also had a very important part to play in advising on the development of indigenous broadcasting services. By 1957, and in close co-operation with the Colonial Office, the BBC had supplied on secondment 45 members of staff to manage and oversee programme, engineering and administrative arrangements[12] in, for example, Nigeria, Sudan, Uganda, Gold Coast, British Honduras, Sarawak and Kenya. This rather considerable drain on BBC resources was, by the middle of the 1950s, something of a problem requiring the Corporation to establish a training programme for the Colonies which brought together students from the West Indies and Africa. As a consequence, the imprint of BBC public service principles and practice was left on broadcasting organizations in many of these newly independent countries over the course of the next generation.

Colonial broadcasting also gained an added significance in the context of the Cold War where the idea of 'colonialism' was used as a persistent and potent criticism of Britain by the Soviet Union. Responding to Moscow's charges that 'the social foundations of African colonies were rotten', in March 1950 the BBC commissioned Martin Esslin and Walter Kolarz of the European Services to travel to West Africa, Tanganyika and Northern Rhodesia to collect material for a series of 15 talks and five features that would refute these allegations and reveal the reality of colonial administration.[13] This was followed, as the colonial Cold War gathered pace, by four talks dealing with 'the strategy and tactics of the Communists in the Colonial Field' and a series of around twenty talks for mainly non-European services titled 'This is Communism'.[14] A renewed appetite to refute Soviet allegations subsequently found expression in early 1951 when J. Sherwood and Anatol Goldberg were sent to cover the creation of the Colombo Plan for Cooperative Economic Development in South and Southeast Asia.[15] Reporting from Ceylon, Malaya, Burma, India and Pakistan, their programmes were explicitly intended to counter Soviet propaganda to Europe about conditions in the region.[16] Meanwhile, the 'positive achievements and purposes of the British Commonwealth and Empire' were regularly juxtaposed with 'the Russian record of dealings with subject peoples' in Central and Eastern Europe.[17] And it was in the context of the European radio race that the BBC had, by this time, been conducting a rather curious broadcast experiment.

Western Union broadcasting

When presenting his argument to the Cabinet for an anti-communist publicity policy at the start of 1948, Ernest Bevin had expressed his belief that it was up to Britain 'to give the lead in spiritual, moral and political spheres to all the democratic elements in Western Europe'.[18] 'In short', he told ministers, 'we should seek to make London the Mecca for Social Democrats in Europe' as part of a wider conception of a Western European 'Third Force' to act as a global balance between the laissez-faire capitalism of America and the expansionist communism of the Soviet Union.[19] In March 1948 Christopher Warner enquired of Jacob how the BBC was 'reflecting in their overseas broadcasts the changed international situation resulting from the recent events on both sides of the Iron Curtain'.[20] In terms of European recovery Jacob noted that 'until fairly recently the work of the European Service was hampered because the facts of the situation in this country and in Western Europe could barely support the theory that Western democracy was capable of standing on its own legs and fighting for something positive'.[21] However, since the announcement of Marshall Aid and the setting up of the Organisation for European Economic Cooperation (OEEC) to oversee its distribution, the failure of the Foreign Ministers Conference in November 1947 and the 'call to action' in Western Europe made by Bevin, Jacob felt that 'the momentum of events has steadily increased, and we now have a tremendous story to tell'.[22] But to what extent would the BBC allow itself to deliver this, essentially political, narrative? This was a question Jacob put before the Board of Management in April when he asked 'what part broadcasting should play in furthering the general aims of Western European recovery'.[23] Was it really the job of the BBC, he wondered, to 'offer the same leadership in the field of radio that the country as a whole has offered in the field of economic cooperation'?[24] Two days after the creation of a Western European Union with the signing, on 17 April 1948, of the Treaty of Brussels by Britain, France, Holland, Belgium and Luxembourg, Jacob got his answer. With the 'unity of Western Europe being of paramount importance', the Board was in 'general agreement that the BBC had a duty to take the initiative'.[25]

Already by the beginning of March the Dutch had proposed co-operative broadcasts among Britain and the Benelux countries, suggesting simultaneous broadcasts of music, short talks by a British speaker to be transmitted on the Dutch domestic KRO network and a feature programme describing the progress of European recovery.[26] These ideas chimed not only with the development of plans within the BBC but also, it appeared, with the wishes of listeners across Europe. As Lean told Jacob, there was a new demand for a Western Union Programme which was supported by a great deal of correspondence from the European audience.[27] Following the consideration of proposals by Lean and the Head of European Productions, Camacho,[28] the Board of Management established a Committee on Cooperative European Programme[29] – otherwise known as the Western Union Committee – to examine co-operation between the broadcasting organizations of Western Europe in order to 'put programmes on the air designed to support the common purpose, economic, political and cultural, of Western Europe'.[30]

Before final proposals could be made about content, however, it was necessary to deal with a number of other considerations. For example, which countries in Western Europe should be included, or would wish to be included, in such a scheme? The first meeting of the government's Working Party on Spiritual Aspects of Western Union in February had concluded that 'the 16 ERP countries should be taken as a starting point'.[31] This view was generally accepted at the BBC, but a series of obstacles soon emerged to cast doubt on the practical viability of such an approach. Such integrated planning required both a relatively high level of expertise on the part of the broadcasting organizations involved as well as a formalization of relations between them. Both of these conditions, however, militated against a scheme involving all sixteen of the Marshall Aid countries. Despite the desire of the Board of Management to get 'the broadcasting organisations of the sixteen countries adhering to the Marshall plan to co-operate', it was argued by Lean and colleagues on the Western Union Committee, and accepted by the Board,[32] that 'for reasons of manageability' a conference should be called of the Western Union countries (incorporating Britain, France, Belgium, Holland and Luxembourg) while 'keeping the ground clear from the start for expansion at a later stage'.[33] Christopher Mayhew at the Foreign Office (FO) was of a similar view and informed the Working Party on Spiritual Aspects of Western Union that 'making a start with the Five Powers would not prejudice any eventual extension of co-operation to the whole sixteen'.[34]

In addition to who should participate, there were other issues that needed to be resolved, not the least of which was who the audience for these co-operative programmes was intended to be. Lean had been keen to stimulate 'the idea of Europe as a good investment' in the Western Hemisphere while in Eastern Europe 'one would hope for a sense of envy, admiration and something more disturbing than respect'.[35] This wider analysis was also reflected in a Cabinet paper by Clement Attlee on European Recovery Programme Information Policy. Here he identified five principal audiences for 'publicity from British sources about the European Recovery Programme . . . the publics at home, in North and South America, in Western Europe, the Dominions, and the Colonies'.[36] In relation to the United States, he felt there was 'a specific obligation to give publicity to the benefits received under the European Recovery Programme', especially as examples of the use being made of US aid 'will be listened for in America'.[37]

Decisions were also required on two essentially constitutional matters before the idea of Western Union broadcasting could be taken any further. Co-operative European programming challenged the concept of national sovereignty by diluting control within a multi-national framework. It was decided, however, at a meeting of senior programme staff that 'on a voluntary basis and by mutual agreement' the preparation of scripts for co-operative transmissions should allow a loosening of the Corporation's national jurisdiction.[38] Henceforth, the voice of Britain would, at certain times, be required to transform itself into the voice of Western Europe.

The second matter related to the quality of output and the policy governing the acceptability of shared programming. There had been little history of programme exchanges between the BBC and other broadcasters in Europe other than the supply of programmes for relay which was characterized by an overwhelming net export for the Corporation. For example, in 1947 the number of outgoing relays had been 442 while those being taken by the BBC was only 112,[39] the majority of which were made up of news despatches and correspondent's reports.[40] The 1946 White Paper on Broadcasting Policy had 'expressed the desire that the Corporation should accept suitable foreign programmes for rediffusion in this country'.[41] Until 1948 this sentiment remained an intention, as yet unfulfilled. Not only did the BBC feel the need to respond to the political desire for collaboration with Britain's nearest neighbours, but co-operative endeavours of this nature, as Mayhew reminded members of the Spiritual Union committee, were now backed by international agreement as Article III of the Brussels Treaty demonstrated: 'The High Contracting Parties will make every effort in common to lead their peoples towards a better understanding of the principles which form the basis of their common civilisation and to promote cultural exchanges by conventions between themselves or by other means.'[42] Broadcasting, and the BBC in particular, was ideally placed to undertake such a task and the committee discussed radio 'as a medium in which 5-Power cooperation was both "possible and desirable"'.[43]

Programme quality had been the defining criterion of the BBC's broadcast output, but Jacob now posed the question of whether 'what might be called diplomatic instead of merely programme consideration would be given to all offers of programmes for relay'.[44] As such, 'each case would be assessed in relation to its effect upon the total responsibilities of the BBC'.[45] Jacob acknowledged the concern that 'the effect would be to debase programme standards by introducing political considerations', but in what was a surprisingly frank assessment of the relationship between the Corporation and the government, he argued that 'this is in fact a process that goes on all the time, since the BBC is an instrument of national policy and not merely a programme making body'.[46] The BBC Board of Management agreed that 'the process is justified by the belief in the intrinsic value of programme exchanges'.[47] Accordingly, the exchange of programmes between the broadcasting organizations of Britain, France, Holland, Belgium and Luxembourg was embedded into the wider conception of Western Union broadcasting.[48] What, though, was to be the detail of the co-operative venture? The Western Union Committee suggested two types of transmission and at the end of May the Board decided that the co-operation of the Western Union countries should be sought for the planning of a single pooled 'symbolic' programme to be broadcast by all the participating organizations (and, where possible, simultaneously).[49] A further step would be to add a 'mutual aid' programme which would encourage co-operation 'in obtaining and distributing basic material' with which the different broadcasters could 'independently edit and produce separate versions which they commit themselves to broadcast at significant times'.[50] Consequently, on 1 July 1948 representatives of the five Western Union broadcasting organizations arrived at Broadcasting House for a two-day conference 'to discuss the possibility of arranging in cooperation with one another programmes whose object would be to underline the community of interest and the importance of cooperation between their countries, and to bring about increased understanding between their peoples'.[51]

Indicative of the way this initiative cut across the boundaries between home and overseas broadcasting, the BBC Director of the Spoken Word, George Barnes, chaired this first conference. And it was here that the Board of Management's proposals received approval. As a result, agreement was reached by all broadcasters that each country would arrange, in turn, a talk by a non-official speaker on a subject of topical interest for ten minutes over a ten week period in a series entitled 'Western European Commentary'.[52] These commentaries would then be broadcast in all countries during the same week either in the language of origin or in translation (or a combination of both). Participating countries would also broadcast, in their own language, a discussion between speakers from the five countries on 'The Future of Germany'. In addition, a 'European Concert' (a symphony) would be broadcast by one country at a time and relayed at the same time by the others. It was further agreed that 'any music programme in which the five countries could take part simultaneously was likely to contribute towards a feeling of community' and should be arranged.[53]

A great deal of effort was invested in this project along with an unprecedented level of planned co-operation between European broadcasters. Driven by an enthusiasm for telling the story of Western European unity, it quickly transpired this was a story very few people actually wanted to hear. Preparing for the fifth Western Union Broadcasting Conference in May 1950, George Barnes informed his colleagues that 'cooperative broadcasts have not succeeded' and that the BBC should 'make the others face the fact'.[54] Consequently, it was decided among the broadcasters that 'Definite programme commitments of any kind should not be undertaken but that there was a general obligation to interest our listeners in the life and activities of the other countries both individually and collectively considered as parts of Western Union.'[55] This was a far cry from the rhetoric of spiritual union used a couple of years earlier with, in the intervening period, further examples of practical union in Western Europe with the establishment of the Council of Europe and the signing of the North Atlantic Treaty. So what had happened in the meantime?

The real problem lay with the simple proposition that people in one country would have a genuine and continuing peacetime interest in the domestic activities of their near neighbours. The question of whether there was a sufficient appetite among the audiences for this kind of programming had always come second to the political taste for Western Union. Accordingly, the way Barnes assessed the first six months of the project prior to a third conference was a rather curious balance of principle exceeding reality. European co-operation, he explained, 'is now a fact in defence and in trade, and a closer and wider union, even a political one, is being discussed. Thus the broadcast project is now part of a whole.'[56] But, he continued, for the British listener the programmes had been 'a complete failure'.[57] The reason for this was twofold: 'The programmes have hitherto had little unity to reflect, and have had to communicate an idea much more unfamiliar to the British than to the Europeans'; 'Broadcast programmes are successful only when they are addressed to a particular audience and it is very difficult to address five national audiences simultaneously.'[58] And yet he thought that 'the need to continue what we have begun seems to me axiomatic', as it did to the rest of the Board of Management.[59] Among their international colleagues Belgium and Holland were keen to continue as was Luxembourg, as long as the project did not conflict with its saleable air time. Radiodiffusion

Française, though, was of the opinion that bilateral as opposed to multilateral exchanges would be more profitable.[60] By the time of the next conference in Luxembourg in October 1949, plans for expansion evaporated in the light of unfulfilled expectations. The Western European Commentaries 'were agreed without any dissenting opinion to have been a failure' and were dropped.[61] And although co-operative plans for music programmes (classical, light and folk) remained active, imaginative responses to the problems raised by collaborative broadcasting failed to materialize.[62]

By 1950, by which time the European Broadcasting Union (EBU) was established and fulfilling the requirement of a technical centre for Western Europe, the Western Union broadcasting effort was effectively in a state of care and maintenance. The tempo of co-operation had reduced significantly and the BBC now proposed revised terms for working together in which 'we will each in our own way with our own resources, in the light of our own knowledge of our listeners' tastes and as often as we judge to be useful, put on programmes whose object will be to strengthen the links between the five countries'.[63] Within the space of two years, multilateral collaborative action in support of European unity had given way to unilateral determinism.

The British government's focus on a Western European Union was naturally political and strategic in its intent. The BBC's response to this foreign policy initiative had been swift and practical. While changes in its broadcasts to Eastern Europe as a result of the Cabinet's anti-communist publicity policy took time and required a great deal of negotiation between Whitehall and the BBC, broadcasting initiatives in relation to Western Europe were much more forthcoming and appeared, at first sight, simpler to design. It was the reorganized services to Central and Eastern Europe, however, which endured in a more complete form than the experiment of Western Union broadcasting. It was, nonetheless, an important enterprise that engendered a sense of closer co-operation between broadcasters and an understanding of each other's needs and abilities that would assist in future co-operative programme initiatives. For example, the EBU's greatest popular achievement, the Eurovision Song Contest, which began just a few years later in 1956, would have been unimaginable without the experience of Western Union broadcasting in terms of its technical requirements, the focus on simultaneously broadcast music and its symbolic and political ethic. Ernest Bevin could not have imagined this as a lasting legacy of his combined drive for a strategic Third Force and emphasis on anti-communist publicity, but its lineage is as undeniable as it is surprising.

7

Austerity

Changes in the tone of broadcasts over the Iron Curtain were defining characteristics of the External Services' output into the 1950s, as the imperatives of the Cold War were knitted into its remit. Meanwhile, the fiscal relationship between the BBC and the government was the cause of constant instability and uncertainty. From the enshrining of peacetime Grant-in-Aid funding for the BBC's overseas transmissions in 1947 to the renewal of this arrangement under a new Charter five years later, the amount of money provided by government and the means by which it was calculated were subject to the vicissitudes of the political and economic climate of the time. The cost of domestic policy initiatives such as welfare reform and nationalization, the increasingly complex pressures arising from Imperial, Commonwealth and European responsibilities, the slow recovery from war and the effort of reconstruction both at home and overseas resulted in economic crises that stretched the nation's financial resources to breaking point. Added to these were the almost crippling costs of the escalating conflict between East and West (and the re-emphasis on defence spending) in which Britain attempted to maintain its position as one of the Great Powers. It was among this mêlée of competing financial priorities that the External Services sought its slice of the Exchequer's cake.[1]

At a meeting on 12 March 1947 attended by the Treasury, the Foreign Office, Dominions Office, Colonial Office, General Post Office, the Service Departments and the BBC, a reduction of £100,000 in the External Services budget was agreed on the basis of proposals submitted by the Deputy Director of Overseas Services, J. B. Clark.[2] This was the first step in a process of negotiation and renegotiation concerning the Grant-in-Aid over the next few years that pushed the External Services to the limit of their operational capacity and engendered an acute disagreement between the Corporation and the Treasury over the value to be placed on overseas broadcasting. By the end of 1947, BBC spending plans were again revised to accommodate a government request for a ten per cent cut in the overseas budget.[3] As a consequence, from 1 April 1948 overseas services were forced to make major reductions in output.[4] Although lunch-time broadcasts to Europe were saved, a revised External Services budget for 1948/49 of £4,025,000 saw daily programme hours for non-European Services cut by 20 per cent with a 25 per cent reduction in overall transmitter hours.[5] The section which bore the brunt of this and future reductions was the Latin American Service, where daytime broadcasts were abandoned. Other government reductions had already led the British Information Services and the British Council to close down in four Central American countries, the Dominican Republic and Paraguay. The result was a major loss of influence for Britain in the region, with BBC bulletins unavailable as 'an important source of news guidance for the afternoon Press in Latin America', and with 'no one to look after the distribution of transcription material and the *Voz de Londres* in these countries'.[6]

In the summer of 1948, just as the European Services were working towards an accommodation with the Foreign Office (FO) as to the tone of Britain's voice abroad, there was increasing pressure within the Cabinet to examine the cost of the government's overseas information services, of which the External Services were a key part. Still reeling after the end of Lend-Lease three years earlier, and having spent the majority of the $3.7 billion American loan negotiated by John Maynard Keynes by the summer of 1946, the implementation of sterling convertibility in July 1947 (a condition of the Bretton Woods conference of July 1944 which led to the establishment of the International Monetary Fund a year and a half later) had induced an economic crisis in which a dollar drain of $650 million was lost before convertibility was suspended the following month.[7] Over the next three years Britain received $2.7 billion of Marshall Aid but the government's relative inability to exercise control over its macro-economic environment compounded the problems it had in meeting the needs of its micro-economic responsibilities.[8] This meant that by the time of the Berlin blockade in June 1948 the government was increasingly willing to re-examine its spending plans and realize savings. For its information services, this was to result in harsh budget cuts.

A Cabinet memorandum by the Chancellor of the Exchequer, Stafford Cripps, put the cost of overseas information services in the summer of 1948 at £11,621,700, over a third of which went to the External Services via Grant-in-Aid.[9] When added to the £5 million spent at home, he argued that 'the total expenditure on these services had now reached a level which exposed the Government to risk of public criticism'.[10] By the time this submission was considered by ministers at the end of October, much had been done by overseas Whitehall departments to orchestrate their response to Cripps. In July the committee of senior ministers on Anti-Communist Propaganda had decided to set up a small body consisting of the Parliamentary Under-Secretaries at the Foreign Office, Commonwealth Relations Office and Colonial Office, at the latter's suggestion, to 'co-ordinate the collection and presentation of publicity material regarding British Colonial policy and administration'.[11] It was intended that it would present Britain's activities in this field as progressive and constructive while, in a more destructive vein, 'give the world a true picture of Russia's conduct in Eastern Europe and its own territories'.[12] This was the beginning of the Colonial Information Policy Committee (CIPC) and added to its permanent membership were the head of the COI, Robert Fraser, and Ian Jacob from the BBC. Consequently, by the time ministers discussed Cripp's challenge to the overseas information services budget in October, CIPC was beginning to play a key part in prosecuting the government's campaign against communism and would provide a galvanizing forum in which to mount a counter-attack against Treasury plans.

On 22 September, Bevin wrote to the Secretary of State for Commonwealth Relations, Philip Noel-Baker, requesting that CIPC 'consider whether the work of our Information Services in and about the Colonies and in the Dominions, especially India, Pakistan and Ceylon, should not also be much expanded. The Under Secretaries would then draw up a three-year budget of expenditure on overseas publicity.'[13] This move coincided with a subsequent development whereby the activities of CIPC were widened to cover 'the whole field of overseas propaganda, with the object of repelling Communist campaigns by both positive and destructive counter-propaganda'.[14] Mindful of being outmanoeuvred in this deliberate attempt by overseas departments to seize the initiative for setting the information services budget away from the Exchequer, Cripps appointed to the committee, with Cabinet approval, the Financial Secretary to the Treasury.[15] When the Cabinet came to consider the Chancellor's memorandum on 25 October, ministers were also informed of the Foreign Secretary's view that far from being cut back, the work done by the overseas information services should be enhanced.[16] This, however, was a difficult argument to make in light of the fiscal pressures on the Treasury and a final decision was put in abeyance. Nonetheless, by the end of the year overseas departments had control of an increasingly important part of the government's anti-communist machine and, in the shape of CIPC, a vehicle from which a defence of the information services could be mounted.

A consequence of the widening remit of CIPC was the removal of Jacob and Fraser from its permanent list of members. Jacob, though, remained in close contact with the work of the committee and still received its papers (except for those put in a confidential annex) and continued to attend meetings at which matters affecting the BBC were discussed.[17] As such, he was an influential occasional member of the committee. Meanwhile, as forecasts were made about the future of the government's information services in Whitehall, more immediate concerns were raised at Bush House when at the start of 1949 the Treasury asked the External Services to accept a further cut of £280,000 for the coming financial year, later reduced to £250,000.[18] Although this was achieved by deferring capital projects amounting to £200,000 and by making further 'unspecified savings',[19] Jacob made it clear to the BBC Governors that 'we shall be hard put to make two ends meet and any new developments will certainly have to be financed by reductions elsewhere'.[20] The finances of the External Services had reached a precarious balance and although a great deal of effort had been put in to carry out organizational and administrative efficiencies, any slack there may have been was fast disappearing. A ten per cent cut the previous year followed by a further reduction on that figure of around seven per cent left almost no room for manoeuvre.[21]

The devaluation of sterling in September 1949 from $4.03 to $2.80 proved to be an additional headache for the External Services with a special BBC Board of Management meeting required to approve 'proposals which would at the least keep the expenditure in foreign currencies to the present authorised sterling totals and, wherever possible, reduce them below these totals'.[22] The result was a £12,000 cut in programme allowances and the need for savings of £42,000, out of a total spend of £94,000, on offices in New York, Colombia, Mexico City, Brazil and Argentina.[23] Following discussions with the FO, who considered the already badly hit BBC services to Latin America 'as the principal agent of Britain in the information field there', it was decided that the 'surfeit of radio, press and magazine fare which surrounds the people of the United States, the great distances, the immense population, and the absence of any centralized broadcasting system into which we might gain entry, make it a somewhat unprofitable field for work'. Accordingly, a 50 per cent reduction in expenditure on the New York office was made by cutting staff from 29 to 14 and putting an end to 'specialised projects in the North American Service'.[24]

The competing visions of the residents of King Charles Street (the road dividing the Treasury and the Foreign Office) on the future of the overseas information services resulted in a state of relative inertia as the strategy governing funding requirements remained unresolved while the annual bunfight for resources continued. In preparation for the 1950/51 financial year the BBC argued that the External Services would need an increase in its Grant-in-Aid of between £200,000 and £300,000 on the previous year.[25] This was reflected in an overseas information services budget estimate for that year of £11 million proposed as part of CIPC 'Three Year Plan'. However, this found itself at odds with a new financial ceiling of £9.5 million for all services put forward by the Chancellor.[26] Attending the CIPC in November 1949 Jacob explained that a reduction in line with the Treasury's figure would mean cuts in programme quality, time on the air, and the cancellation of complete services, 'for instance, the whole of the dawn transmissions for Europe' which was 'our only way of reaching the skilled workmen class in a number of countries. . . . These would be serious disadvantages to set off against the financial savings that would be made.'[27] To underline his point and with the next year's budget pending a decision, Jacob ordered a standstill on the construction of a major transmitter station being built in Singapore. This was a long-term and important capital project for both the government and the BBC and one CIPC had considered as 'axiomatic that the BBC should proceed with'.[28] It was hoped a meeting of the Committee on Anti-Communist Propaganda on 19 December would bring matters to a head when it considered CIPC's three-year plan for overseas publicity.[29] In addition to the Prime Minister, the Foreign Secretary and the Chancellor, attending the meeting were Albert Victor 'A.V.' Alexander (Minister of Defence), James Chuter Ede (Home Secretary), Arthur Creech Jones (Secretary of State for the Colonies) and Philip Noel-Baker (Secretary of State for Commonwealth Relations). Following Jacob's lead, CIPC's paper took the line that 'a broadcasting service is not something that can be turned on and off like a tap, since its audience and its reputation can only be built up slowly and laboriously'. Moreover, radio 'is our only means of injecting anti-Communist publicity into the "iron-curtain" countries' and that 'any reduction in the output of the BBC's foreign language services at this juncture would be a false economy and would result in a loss of British influence which would take many years to recover'.[30]

Although compelling for those engaged in the making foreign policy, the External Services' case was not received with similar enthusiasm by ministers with a domestic portfolio. Cripps, for example, was possessed of a far more protean view of the aims and means of broadcasting to other countries. In the present context he viewed 'the Overseas Information Services . . . as an aspect of defence', and as defence spending at that time was also being reduced (before the flames of war flickered on the Korean Peninsula) so must that of these services. It was far better, he thought, 'that we should concentrate largely on the anti-Communist side of overseas publicity and should consider abandoning certain spheres of operation altogether, e.g. Latin America'. Similarly, Attlee felt 'that we should concentrate on the most dangerous areas. Could we not consider abandoning Information Services altogether in such parts of the world as Scandinavia?'[31] This segregation in policy terms between anti-communist objectives and the rest of the world had clear implications for foreign language broadcasting (as opposed to English output and its associations with empire and commonwealth) and would prove to be the crux of the Grant-in-Aid funding issue for the following decade.

By the end of the meeting a compromise was reached whereby expenditure on the Overseas Information Services would be restricted 'to as low a figure as possible between £10 and £11 millions'.[32] Nevertheless, it did illuminate a clear divide between home and overseas departments in which the final arbitrating voice, that of the Prime Minister, was in sympathy with the views of the former. However, a period of extra time had been given to this debate and the scene was now set for some very hard bargaining over the next year and a half. In the meantime, as an overall budget decision hung in the balance, operating estimates had to be set for 1950/51. In this the External Services, perhaps as a result of Jacob's special pleading, received a net increase of £195,000 (unlike other elements of the government's information machinery) which went some way to maintaining the status quo at Bush House. The future, though, remained uncertain with next to no reserve funds, rising annual costs, the expense of countering Soviet jamming and ageing technical stock. As Jacob informed the BBC Governors in the spring of 1950:

> As it seems unlikely that we shall be given any more money in the future than we have now, some axeing of the less essential Services to make room for necessary improvements seems unavoidable.[33]

The failure of CIPC's three-year plan to be formally accepted as a basis for future planning was a significant but unsurprising blow to the BBC as was the *de facto* acceptance of an annual budgetary ceiling for all overseas information services as the practical method of establishing expenditure. For 1950/51 this was initially set at £10.82 million with a subsequent agreement to keep costs down to £10.5 million.[34]

The External Services had so far avoided the severest cuts which had been borne, for example, by the British Council and the Foreign Office Information

Services. But as an estimate between £5.2 and £5.3 million for 1951/52 was prepared by Bush House it was clear that BBC services would face major reductions unless there was a fundamental rethink in Whitehall of the whole basis of government accounting for the overseas information services.[35] It was with this threat in mind that Jacob, along with the FO and others, set about challenging the prevailing budgetary mindset.[36] At a meeting of CIPC on 20 June 1950, Jacob launched the fight back against year-on-year cuts by suggesting a new line of argument which put the case for expansion rather than trying to hold back the tide of cuts. As he told his CIPC colleagues, 'the £10.5 millions provided for overseas information work was insignificant compared with the £700 millions for defence; the Information services could do much towards winning the Cold War, but if that was lost all the money spent on defence would have been wasted'.[37] In this way, Jacob sought to change the terms of the debate over the cost of overseas publicity and in doing so take the initiative away from the Treasury.

Jacob's thoughts were fed through to the Working Party of CIPC where they were co-ordinated with the needs of the other information services. In this forum Jacob and the Chair of the Working Party, the Head of IRD Ralph Murray, worked together on a paper that focused on getting the principle of an overall ceiling removed. This they did by arguing that rising costs produced not stabilization but progressive run-down, and that extra finance, not less, was needed as 'a means of political warfare to strengthen the forces of democracy wherever they are most threatened'. The Korean War had 'quickened the tempo of the struggle against the Kremlin and increased the importance of the role of overt as well as covert information work'.[38] 'The prime need', Jacob argued, 'was to persuade Senior Ministers to adopt an entirely new attitude towards the overseas Information Services and to agree that a considerable increase of effort was necessary'. Money spent on information services should be regarded as a 'form of insurance' against greater expenditure if they did not play their part in the struggle between East and West:

> The Information side of the "Cold War" . . . might be likened to a campaign which we must fight as efficiently as possible; and, as in a military campaign, it was necessary for us to have the funds readily available, so as to seize each opportunity as it presented itself, without being subject to long delays required to obtain Treasury approval for each item.[39]

Consequently, the three overseas ministers approved the recommendations that a reserve fund should be established to allow for contingencies and that ceilings on expenditure should be removed 'and a return to the more normal practice whereby the estimates are worked out in conjunction with the Treasury on the basis of the requirements which the Committee consider necessary'.[40] With strong opposition to these measures from the Treasury, Attlee called a meeting between the Exchequer and overseas ministries in an attempt to once again resolve the matter.

Just a month after succeeding Cripps as Chancellor, Hugh Gaitskell informed fellow ministers on 14 November 1950 that he was 'contemplating a decrease which might amount to about £2 million',[41] on the basis that while there 'was value in some aspects of propaganda, particularly in the front line of the anti-communist campaign' he felt that the government 'could afford no "frills" at the present time'.[42] Such frills included, for example, services to Latin America. It was also suggested by the Treasury that the BBC External Services budget for 1951/52 should be reduced to £3,750,000, £1.55 million short of the BBC estimate.[43] The Chancellor was 'not convinced', when the matter was referred to the Ministerial Committee on Information Services (ISC) in February 1951, the External Services 'have been reorganised on to a new basis appropriate to even the present' while overseas ministers noted that when it came to costs, 'the floor rose while the ceiling came down'.[44] The British Chiefs of Staff had already been drafted in to support the case for overseas broadcasting, concluding that 'it was most important to maintain to the fullest possible extent the Overseas Services of the BBC on account of their value in the prosecution of the Cold War'.[45] Following up this military analysis the Minister of Defence informed ISC members that 'the Chiefs of Staff have once more drawn my attention to the damaging effects of a change of policy' that 'could not fail to cripple the BBC's efficiency as a Cold War instrument'.[46] Needless to say the BBC had been at pains to canvas opinion at the War Office in advance of this meeting and had arranged an informal briefing at Langham House to highlight the type of cuts the Corporation might be forced to make.[47]

Critical to the BBC's case, and that of the overseas information services, was an appeal to view their influence, and consequently their value, as to some extent dependent on their global reach. Their credibility was enhanced as much by engaging with publics overseas as a cohesive force as it was by exploding the myths of Soviet communism. Sympathetic cultural ties, alongside more aggressive tactics, could deliver significant dividends as part of a defence spending strategy as well as giving the British government direct access to a genuinely worldwide audience. This type of effort and the influence derived from it took time to establish and once dismantled, could not easily be rebuilt. It was on this basis that they hoped to respond to Cripp's earlier linking of a reduction in defence spending with one applied to the information services. However, in a reversal of misfortune the sheer scale of expenditure on the Korean War and the rearmament programme this galvanized meant that reductions in the budgets of other departments and dependent organizations were inevitable. In a report for the Board of Governors, Jacob seemed taken aback by what was happening:

> It seems hardly possible that His Majesty's Government would proceed in this drastic fashion at a time like the present, particularly as any Services now abolished would have to be started up again if there were a war, and in the meanwhile we should have lost the frequencies, the staff and the audience.[48]

Continuing negotiations in search of a budgetary settlement before the start of the 1951/52 financial year saw the Treasury offer an overall spend of £9.8 million (£4.4 million for the BBC)[49] while the overseas departments countered with a figure of £10.8 million, the amount originally agreed for the previous year.[50] By the time of the decisive Cabinet meeting on 2 April 1951 Gaitskell had adjusted his offer to £10.15 million, with £4,750,000 authorized for the External Services, leaving the overseas ministers to argue that counter-jamming measures and planned improvements in services to Far Eastern and Arabic audiences along with European services would be badly affected.[51] For his part, the Chancellor believed 'some overseas services could be reduced or even abolished without serious loss to the national interest'.[52] In truth, the die had been cast even before Ministers met. On 9 March 1951, Ernest Bevin, whose health had been failing fast and whose once formidable presence in the Cabinet was in decline, was made Lord Privy Seal. Although he was given responsibility for questions concerning broadcasting policy, real influence for overseas operations passed to his successor as Foreign Secretary, the former Lord President, Herbert Morrison. Morrison took a different approach to the financing of the information services and had a year earlier 'indicated to the Prime Minister his view that, on the merits of the case, the Chancellor of the Exchequer was right'.[53] When the problem was brought before the Information Services Committee, which Morrison chaired, he was left unconvinced by the arguments supporting the External Services' estimate believing 'the targets of overseas broadcasting should be more carefully selected'.[54] As he informed colleagues around the Cabinet table, he had 'discussed this matter further with the Secretaries of State for the Colonies and Commonwealth Relations, and had persuaded them to accept the lower figure proposed by the Chancellor'.[55]

The attempt by the BBC and its partners in Whitehall over the course of three years to re-engineer governing perspectives and argue against successive reductions in the overseas information services budget and the BBC External Services Grant-in-Aid had ended in failure. The result for the BBC was extremely painful, coming so soon after the cuts of the previous year.[56] The following month the General Overseas Service in English was reduced from a round-the-clock operation to 21 hours a day. Spanish output for the Latin American Service was cut from five and three-quarter to three and three-quarter hours a day and Portuguese from three and a half to one and a half. Greek for Cyprus was stopped altogether and Afrikaans reduced from 45 minutes to 15 minutes a day. In services to Europe, French was cut by three-quarters of an hour a day, as was German for Germany, German for Austria by quarter of an hour and Dutch by six minutes. In all 40 staff posts were lost.[57] Meanwhile services to East Germany were increased from five to seven days a week and an extra hour was added to the Arabic Service.[58] Arguing for the wider expansion of the overseas information services budget had been an ambitious plan but with Bevin as Foreign Secretary one worth pursuing. With Morrison in the chair there was little sympathy for the concept that lay behind it and Jacob and Gaitskell were left at loggerheads as the financial will of the Treasury exercised its control over the Grant-in-Aid. Would, though, a Conservative administration have responded differently? Jacob and the BBC did not have to wait long to find out.

Drogheda

It soon became apparent that the same critical tension in relating value to expenditure existed regardless of whether Clement Attlee or Winston Churchill occupied No. 10 Downing Street. In February 1951, the senior Conservative, Richard (R.A.) Butler had argued, in response to the announcement that the External Services budget was to be cut again, that 'this arm of broadcasting is one of the most vital that we can use in our general defence arrangements'.[59] Likewise, there was derision in the press over this latest funding decision with the *Daily Mail* noting, 'The "Voice of America" booms, the Voice of Stalin roars, the Voice of Britain must whisper.'[60] Nine months later, however, the Conservatives also found themselves looking for a mechanism that would unlock the problem of funding in the context of vastly swelling defence expenditure as a result of the Korean War and a consequent desperate need to exercise control over the public purse.

To this effect, the new Conservative government established a small Ministerial Committee to 'examine the requirement for Overseas Information Services for the coming year' under the Lord President of the Council, Lord Salisbury. In truth, the committee had been given the task of cutting £500,000 from the overall budget which was done by squeezing even further the resources of the British Council and the COI.[61] Nevertheless, the decision of the government in early 1952 to freeze the overseas broadcasting budget for the coming financial year at £4,750,000 resulted, according to Gerard Mansell who would take charge at Bush House in the 1970s, in 'the most serious blood-letting the External Services were ever to know'.[62] This was no understatement. Further cuts were made in Portuguese and Spanish services to Latin America along with the closure of the four remaining BBC offices there. The majority of breakfast and lunchtime broadcasts to Western Europe were eliminated with services to Belgium discontinued completely. In addition, the *Arabic Listener* ceased publication (a decision the government would come to rue four years later), and nearly all capital expenditure, desperately needed to update ageing transmitter stock, was deferred. Finally, and most dispiriting, 130 posts were abolished.[63] As Jacob informed the BBC Board of Governors in February 1952, 'there is a real danger of our becoming inaudible in various parts of the world unless we take steps to regain our position'.[64]

Deeply frustrated by the course of government inaction, Jacob agitated for an independent enquiry to help resolve this unsatisfactory state of affairs. Concerned at losing political control and the financial implications of such a move, the government resisted. However, the increased cost of jamming and the impact on domestic opinion of the External Services' swingeing cuts forced a change of approach in Whitehall. In the face of increasing public criticism the Parliamentary Under-Secretary of State for Foreign Affairs, Anthony Nutting, announced to the House of Commons on 2 April 1952 the government's decision to set up an interdepartmental Committee of officials:

> Each successive year the Overseas Information Services have been subjected to the over-riding requirements of finance. . . . It is high time, in my view, that an enquiry was made into the political aspects of this field. We have, therefore, already taken steps to invite the departments concerned, together with the British Broadcasting Corporation and the British Council, to consider the whole range of our overseas information services from the political and strategic aspects.[65]

This committee, chaired by Jack Nicholls of the Foreign Office who had taken over from Christopher Warner as Assistant Under-Secretary superintending information services was, perhaps surprisingly, not designed to find a solution. Rather it was a way of buying time and once again a means to generate a consensus of opinion with which to mount an assault on Treasury intransigence. It was to this effect that the committee reported on 14 July:

> We believe we have established the necessity for, and the advantages of, efficient overseas information work. . . . We are clearly not qualified to express any opinion on the proper distribution of the national resources; we must therefore confine ourselves to saying that in our view the international situation, the Communist ideological onslaught on the free world, the need to right the balance of payments and the necessity of maintaining Commonwealth relationships, all demand an intensification of overseas information work and a measure of continuity in its financing, in order to permit operations to be so planned as to produce their full cumulative effect.[66]

Two weeks later Nutting announced in the Commons, in response to a question put by the Labour MP Ernest Davies, the government's decision to establish 'a small expert advisory committee of independent people outside the Government service' to make recommendations on the long-term policy of overseas information services.[67] The stage was now set for just the type of enquiry the BBC hoped would bring an end to the suffocating inertia of the previous years.

Under the chairmanship of the House of Lords' Deputy Speaker (Lord Chairman of Committees) and former Director-General of the wartime Ministry of Economic Warfare, the Earl of Drogheda, the committee began its work in October 1952 having been asked

> To assess the value, actual and potential, of the overseas information work of the Foreign Office, Commonwealth Relations Office, Colonial Office, Board of Trade and Central Office of Information; the External Services of the British Broadcasting Corporation; and the work of the British Council; to advise upon the relative importance of different methods and services in different areas and circumstances and to make recommendations for future policy.[68]

In order to do this, the Drogheda Committee set about establishing general principles that should guide its analysis of the various parts of the government's overseas information services. For example, it was thought that 'The aim of the Information Services must always be to achieve in the long run some definite political or commercial result.' Equally, it was considered that 'Information

Services should be directed at the influential few and through them at the many.'[69] With regard to the BBC's External Services the Committee thought that the value of overseas broadcasting would be further determined by three additional considerations: first, the extent to which listeners in reception countries had access to alternative and reliable sources of news; secondly, whether people in another country look to the West for 'encouragement and guidance' and; finally, where local broadcasting systems relied on the External Services to supply programming for output and where the BBC 'performs an essential role as the centre of a broadcasting network which brings the voice of Britain to countries which naturally look to London for news'.[70]

During the course of its deliberations, the BBC put a great deal of effort in furnishing the Committee with ample information supporting its argument in favour of increased financing. This work was led by the new Director of External Broadcasting, J. B. Clark, after Jacob's departure in June 1952 on a six-month secondment as Chief Staff Officer to the Minister of Defence, at Churchill's personal request, before returning in December to replace William Haley as Director-General.[71] Clark noted that in his dealings with the committee the 'atmosphere has been markedly receptive to expressions of anxiety at the limitation of BBC activities' and both 'collectively and severally all the members of the Committee seem well disposed to the BBC External Services'.[72] Consequently, it was felt that the Corporation 'has had a fair and full hearing at its various sessions with the Committee'. However, on the eve of the Committee presenting its Report to the government, concerns at the BBC started to emerge about 'a somewhat dangerous and unwelcome inclination to contemplate the curtailment of services to Western Europe'.[73]

The Report of the Drogheda Committee, which was declassified and released only in September 2008, was presented to the government on 27 July 1953, a year on from the report of the committee of officials.[74] Both the BBC and the FO had hoped 'to use the weapon of the Independent Inquiry as a means of persuading the Treasury to make increased grants to cover rising costs for the maintenance of the existing services'.[75] However, as the Report's recommendations revealed, such a clear strategy was no longer applicable. With respect to the BBC, the Drogheda Report recommended the return of the General Overseas Service to a round-the-clock service. Broadcasts over the Iron Curtain should be maintained and effective counter-jamming measures continued. Services to the Middle East in Arabic should be extended with those to the Far East further strengthened. The Latin American Service should be restored to previous levels and programmes to North America and the Colonies maintained at present levels. It was on the issue of Europe, as the BBC had feared, that the Committee had less palatable news. While it was recommended that services in English, German, Austrian, Finnish, Spanish, Turkish, Yugoslav and Greek should be kept, because of their political importance, it was proposed that others in French, Italian, Danish, Dutch, Norwegian, Portuguese and Swedish should be eliminated.[76]

The Report presented a genuine dilemma for the BBC. The Corporation had presented a robust case and felt that it had had a fair hearing. The Committee paid tribute to the BBC's 'high reputation as a news source, to its penetrative power though the Iron Curtain, its influence in the Middle East, the value of the General Overseas Service and the importance of the Far Eastern and Latin American Services'.[77] In addition, by recommending an annual spend of £500,000 over five to ten years on capital investment to improve ageing technical stock, the Committee was clear in its support of the long-term future of overseas broadcasting. However, services to Western Europe had been evaluated, the Corporation felt, on the basis of 'irrelevant principles . . . made to apply to broadcasting as if they were native to it'.[78]

In its defence of broadcasting to Western Europe the BBC argued strongly against the fifth principle laid down by Drogheda – that information services shall be directed at the influential few and through them at the many. This, it felt, was more suited to the choice of student for a British Council course or the activity of a British Information Officer among contacts in a foreign capital. Meanwhile, it utterly failed to appreciate or take advantage of 'the greatest development in the propaganda field in the past century', namely, that 'Wireless has given to governments for the first time direct means of access to audiences overseas, which enables them to influence foreign governments by and through direct contact with the masses.' In the case of France, it was as if the British government possessed in its own right a daily newspaper with a circulation equivalent to *The Daily Telegraph*. As such, the BBC argued, 'any information service which is in daily touch with five million people is itself in a position "to make policy or mould public opinion"'. To disrupt the global flow of the External Services for tactical purposes, they said, would have a deep impact on the hard earned reputation of the BBC abroad as listeners had become well aware of the political considerations pertaining to overseas broadcasting: 'Audiences are quite clear as to the motives for treating them in this opportunistic manner, and the BBC would in the shortest period acquire a new reputation.'[79]

This dilemma was mirrored in Whitehall where a virtual impasse had been reached between the Treasury and overseas departments. Echoing the approach taken by Jacob and others on the CIPC, the Report recommended the removal of the information services financial 'ceiling' and proposed a substantial increase in overall funding. In addition to the increase in capital expenditure for the BBC it was proposed that annual revenue should also see an uplift of £485,000 to compensate for the erosion caused by under-funding in previous years. These were measures that the Treasury, under current fiscal pressures, did not feel it could nor should accede to and as Prime Ministerial thoughts focused on the challenges and associated costs of the country's thermo-nuclear future and maintaining Britain's position at the top table of international diplomacy, the necessary executive direction was lacking to enforce a resolution. Accordingly, a White Paper based on the Drogheda Report was not published until April 1954, and then without a commitment from government to enact any of its recommendations.[80]

In November the Foreign Secretary, Anthony Eden, eventually conceded that the government 'have accepted the broad principles set out in the Drogheda Report', but would not commit to a schedule of implementation.[81] It was another month before it became clear that the government really did not intend to act on the Report any time soon. In a debate in the House of Lords the Minister of State for Foreign Affairs, Lord Reading, noted the decision 'not to abolish for the next year any of the Western European Services'.[82] While this was a welcome reprieve for the External Services it also indicated that Bush House would not benefit from any of the increases in expenditure and expansion recommended by Drogheda. It also made plain that the strategic reorganization of overseas broadcasting was to be postponed at least until 1956 – an unfortunate legacy as the Corporation would duly find out.

The equivocal nature of these public announcements could scarcely conceal the genuine conflict of opinion among ministers. In the meantime, Whitehall's continued indecision meant that Bush House, unable to make plans for the future, was once again forced to prepare for further cuts as the annual horse-trade among it, the Foreign Office and the Treasury returned to its normal attritional pattern. As J. B. Clark noted of the latest round of budgetary negotiations in November 1954, 'the recommendations of the Drogheda Committee, which on balance called for considerable expansion of the External Services, has so far had no application to the BBC. On the contrary, we are now going slightly into reverse.'[83] Nevertheless, while on the surface inertia seemed to rule, there was a subtle change occurring in official attitudes on King Charles Street that although not fully appreciated at the time would, in the course of the next year or two, come to be hugely significant in Whitehall's attitude towards overseas broadcasting.

In negotiations with other departments the FO had consistently supported the BBC's argument 'to maintain the status quo in relation to the overall scope of the External Services'. This was the line it had pursued at meetings of the Treasury Working Party on broadcasting services at the end of 1954.[84] However, debates within the department revealed the emergence of a far more pragmatic flexibility concerning the range of services broadcast overseas by the BBC. Prior to the publication of the White Paper and with government discussions, both within the Cabinet and in Ministerial Committee, stuck in departmental deadlock the FO was forced to reconsider its position. As a result, the BBC was informed that while the Foreign Office,

> would not have taken the initiative in suggesting the elimination of services to the free countries of Europe, they feel that the position is one in which they may have to accept this unwelcome proposal in order to save the many good things elsewhere in the Committee's Report. The alternative . . . might lead to a virtual disregard of the entire Report.[85]

The practical acceptance by government at the end of 1954 of the latter course appeared to have made such a compromise unnecessary. This nevertheless masked the beginnings of a very real change of attitude in the FO where ever-worsening departmental budgetary constraints meant the BBC's continued defence of its global remit would increasingly be judged against the more immediate diplomatic, political and economic imperatives facing the government. As Clark noted, Drogheda 'has not allayed the recurrent budget troubles which it was really called into existence to cure'.[86] It had, however, planted the seeds of future discord that would contribute to the breakdown of relations between the FO and the BBC External Services just a few years later.

Part Four

Battlefields

8

The Soviet Challenge

On the eve of what would be a most traumatic and momentous year for both the British government and the Corporation, the BBC Governors hosted a dinner on 8 December 1955 for the Foreign Secretary, Harold Macmillan, at Broadcasting House. With the Director-General, Sir Ian Jacob, and senior overseas staff also in attendance, conversation focused on the challenges facing the External Services.[1] It was suggested that the recent Council of Foreign Ministers meeting in Geneva heralded a 'revived hardening of the cold war' and that the Russian refusal to agree to closer cultural relations increased more than ever 'the value of broadcasting as a means of communication which, despite the jamming, remains almost the only one open to the West'.[2] It was clear, however, that what really exercised the minds of BBC management were the domestic challenges facing overseas broadcasting and the future of relations with the British government.

The shadow of the Drogheda Committee continued to hang over any consideration of the strategic purpose and scope of the External Services. Although the BBC claimed that its continued non-implementation should mean that its Report be considered 'obsolete in detail', the Corporation could not escape from the threat it represented to remake the External Services as an organization predisposed to servicing the foreign policy and trade requirements of the British government. Anxieties were compounded by the fact, pointed out to Macmillan, that in the last eight years 'overall costs have risen in this country by about 50%, whereas the grants for revenue expenditure on the External Services have risen by only about 20%'. As a consequence British overseas broadcasting had become an impoverished enterprise when compared to its American and Russian counterparts: 'our Services have been curtailed or eliminated in order to make ends meet, during the very period when the Cold War has been raging'.[3]

However, while the BBC was seeking a fiscal stimulus to enhance its remit, the Foreign Office (FO) was beginning to argue for a more selective assessment of the value of broadcasts.

On 20 February 1956, Paul Grey of the FO's IPD attended a meeting chaired by Anthony Nutting at which the Minister of State emphasized, in light of the government's commitment to reduce public spending by £100 million, 'the need for fresh thinking and for concentrating our resources on essentials'. Grey was asked whether he was 'satisfied that no reallocation could be made in our own overseas information vote to meet the special threat of Soviet propaganda'?[4] Was there, Nutting wondered, 'any rearrangement which could be made in the information services . . . in particular, the BBC transmissions to Europe'?[5] This was just the opportunity that many Foreign Office officials had been waiting for to reopen, under ministerial cover, the debate on overseas broadcasting that had been stuck in a state of inertia since the Drogheda Committee reported in 1954.

While protective of the overall information services budget – 'I am sure that we cannot make further significant savings in our general information and cultural effort without destroying our basic propaganda machine' – Grey offered to look again at 'the question of the BBC'. It was not just the 'value for cost of our broadcasts to Russia' that Grey felt needed review. He argued that a wholesale study should be employed to 'show how much would be saved by cutting out broadcasts to various countries or groups of countries'. Grey had seized the initiative and with the support of his colleagues began sweeping aside official nervousness at addressing the perceived inadequacies of BBC services abroad.[6] From now on, they would be considered essential only where it was possible for a positive contribution to be made to government publicity objectives and anti-communist work in particular. As in 1948, the broadcast environment was changing. The Corporation, Grey argued, was 'holding on to what is largely a fetish' by believing it had an unassailable right to a global broadcast remit.[7]

Cultural rapprochement

The decision to embark on a cost-benefit analysis of the BBC External Services was as much a response to the inconclusive outcome of the Drogheda Committee as it was a reaction to the perceived requirements of overseas broadcasting in the current political and diplomatic climate. The added impetus in the spring of 1956 was the determination of officials to reinforce the BBC's programmes to Russia and by extension to maximize the dividend realized from broadcasting to Central and Eastern Europe.

The triumvirate post-Stalin leadership of Nikolai Bulganin, Nikita Khrushchev and Georgy Malenkov suggested a new direction in the management of Soviet affairs.[8] The continuing process of de-Stalinization implied a marginal loosening of central control over life in the Soviet Union while the rapprochement in May 1955 with Yugoslavia had given currency to the idea of 'national roads to socialism' within the Soviet orbit. In the same month the signing of the Austrian State Treaty, the Geneva Conference in July and, later in 1955, trips to Afghanistan and India were evidence of a re-engagement by the Soviet leadership with the world beyond the Iron Curtain.[9] There remained, however, continuing trends that pointed towards a more orthodox interpretation of Soviet objectives and methods and generated a deep scepticism in British official circles towards these events at the beginning of 1956. Not the least of these was the emergence of a Soviet thermo-nuclear capability, increased Russian penetration of the Middle East and North Africa, the signing of the Warsaw Pact and the continued propaganda attack on the West in general and British 'imperialism' in particular.[10] In the face of this evidence, and underlined by the brusque and uncooperative manner in which Molotov had brought the second Geneva conference to a close, the FO considered that even greater effort should be put into meeting the 'special threat of Soviet propaganda'.[11]

Naturally, the BBC was intended to be a central player in this renewed counteroffensive, but there existed at the heart of the relationship between Whitehall and Bush House a long-term difficulty in the handling of Russian output. The accommodation reached between the two in the years following the 1948 Cabinet decision on foreign publicity policy had, by the mid-1950s, begun to splinter and significant divergences of opinion on the tone used in broadcasts to Russia contributed to an increasingly dysfunctional relationship between officials and broadcasters in this respect. Indeed, the BBC's Russian programmes had been 'the subject of discussion between the department and the BBC for the past three years in an attempt to improve them', but without, from the Foreign Office's perspective, success.[12] In particular, it was felt that 'in their anxiety to appeal to the Soviet intelligentsia and to create a mental and emotional bridge across the Iron Curtain, the Russian Service have tended to blur their presentation of the British case by trying to be too conciliatory'.[13]

Several years' worth of experience of transmitting over the Iron Curtain had produced two distinct doctrines of how best to maximize the effectiveness of broadcasts in Russian. For the Foreign Office, the BBC's programmes were excessively 'dry and dull' and therefore lacked the necessary edge to be an effective form of propaganda, opening the ears of listeners to the world outside and exposing the inequities and hypocrisies of Soviet communist rule as seen from the West.[14] For example, there was concern that recent 'talks on the Rembrandt exhibition in Amsterdam, one on the Schumann centenary and another on the merits of the Tunisian Prime Minister would seem, given our relatively short broadcasting hours, to be only justifiable if there were a drastic dearth of interesting material'.[15] The BBC, as Ian Jacob pointed out, had developed a rather different approach. 'The art of broadcasting successfully to foreign audiences', he explained in a paper for the FO, 'lies in estimating how best to secure their friendly interest.'[16] This echoed the personal style of the Russian Service Programme Organiser (head of the service), Anatol Goldberg, and although Russian output did not eschew critical commentary – indeed it had become a fact of Cold War broadcasting life – the BBC sought to couch it within an empathetic framework rather than a more aggressive and potentially alienating one.

What made this difference of emphasis particularly difficult was that it centred on an issue of editorial tone – a textural dispute. This fact was, of course, well understood by both sides and helps explain why, after three years of debate, the FO felt that it had failed to realize the desired changes in output. Actual editorial control, as opposed to instructions concerning where and when to broadcast, was the emblem of the External Services' independence from the British government. It was also, the BBC maintained, the preserve of the broadcast specialist, not the realm of the policy analyst, and a strict interpretation of the BBC's Charter would confirm this constitutional and practical position. And yet, it was also understood that the BBC, under the rubric of the national interest, had a duty to protect and present Britain's interests overseas. To do this successfully required negotiation with the FO over the strategic direction of broadcasts abroad. This had been the case in 1948 in terms of the external threat that communism posed Britain, and now in 1956 another such reorientation was on the cards.

Rather than continuing to push for a gradual editorial overhaul, by the spring of 1956 the FO was planning a radical shake-up of the External Services. What remained to be seen was whether common ground could be found between Whitehall and the BBC on the direction to be taken. However, before this process had a chance to gain purchase it was overtaken by a hugely significant development: the cessation of the jamming of BBC programmes in Russian. The trigger for this was the arrival in Britain of Khrushchev and Bulganin. On 18 April 1956, the first day of their visit, the BBC noticed 'that a very substantial proportion of the jammers located in the USSR were no longer attacking these particular broadcasts'. Among the western radios transmitting in Russian – America, Canada, Italy, Turkey, Spain, France, Israel and the Vatican – only the BBC was given this reprieve.[17] There was an obvious and immediate political and diplomatic dividend for the Soviet leaders in having the jamming suspended both at home and overseas. On the one hand, it demonstrated an intention for cultural co-operation with the United Kingdom at the start of an historic visit, while on the other, it allowed the BBC's Russian audience to glimpse their leaders on the international stage as reported independently and freely by the world's press through the BBC. It is also important to recognize that there were other, more rooted, reasons for the cessation.

Central among these was the desire within the Soviet leadership to promote their vision of peaceful coexistence as the future for Cold War relations. And a high profile way of demonstrating this was to shut down some of the jamming operation. In this context, it was ironic that the persistent thread of British government criticism of BBC broadcasts to the USSR – that output was too mild – may have been a compelling facilitating reason on the Soviet side in support of cessation. The fact that the Russian Service was not overly denunciatory in character, that it was in essence a news service, would certainly have made it far less offensive on political, ideological and theological grounds to Soviet Communist Party sensibilities than certain other western broadcasters. Not surprisingly, however, BBC broadcasts to the satellites, which maintained a much sharper attack on Soviet domination and with which the FO were much more satisfied, continued to be jammed.[18] There were also significant logistical reasons for a curtailment of jamming activity. The BBC and the FO were very aware of the cost they (along with the Americans and others) were placing on the Soviet Union in terms of financial expenditure and material resources (including personnel), in maintaining such a major jamming enterprise. And as the dimensions of the radio race between East and West expanded, the reduction of this burden may have been a consideration for the Russians in deciding if and when a reduction in the jamming operation could be made.

A perhaps less well-known contributing factor to this break in jamming was the continued development of co-operative relations between BBC and Soviet broadcasters and a series of discussions that took place between their representatives in 1955 and 1956. In October 1955 a Russian delegation of broadcasters had visited the United Kingdom to discuss mutual areas of interest – technical, engineering, management and output – and the scope for future co-operative development with the BBC. High on the agenda, from the British perspective, was the continued jamming of BBC broadcasts. During this visit the leader of the delegation, Topuriya, the Deputy Minister of Communications (the Soviet department responsible for the technical execution of the directive to jam BBC broadcasts), implied there was room for manoeuvre on the topic. The UK response was not to accept this informal invitation so as to avoid giving the impression of a 'concessionary attitude'.[19] Nevertheless, it was clear that, whatever the Soviet motivation, a shift was occurring in its attitude towards jamming. The visit to London in February 1956 of Mikhailov, the Soviet Minister of Culture (responsible for Soviet Radio), may also have provided another opportunity for official discussion of the culture of jamming and its future direction.[20] As it was, the cessation of jamming was not the complete surprise it might otherwise have appeared. The Director of External Broadcasting, J. B. Clark, when explaining the circumstances to the BBC Governors clearly felt that the reduction in jamming was a consequence of the combined effect of 'Russian détente' and negotiations conducted by himself with the Soviet authorities 'in London and Moscow'.[21] It was, nonetheless, a hugely significant development and marks the beginning of what might be described as a unique period of 'radio détente' between the BBC and Soviet Radio.

In the spring of 1956 the course of radio diplomacy between BBC and Soviet broadcasters in many respects mirrored that of relations between Britain and the USSR. Under the leadership of Khrushchev and Bulganin it was apparent that a significant change in the style of Soviet engagement with the rest of the world was taking place. But there were major doubts, highlighted by the 'imperialist' criticisms levelled at Britain during the Soviet leaders' Asian tour, about whether this represented a change of substance. Nonetheless, the possibility of lessening Cold War tensions provided a compelling reason to explore with an open, though sceptical, mind the parameters and dynamics of the emerging détente. It was in this spirit that the FO had agreed to a return visit to the Soviet Union by a BBC delegation that would be 'prepared to insist on answers to awkward questions', particularly on issues related to jamming.[22] Accordingly, eleven days after the Soviet leaders arrived in Britain a BBC party of seven, led by the Director of External Broadcasting J. B. Clark with the Russian Programme Organiser Anatol Goldberg acting as interpreter, arrived in Moscow.[23] Top of the visitors' agenda on their twelve-day tour (which included visits to Leningrad and Kiev) was the question of programme exchanges between the BBC and Soviet Radio. These had been taking place for some time albeit on a rather uneven basis but there was now a desire, also strongly supported by the FO, to develop the potential for television programme exchanges in addition to extending the trade in radio exchanges. During negotiations the BBC delegation were at pains to stress at every available opportunity 'the fact that the continuance of jamming which was so directly in conflict with the purposes and potentialities of broadcasting bedevilled the whole prospect of cooperation'.[24]

The visit also provided a first rate opportunity to look for evidence of jamming operations – 'mysterious sausage type aerials are visible on a number of buildings' – and to judge the reach and audibility of BBC broadcasts to Russia with the portable medium and shortwave receiver they had brought with them. Neither was easy and Clark noted that it was not possible 'within the limits of tact, to take the receiver in a car some 20 or 30 kilometres out of Moscow to attempt reception of the Russian Service and to confirm that the jammers are only effective in the main centres of population'. Nevertheless, they were able to conclude that the western areas of the Soviet Union provided good shortwave reception from most parts of the world. The greatest surprise, though, and of quite some importance to the ongoing expansion of English by Radio output in broadcasts to the USSR was the discovery that the English-language General Overseas Service 'was received excellently' even when radiated from the Tebrau transmitter in Singapore which was not directed for reception in Moscow.[25]

Although discussions between the BBC and their Soviet counterparts produced no tangible concessions in the official Soviet argument in favour of jamming (that it was a necessary means of protecting Soviet citizens against hostile propaganda), there was detected in discussions with the Head of Soviet

Radio, Puzin, 'a mood in which negotiation might be possible' and a 'wish on the part of the Soviet Government to make a first step towards some abatement of this major irritant'.[26] As Jacob pointed out to the Governors in the summer of 1956, 'plans for future liaison are based on the assumption that the recent reduction in jamming will continue.'[27] Clark, however, sounded a note of caution about the long-term implications of this apparent breakthrough in his report on the trip of the BBC delegation:

> The elaborate and obviously carefully engineered jamming installations . . . and the importance clearly attached to the control of listening inherent in the act of jamming, yields no indication that the Soviet authorities are likely to dismantle or abandon the means of jamming, whatever bilateral or multilateral arrangements they may make. It would be wishful thinking to imagine that, in the context of their present more cooperative attitude in broadcasting as in other fields, they contemplate depriving themselves of the jamming weapon – at least for many years to come.[28]

This sober, though entirely accurate, assessment was a useful reminder of the geopolitical context within which these discussions were taking place.

It was, nonetheless, a very successful visit and the source of a real improvement in relations between the two broadcasters with an agreement, in principle, reached 'on the basis of collaboration which will cover the exchange of programmes on an entirely satisfactory basis and liaison in other matters of mutual interest'.[29] The trip had also been very useful in terms of gaining an assessment of the potential of the BBC's audience in the Soviet Union – a field that had lacked illumination for some time. Out of a total of 35 million licensed receiving installations, 10 million wireless sets were produced by the Ministry of Radio Engineering Industry.[30] Therefore, the need to maintain a domestic broadcasting service across the vast distances of the Soviet Union provided wireless receivers with a short-wave range capable of picking up BBC broadcasts in Russian. The Soviet authorities were, in effect, manufacturing wireless Trojan horses which gave the BBC access to an audience of millions deep behind the Iron Curtain which were otherwise untouchable from the outside. Both Bush House and the Foreign Office were quick to identify the 'immediate and striking opportunities . . . now presented by the lessening of jamming of BBC broadcasts' to penetrate Soviet minds as never before.[31]

Indicators of change

The 'unparalleled opportunity', as IPD's Paul Grey described it, to address Russian listeners unimpeded now gave greater impetus and direction to the FO's editorial re-engagement with the BBC External Services' output, and broadcasts in Russian in particular.[32] It also provided the BBC with a chance, mindful of official views on King Charles Street and keen to retrieve the initiative, to re-engineer its programming over the Iron Curtain in line with the new listening conditions. In a very important memorandum for the FO in May 1956 the Director-General, Ian Jacob, evinced the latest BBC thinking on Russian-speaking audience requirements. The listener, he wrote, 'will be in receptive mood, and avid for knowledge and stimulation. In place of the bare presentation of facts and argument which is all that has been possible in the face of the jamming, a more elaborate programme will be necessary in order to follow up and develop our advantage.' New series of talks would be commissioned 'to correct the distortions and gaps in knowledge'. The teaching of English by Radio would be increased and the 'music, entertainment and the ordinary sounds of this country will need to be put across for the first time'.[33] What Jacob was talking about amounted to an educational agenda to engage the people of Russia with a more composite programme, indicative of wider social trends within British society, than had been possible before.

The FO, too, was focused on re-educating a Soviet audience that had been 'cut off from information about the West for so long'. However, their educational zeal was punctuated by more pressing political concerns than that of the BBC. Increasing the range of output to give a genuine picture of life in Britain, they argued, 'did not mean to imply that we should abjure all criticism of Soviet policy. . . . Indeed projection of Britain and criticism of Soviet behaviour must often go hand in hand; the one will not be effective without the other.'[34] As such, while BBC plans for the broadening of Russian Service programme content were considered by the FO to be 'plainly on the right lines', there was a strong belief that the Corporation was simply not making the most of the opportunity the cessation of jamming presented. As Cosmo Stewart, the head of IPD, put it in an internal briefing note, there was an 'intellectual softness' at the heart of the BBC's operation that prevented the British point of view from being presented more forcefully. Broadcasts were characterized by 'too much hedging, ambiguity and oversubtlety'.[35]

A good, if rather curious, case in point had been the arrest in the summer of 1956 of the Russian discus-thrower, Nina Ponomareva, for stealing hats from *C & A Modes* in Oxford Street while in London with the Soviet athletics team for the White City Games. The ensuing crisis – the Soviet team's withdrawal from Games, Ms Ponomareva's initial failure to attend her bail hearing and six week confinement at the Soviet Embassy until she was finally permitted to go to court – was fully reported, often through eyewitness accounts, as was her conviction and non-custodial sentence of a payment of three guineas. The Director of External Services, J. B. Clark, noted at the time that

> comment in the BBC's Russian broadcasts confined itself to a calm exposition of the facts, explaining the independence from political interference of the legal processes that had been set in motion, coupled with regret that political prejudice had again been injected into a field which had been pleasantly free from it in recent months.[36]

This treatment of the case exemplified the nature of the FO's criticism of the present balance in Russian output. On the one hand, the opportunity taken to explain the principles and operations of the British legal system, particularly when contrasted with the Soviet judiciary, was well realized. On the other, the FO believed there had been a failure to 'firmly condemn Russian nonsense': 'We fully recognise that there is scope for subtlety in penetrating Russian minds, but the prime purpose must surely be to state our views unambiguously, and this means that if the Russians behave badly at our expense we should not shrink from telling them so plainly.'[37] Where the BBC had shown regret over the course of Soviet actions the FO wanted condemnation.

The debate over broadcasts in Russian stood in contrast to that concerning services to the Soviet satellite states which the FO considered far more satisfactory. The reason for this was the convergence of respective appreciations of the interests, needs and tolerances of the listening audience. Since 1948/49 when the editorial policy towards the satellites was first fixed in its Cold War mode, Soviet domination over the internal affairs of these territories had provided a central and rich theme which the BBC, after careful negotiation with Whitehall, was willing to exploit. As Jacob noted of overseas listeners in the summer of 1956, 'It may in some instances be best to enlist their support against the regime in which they live, as in Germany during the war, or in the Russian satellites.' This was a strategy that made sense in broadcasting terms because there already existed a cleavage between the people of Central and Eastern Europe and their Moscow-sponsored communist leaderships. Consequently, programmes that highlighted, in their coverage of current events and world affairs, the nature of Soviet oppression had a ready audience and a chance of gaining purchase. Although not liberationist, these broadcasts did seek to extend the emotional and political distance between the people and their leaders. As a result, the theme of Soviet imperialism, in contrast to national or regional self-determination, was seen in Bush House as a fruitful and worthwhile target in a way that just did not translate to the Soviet context where history and culture were against it. For Jacob nothing was to be gained by 'alienating the listener or his nation as a whole'.[38] The fear at the BBC was that to follow a highly critical and denunciatory policy in its broadcasts to Russia would run the risk of doing just that.

Aggressive broadcasting which challenged the listeners' loyalty to their homeland weakened the broadcast authority of the BBC, it was argued, whereas attacks on the Soviet system in the satellites where there was growing hostility towards Russian domination made the central control exercised by Moscow a weakness that could be legitimately targeted. This convergence of purpose on Central and Eastern Europe reflected a consensus, in this sphere at least, of what it meant to broadcast in the national interest. It was based on a calculation that took into account UK attitudes, government opinion, as well as the cultural, political and emotional needs of audiences whose national identity was made subservient to Soviet regional aims and who lacked an independent media.

As Jacob pointed out in the summer of 1956, the value derived from this approach rested on the application of a consistent editorial strategy over a long period of time.[39] Strong support for this view was evident in a contemporary Radio Free Europe (RFE) report on listening in Poland which had concluded that the BBC's popularity, which exceeded that of RFE, Radio Madrid and VOA, was predicated on 'its reliability and tradition dating back to the days of the German occupation, which accounts for the listeners' attachment to the BBC'.[40] Accordingly, when Jacob laid out for the FO the editorial strategy for broadcasting over the Iron Curtain he was able to point to six major themes that had formed the basis of critical attacks on the Soviet regime 'during the past decade':

1. The rigid insistence on the doctrine of Marx and Lenin (in its Stalinist version) coupled with total control of the press and suppression of criticism

2. The arbitrary powers of the state police
3. The detention of prisoners after faked trials or without trial
4. The forced labour camps and the exploitation of ordinary labour by Stakhanovite campaigns
5. The collectivization of agriculture
6. The refusal or effective discouragement of travel facilities outwards from Russia or inwards to Russia[41]

In reflective mood, Jacob wondered whether it was 'a coincidence that the work of a decade on these themes by the BBC has been followed by major admissions and modifications under each of these headings, with a resultant loosening of the whole regime'. Leaving his Whitehall readers to contemplate the consequences of this claim, his comments brought into focus a highly important conclusion being drawn in the West in the early summer of 1956: that the Soviet Union was experiencing highly significant problems in managing internal dissatisfaction within its satellite system. In this context, did the BBC have a role to play in amplifying the pressures being felt in Moscow? Jacob seemed to think so:

> While the future will establish how much the cracks spreading across the Communist façade have been due to broadcasting from without. . . . The cracks which have appeared must now be prised further open and prevented from closing again. The Soviet domination of Eastern Europe must be further weakened and its recovery prevented.[42]

By 1956 the Soviet Union had been coming to terms with the political and doctrinal legacy of Stalin's death for nearly three years. The competition for the Soviet leadership – involving, principally, Malenkov, Bulganin and Khrushchev – had mirrored the unsettled direction of the USSR's ongoing ideological strategy and its practical application. By extension, the nature of Soviet control over the satellites became inherently bound up in the vicissitudes of the leadership race. At the Twentieth Congress of the Communist Party of the Soviet Union in February 1956 a vision of the future did emerge out of a dramatic critique of the past that was to have a seismic impact on relations between the Soviet Union and her satellites and provide an organizing theme around which broadcasts over the Iron Curtain were thereafter framed. In a closed session on the last day of the Congress, the ascendant Khrushchev delivered a long and wide-ranging speech that at its heart sought to cut the Soviet leadership free of the previous twenty years of Stalinist rule. Khrushchev's purpose, in what was a carefully calculated, but none the less daring, speech was to effect a decapitation of the old order and revitalize the governing communist tradition, with himself at its head.[43]

In what must have been a shocking and unsettling break from normal practice for delegates, Khrushchev came to bury Stalin, not to praise him. And this he did with a penetrating piece of character assassination that, on the one hand, acknowledged officially for the first time what many had privately known or suspected about the terror of previous decades while, on the other, consigning this problematic past to the history books along with its chief architect in what was a calculated act of flagellation to effect political renewal. Stalin, he argued, had violated principles of collective decision-making and fostered the 'cult of personality' as an adjunct to power. What was now required was a return to 'Leninist principles of Soviet socialist democracy' which would be 'characterised by the wide practice of criticism and self-criticism' – something that had been conspicuous by its absence under Stalin.[44]

This was a step into the unknown for Khrushchev and other senior officials. The notion of criticizing the state, self-criticism indeed, had been absent from Soviet life for a generation and sat incongruously with the idea of an infallible and historically determined system which had become an inherent part of the projection of Soviet identity both at home and overseas. It was a message that needed careful dissemination if the Soviet leadership was to control the course and consequences of the debate it had started. Developments over the next few months, however, led the BBC to conclude that Khrushchev had opened the floodgates and could not now easily stem the liberalizing sentiment flowing through some of the satellite states. As the Hungarian Section Programme Organiser, Ferenc Rentoul, succinctly put it in a General News Talk for the European Services at the end of June: 'Like the sorcerer's apprentice who had released forces he could not later control, the Communist regimes of Central and Eastern Europe are in difficulties.'[45]

Far from being passive observers of the dramatic changes taking place in the Soviet Union, the BBC and other broadcasters, in particular RFE and the VOA, put a great deal of effort into influencing the way in which these shifts were interpreted by satellite audiences. As Clark noted, 'Khrushchev's admission that the Stalin regime had been a tyrant-ridden nightmare was persistently underlined in comments in the days and weeks that followed.'[46] This critique was considerably enhanced when the text of Khrushchev's speech was leaked by the CIA (who had obtained a Polish copy in April from Israeli Intelligence) to the *New York Times* and published on 2 June.[47] Now it was possible to broadcast 'extensive extracts . . . to those countries without a free press'. Consequently, publication of the speech dominated output of the BBC, RFE and VOA. As Clark pointed out for the BBC Governors, despite the lack of publication within the Soviet Union, 'there is no doubt that everyone who listened to the BBC broadcasts over this period was able to get a clear understanding of what is certainly one of the most remarkable episodes in the history of Communism'.[48]

9

Hungary

Events in Central Europe in the autumn of 1956, in part fuelled by Khrushchev's secret speech the previous February, would prove to be the defining moment for the conduct of intra-Soviet affairs in this period and for the wider perception of international communism. Following months of civil unrest in the region a demonstration organized by Hungarian university students on 23 October sparked a wave of discontent that within a matter of hours escalated into a full-blown revolution. Demanding greater political, economic and democratic freedoms, such as an end to one-party rule, several thousand converged on Budapest's Bem Square before marching through the city. A few hours later, joined by ranks of workers returning home at the end of the day, an estimated 200,000 arrived in Parliament Square – a critical mass full of resentment – with a thirst for change.[1]

Indicative of government confusion about how to respond to these events (the Hungarian leader, Erno Gero, was at that time on a visit to Czechoslovakia), the right to protest initially appeared to be sanctioned by the Hungarian authorities. On the morning of 23 October the official *Szabad Nep* newspaper published a list of ten reforming demands drawn up by an association known as the Petofi Circle while Budapest Radio pledged its support for the student demonstration that afternoon. This was contradicted by a Ministry of Interior ban on all public meetings which was itself withdrawn in a subsequent radio announcement.[2] Either way, the pace of events and the public spilling over of a visceral anger at the Hungarian authorities pushed the machinery of government into a state of panic. At this critical juncture, protestors split into two groups with a large contingent marching on the offices of Budapest (Kossuth) Radio, the audible reminder of Hungarian state control.[3] It was here that broadcasting took centre stage for the first, but not the last, time and heralded the moment of revolution. As negotiations were under way between demonstrators and radio managers for the broadcast of the students' demands, drafted the previous day, the voice of Erno Gero, hastily returned from Prague, rang out from radio sets across the country. To the disbelief of those listening, especially in the capital and around the Budapest Radio building, Gero denounced protestors as 'counter-revolutionaries' and accused them of perpetrating 'impudent lies – hostile propaganda that does not contain a grain of truth'.[4] As the BBC's George Mikes reported from Budapest shortly afterwards, 'it was this speech that pulled the trigger'.[5] In the confusion that followed members of the AVH secret police, who had been posted to the radio station, attempted to disperse the crowds using tear gas and in the ensuing struggle what had begun as a peaceful yet impassioned protest quickly became an armed insurrection in Budapest and beyond. During the following two weeks of the uprising around 2,700 people were killed as first Hungarian, and then Soviet troops sought to extinguish the revolt and the ultimately doomed fight for the right to self-determination.[6]

The cry of 'Russians go home' was a prominent feature of the demonstration that day and reflected a basic rejection of Soviet control over Hungarian affairs.[7] This was a deep-rooted objection to the exercise of external influence that had characterized much of life in Hungary after the Second World War. More recently, the turbulence that accompanied Moscow's battle of succession after the death of Stalin in March 1953 was reflected in the political uncertainty experienced in Central and Eastern Europe at the time. This was the case in Budapest where, in June 1953, Matyas Rakosi was dismissed as Prime Minister (though he retained his position as First Secretary of the Hungarian Workers' Party) by a Moscow leadership eager to rein in the Stalinist tendencies of communist leaders like him. His replacement, the former Minister for Agriculture Imre Nagy, quickly introduced a 'New Course' of economic, social and political reforms in addition to the abolition of internment camps and an amnesty for many political prisoners.[8] Politics in Hungary seemed to have regained a semblance of self-determination within the broader Soviet system. The political wind in Moscow, however, was never still and by January 1955 it was Nagy's turn to be denounced by the Soviet Presidium for rightist deviationism. The charge of industrial and agricultural mismanagement and consequent social dislocation echoed Rakosi's dismissal a year and a half earlier. The result was a return to stricter controls over satellite affairs from Moscow and the replacement of Nagy with András Hegedus.[9]

However, the space for critical debate encouraged by Nagy's brief rule had given sections of Hungarian society both the confidence and a platform from which to tentatively question the priorities and direction of Hungarian politics. This could be seen, for example, in the dispute between the Hungarian Writers' Association, following the dismissal of the editor of its journal *Irodalmi Ujsag*, and the Hungarian authorities in the autumn of 1955 which resulted in a public statement criticizing the 'anti-democratic methods which cripple our cultural life'.[10] By Christmas 1955, Bush House was reporting the 'revolt of the literary men' thanks to the valuable local information provided by the British Legation in Budapest.[11] Quite a number of programmes by the BBC Hungarian Section were devoted to the 'Writers' Revolt' with particular prominence given to Laszlo Szabo, a Hungarian poet working in the External Services who was considered to have a substantial audience among Hungarians: a good example of how Bush House attempted to promote the intellectual bond between the External Services and audiences behind the Iron Curtain.[12] As the BBC's Head of Central European Services, Gregory Macdonald, remarked soon afterwards,

> the most important single development . . . is the way in which criticism of Stalinism developed into a full-scale attack on Rakosi personally, coupled with the welcome readiness of party members at all levels to criticise rationally rather than dogmatically not only the misdeeds and mistakes of the past nine years but the present situation.[13]

It was not communism *per se* that was the focus of criticism, rather communism with a Soviet face.

Throughout this period, relations between Bush House and the Foreign Office (FO) on the question of broadcasts to the Soviet satellites were extremely co-operative. When, in 1955, IRD suggested 'laying particular stress at the present time on what the removal – and even the decrease – of Russian influence might mean', the always receptive Macdonald was in 'full agreement' and thought the idea, which had come from the British Legation in Budapest, 'entirely in line with our tradition of broadcasting to Hungary'.[14] In particular, Macdonald thought that pursuing 'the theme of comparison with West Germany, Austria and Yugoslavia may be the most vivid and the most rewarding'. The Hungarian Programme Organiser, Ferenc Rentoul, duly made a trip to Yugoslavia in July 1955 'to make contacts and get reactions from Hungarians' for the very purpose of obtaining 'points of comparison'.[15] Meanwhile, despite the limited transmission time available, room was found for a series of talks on life in Austria by Karl Brusak after the signing of the State Treaty – which established its post-war independence and neutrality – and another on Yugoslavia by the head of Bush House's Central Research Unit (CRU), Walter Kolarz. Brusak's work closely echoed the Legation's suggestion 'to contrast the general scene in Austria and in Hungary to show how the two countries so closely associated in the past, and with such similar backgrounds, have gone different ways because of Communism'. Likewise, Kolarz's scripts emphasized, as had been proposed, 'how a country can become more prosperous, happier and freer when it throws off Moscow's domination and is able to enter into normal relations with the outside world'.[16] In fact, Kolarz had been provided with 'special knowledge' via the FO for the purpose of producing these talks.[17] As the Legation later pointed out, both sets of programmes 'are quite excellently done and will, I am sure justify the considerable amount of work which has gone into their preparation'.[18]

By the summer of 1956 the 'constituency of dissent'[19] evident in Hungary was reflected in the activities of the Petofi Circle, a debating club created the previous year and named after Hungary's national poet, Sandor Petofi, who fought in the 1848–49 War of Independence against the Habsburg Empire and who died at the hands of Russian troops. Symbolically, a Petofi debate on 27 June about Hungarian information services, censorship and the press attracted a crowd of 5,000 or 6,000, requiring an alternative venue and loudspeakers. As speeches pressed the case for cultural and political freedoms ever more vehemently, so the clamour for change demanded by those present and the wider community of interests they represented became ever more potent.[20] The BBC monitored these events closely with its Hungarian Section, led by Rentoul, developing a scripted thesis on the rise of national communism in Central Europe and its undermining of Soviet controls. There was even a 'reconstruction in a dramatic form of one of the stormiest meetings of the Petofi Club'.[21] In talks entitled, for example, 'Rumblings in Hungary' and 'Communist Conflict in Hungary' listeners were left in no doubt that something truly momentous was afoot. And if they were unsure what interpretation to give to these developments, then the BBC's analysis was clear. There were three important conclusions to be drawn, Rentoul suggested in 'More Hungarian Alarms' on 3 July:

> The first is that the rebellious writers, authors, journalists and so on are themselves Communists. It is they who were demanding a New Revolution and who were saying that the liberation is to begin in real earnest now. The second conclusion

> is that there is undoubtedly strong and by now undisguised opposition to Rakosi continuing as the First Secretary of the Party. He more than any man is a symbol, inside Hungary as well as outside, it now appears, of the Stalin era. And the third conclusion is that no matter from where this demand for more freedom and a real Liberation may have come, no matter by whom it has been voiced, it has undoubtedly found a wide and enthusiastic appeal among the masses.[22]

Mass dissent was also dramatically on display in Poland that summer, underlining the internal challenges facing Soviet control in the region. On 28 June 1956, the day after the Petofi Club's vociferous meeting on press censorship, workers at the Cegielski engineering works in Poznan (the largest industrial plant in the country) marched on the city centre demanding fairer economic and political conditions, carrying banners calling for 'Bread and Freedom'.[23] Over the course of the next two days 53 people were killed, according to official figures, and around 300 injured in clashes with Polish army units and security forces.[24] Moreover, the riots started at the end of the annual International Trade Fair in Poznan when the town was filled with overseas businessmen who observed the violence. They, in turn, became 'stringers' (unofficial reporters) for news agencies around the world.[25] Initially, Premier Cyrankiewicz blamed foreign agents for the violence in Poznan, but the official ruling Polish United Workers' Party (PZPR), reflecting internal divisions of opinion, quickly began to talk in terms of the legitimate complaints of the workers and the responsibilities of the state towards them.[26] The subsequent trials of those accused of taking part in the riots, recordings of which were broadcast by Radio Polskie every evening, were considered by staff at the BBC to demonstrate 'the determination of the Poles, the defence lawyers amongst them – to give the truth to the world'.[27] In contrast, an embattled Rakosi was frantically marshalling the levers of power for an all-out assault against his challengers at home. It was already too late, however, and on 17 July the Soviet Foreign Minister, Anastas Mikoyan, arrived in Budapest and in the car from the airport informed Rakosi of the latter's immediate resignation on health grounds.[28] His successor, chosen by Moscow, was Erno Gero – a Stalinist and former Deputy Prime Minister under Rakosi who was representative of all that had gone before and utterly incapable of managing the tensions that were fracturing Hungarian society.

The defiant and increasingly anti-Soviet sentiment associated with the idea of a national road to socialism then incubating within Central Europe was given extra impetus prior to the uprising by two critical events. First, the attendance of tens of thousands at the reburial on 6 October of the posthumously rehabilitated Laszlo Rajk, former Hungarian Minister of Interior and Foreign Affairs Minister. Second was the success with which Poland's new First Secretary, Wladyslaw Gomulka, had dismissed the Kremlin appointed Marshal Rokossowski as Minister of Defence and seen off a Soviet delegation, threatening military repercussions, consisting of Khrushchev, Mikoyan, and Molotov. Both these events were given wide coverage in domestic and overseas media.[29] Bush House also offered listeners behind the Iron Curtain an external interpretation of the dramatic developments taking place around them. Criticisms of press censorship, the repressive methods of the state police, mass detentions, the use of show trials, and the exploitation of labour and national resources were all used to emphasize the advantages to be gained from the removal of Moscow's influence over political, economic and cultural life and the value of self-determination. By the summer of 1956 this was fertile ground and an atmosphere of hope and apprehension attended the task of broadcasting over the Iron Curtain: hope that genuine freedoms could be won in Central and Eastern Europe, apprehension that such demands might provoke an angry backlash from Moscow.

Broadcast revolution

The Hungarian uprising was a compelling and resonant moment in the Cold War. The emotionally charged narrative arc of the two-week uprising – a battle for freedoms seemingly won against overwhelming odds and then brutally denied – became a defining reference point for people all over the world.[30] In the West, as the Marxist historian Eric Hobsbawm later claimed, 'probably no other episode in 20th Century history generated a more intense burst of feeling'.[31] Radio, both domestic and international, became the cartographer of the revolution, broadcasting its confused and frantic beginnings before mapping the path to its desperate and terrifying end. Radio Budapest, Radio Moscow, the BBC, the VOA and REF not only reported on the uprising, but were, from the beginning, an integral part of it. Journalistic endeavour was mixed with diplomatic and political functions in a unique blend that established, in what is recognizably a modern context, a new relationship between the media and the international events they reported.

Figure 8 BBC European Service News Room, Bush House, February 1945

Sub-editors in the BBC European Service Newsroom put together the latest bulletin in English for retranslation and broadcast by the language services.

Listening to Erno Gero's fateful broadcast on the evening of 23 October, Etele Papp of the BBC's Monitoring Service (BBCM) in Caversham was instantly alerted to the fact that something very unusual was afoot. As further news of an emergency meeting of the Hungarian Central Committee was picked up along with the first casualty figures 'the resources of the Monitoring Service were mobilized'. From that moment on, Papp later recalled, 'the ears of the Monitoring Service were kept on Radio Budapest day and night'.[32] And while teleprinters in Whitehall and Washington sang with the momentous news reported by BBCM, Bush House readied itself for the most challenging broadcasting crisis it had faced in Europe since the Second World War. Armed with the information received from BBCM, the Hungarian Section set about organizing itself into a round-the-clock production centre. As Rentoul recalled,

> we split ourselves into small teams. While a group of two or three people was listening to the latest reports coming out of Budapest Radio and taking hasty notes, others were getting bulletins on the air, translating news from English into Hungarian, compiling reviews from the latest newspaper articles on the Hungarian events and writing comments on the impact and significance of what was happening in Hungary at that particular moment.[33]

The revolution in Hungary 'very soon dominated all the broadcast output, and for a period transmissions in nearly all the languages were wholly concerned with reporting and interpreting its developments'. As the recognized specialists, the Hungarian Section not only had to manage its own programmes, including an extra quarter-hour transmission in the evening from 24 October, but also provide daily bulletins and comments for the rest of the European Services, the General Overseas Service and the BBC's domestic Home Service.[34] At the height of the crisis Rentoul appeared nightly on the Corporation's flagship current affairs television programme, *Highlight*, to explain to domestic BBC audiences the significance and course of events in Hungary.[35]

Radio Budapest was not only at the centre of the uprising, but was the principal source of news on its development and to assist the Hungarian Section its output was fed directly into Bush House – an innovation taken from recent experience covering Poland.[36] Assistant Head of Central European Services, George Tarjan, recalled listening to these broadcasts in the early hours of 24 October and hearing 'untrained voices making sporadic, hasty announcements on the wavelength . . . we knew then that the Communist Government had lost control of the situation despite seemingly confident statements about people laying down their arms'.[37] With this live feed staff could 'interpret minor developments' such as 'delays of incidental music', and the 'fluctuations in the fortunes of the Government and revolutionaries were apparent from the announcements made'.[38] Tarjan also considered it essential to balance editorial assessments in London with a visceral feel for what was actually happening: 'we felt that only by listening ourselves to Radio Budapest could we get near enough to the atmosphere in the Hungarian capital to gauge what events really meant'.[39]

This in-house analysis enhanced the vital flow of information provided by BBCM which, with its resources and depth of coverage, was an important adjunct to the work done in Bush House. There remained, however, one other less visible, but nonetheless essential, internal resource within Bush House for understanding events in Budapest. This was the Central Research Unit (CRU), the External Services' institutional memory-bank headed by the mercurial Walter Kolarz. Filed in CRU was a history of communism in Hungary and around the world with information on 'the names and careers of every insignificant Under-Secretary and most of the Communist Party functionaries, dating back to 1945'. This reference library, as Rentoul recalled, was Bush House's 'self-contained information bureau through all these years and it paid rich dividends when the slow-moving events of the Cold War years suddenly burst into a full national revolution'.[40]

Though well served by its own machinery during the uprising the BBC's Hungarian output would have suffered greatly but for the assistance it received from the FO and, by extension, the British Legation in Budapest. The constant stream of reports (with many carrying the special 'Aside' label intended for BBC consumption) from the Minister at the Legation, Leslie Fry, gave the BBC invaluable on-the-ground assessments from which to paint a radio picture of the revolution.[41] Meanwhile, IRD's Peter Foster had met with Macdonald and Kolarz just five days before the student demonstration in Budapest to discuss the reinstitution of regular meetings between them which had latterly fallen into desuetude. An agreement was reached for these influential members of Bush House staff (or their deputies George Tarjan and Hugh Lunghi) to attend every Friday the FO's daily morning discussions on the day's news and the possible treatment of it 'attended by the Heads of the Soviet and East European Desks, Miss Storey, Miss Korentchevsky and Miss Harris'. This, it was felt, would be 'an opportunity for a weekly round-up and to discuss any current or medium-term projects on which exchange of views might be useful'. In particular, and underlining the often unacknowledged importance of CRU, Foster hoped that 'we may be able to co-ordinate our own output a little more closely with Mr Kolarz's excellent projects and thus save possible duplication of effort'.[42]

Incredibly important flows of information rapidly developed between the Budapest Legation, the Foreign Office and Bush House. Telegrams from Fry reporting almost hourly on the course of events were, depending on the sensitivity of their contents, copied to Bush House and, in a break with normal strict BBC protocols concerning Foreign Office telegrams, distributed among senior members of the Hungarian Section for editorial assessment. In addition regular telephone contact was maintained between the Foreign Office and Bush House for clarification of specific issues or when particular information needed to be passed on especially quickly. This was the case, for example, when IPD's Penney Storey called on 25 October to pass on the news that 'Hungarian tricolours without Communist emblem now flying on many public and other buildings throughout the city', which was subsequently used in BBC programmes.[43] The close-knit nature of this co-operative endeavour, while impressive, did not prevent familiar editorial tensions from coming to the fore. The ubiquity of Budapest Radio as a source of news was an acknowledged problem for the External Services in deciphering the accuracy of events. Fry thought it 'most disturbing to the Hungarian people that the BBC should still be quoting virtually nothing but Budapest Radio' especially when its official claims, for example, that the resistance of revolutionaries was almost over, were 'far from the truth, as of course are practically all the other news bulletins from this city'.[44] In response, Macdonald noted that the 'absence of open sources apart from Budapest Radio (and Vienna Agencies)' meant that

> we had no option but to use the normal procedure of reporting Hungarian news from the one public source available – this was also the source of most of the agency material – at the same time making it clear in every story, even in every paragraph, what the source of the various statements was.

It was true, he admitted, that 'pinning of everything to Budapest Radio meant', as Fry had observed, 'that unwelcome Communist jargon sometimes crept in'.[45]

Fry also felt the BBC should make more use of the front-line details he was providing and believed that 'we should not hesitate to take this magnificent opportunity to discredit the fraudulent regime which is maintaining itself so precariously here by force of Russian arms'.[46] Macdonald, however, stuck to established procedure insisting that Foreign Office telegrams be used as background information and not as news because of 'the cumulative danger over a long period of sources being identified'.[47] On 26 October Fry suggested that the arrival of 'three prominent British journalists in Budapest', all of whom might be able to get their despatches back to London via Vienna, was sufficient cover to use Legation intelligence.[48] The FO eventually concurred and decided to give 'permission for the use of telegrams from Budapest as news'. It was not long though, as the Head of Central European Services had feared, before 'the source became a matter of public knowledge'. Nevertheless, Macdonald was accurate in concluding, despite these tensions, that the BBC was 'magnificently served by Budapest throughout the period'.[49]

A challenge of equal magnitude facing the BBC was arriving at an agreement on the Corporation's own editorial interpretation of events. On the morning of 24 October this was focused on how to interpret Gero's overnight decision to replace Andras Hegedus with Imre Nagy, the titular head of the reform movement, as Prime Minister. Tarjan later recalled that Nagy had from the outset been recognized as a genuine alternative and was given the benefit of the doubt throughout those turbulent days.[50] While this may have been the case by the end of the uprising, attitudes to Nagy and the changing Hungarian leadership within the BBC's Hungarian Section were far more equivocal than Tarjan suggests in those first moments of revolution. Matters were greatly confused with the announcement by Budapest Radio at 08.00 GMT on 24 October that as a result of the 'dastardly armed attack of the counter-revolutionary gangs during the night' the Hungarian government had 'applied for help in accordance with the terms of the Warsaw Treaty to the Soviet formations stationed in Hungary. The Soviet formations, in compliance with the Government's request, are taking part in the restoration of order.'[51] Later that morning Nagy, inadvisably also using the terms 'counter-revolutionary' made a plea to the workers for calm: 'Defend the factories and machines. This is your own treasure. He who destroys or loots harms the entire nation. Order, calm, discipline – these are now the slogans; they come before everything else . . .'[52] Despite a subsequent broadcast in which he announced a programme of reforms and the start of negotiations over the withdrawal of Soviet troops, the strong impression was given that Nagy represented the old regime and had himself issued the invitation for Soviet military assistance. Laszlo Veress, who often found himself in opposition to Tarjan, immediately denounced the new government and held Nagy 'ultimately responsible' for the arrival of Soviet troops.[53] The attendant uncertainty about how to characterize Nagy within Bush House informed the BBC's early coverage of the uprising. As it later transpired it was Gero and not Nagy who issued the invitation to the Soviet Union, first through its Ambassador to Hungary, Yuri Andropov, and then on the phone with Khrushchev himself.[54]

The evolution of the External Service's analysis of Hungarian news mirrored in some respects the changing nature of the revolution as it moved through its different phases. The confusion surrounding its beginnings had given way to a sense that something irrevocable was taking place. On the evening of the 24 October the BBC's Maurice Latey described how the people of both Hungary and Poland must now 'either have better things . . . or be held down with Soviet tanks'.[55] A day later, after the arrival in Budapest of the Soviet Foreign Minister Anastas Mikoyan along with Mikhail Suslov and the massacre of Hungarian civilians by the AVH in Parliament Square, Gero was replaced by Janos Kadar. On 26 October, with Nagy established in the Parliament buildings under his own authority and negotiating with the Russians, a new phase emerged in which the aspirations of Hungarian nationalism began to take shape. Evidence of this materialized the following day when Budapest Radio announced a new government including, for the first time since 1948, non-communists such as Zoltan Tildy and Bela Kovacs. The 28 October brought the most remarkable news yet when Nagy, again on Budapest Radio, announced a general ceasefire and the withdrawal of Soviet troops from Budapest. The seemingly impossible had happened, but a sceptical world waited for Moscow's response. In a broadcast that the Director of the CIA, Allen Dulles, described as 'one of the most significant to come out of the Soviet Union since the end of World War Two', Radio Moscow announced on the evening of 30 October,

> the Soviet Government has given orders to its military command to withdraw the Soviet army units from Budapest as soon as this is considered necessary by the Hungarian government. At the same time, the Soviet government is ready to enter into corresponding negotiations with the government of the Hungarian People's Republic and other participants of the Warsaw Treaty on the question of the presence of Soviet troops on the territory of Hungary.[56]

It was a remarkable broadcast and one that must have had monitors and broadcasters at the BBC listening in near disbelief, but there were surprises yet to come that evening. Budapest Radio, which for so long had been the mouthpiece of repressive and authoritarian government and which had adapted its tone to the varying shades of authority over the previous few days, now transformed itself into the voice of a new Hungary. 'We are opening a new chapter', it announced, 'in the history of the Hungarian Radio at this hour':

> For long years past, the radio was an instrument of lies. It merely carried out orders. It lied during the night and at daytime, it lied on all wavelengths. . . . We who are facing the microphone now, are new men. In future you will hear new voices over the old wavelengths. As the old saying has it, we shall tell "the truth, the whole truth, and nothing but the truth".

They wished, 'to let the Hungarian nation's voice be heard throughout our homeland and the world', and in its subsequent broadcasts to Central Europe and around the world the BBC made sure that happened.[57]

By the time of this broadcast, however, the Hungarian revolution was already entering its final, terminal, phase. A combination of an increasingly radical reform agenda led by Nagy including a commitment to multiparty elections, pressure from the Chinese to put a halt to it, Anglo-French intervention in Egypt and events on the ground, such as the slaughter of a detachment of security police in Budapest on 30 October, led the Soviet Presidium to change tack with a previously uncertain Khrushchev now arguing that 'we should take the initiative in restoring order in Hungary. If we depart . . . the imperialists will interpret it as weakness on our part.'[58] On 1 November, amid reports that Soviet troops were surrounding Budapest and not retreating, Nagy met with Andropov and demanded that they been withdrawn. The following day Hungary unilaterally dissolved its ties with the Warsaw Treaty and declared its neutrality. Once again radio was at the heart of things with Budapest Radio acting as a diplomatic vehicle speaking directly to Moscow, Washington and the United Nations, while the BBC consciously appealed on its behalf when reporting the station's output. One talk, by Anatol Goldberg in his *Notes by Our Observer* series, broadcast on 3 November across Europe and in Russian, was a good example of how Bush House sought to reflect inherent diplomatic sensitivities in its programmes. While on the one hand it re-emphasized Nagy's appeal for the UN 'to uphold the Hungarian Government's decision to leave the Warsaw Pact and occupy a position of neutrality in the international arena', Goldberg was also at pains to assuage Soviet fears of an independent Hungary: 'Every serious politician and observer in the West realises that this is the best solution for Hungary, and that no one is out to entice her into some other camp. The Soviet Union should be pleased with Hungary's neutrality as far as Soviet frontier security is concerned.'[59]

As hope was replaced by a pervasive sense of pessimism and desperation as the Soviet troop build-up continued at the start of November, the BBC broadcast a message it had received from Radio Budapest, initially delivered to the British Legation in Budapest, expressing,

> our appreciation of the London Radio Station, BBC, for the objective information given to the world about our people's struggle. We were particularly pleased to note that there was no incitement to extremism and that the tone of the broadcasts expressed solidarity in our joy over victories and in our sorrow in weeping for our dead.[60]

This message was rebroadcast in all languages by the BBC, as was the Corporation's carefully pitched reply which was designed to show solidarity through the spoken word:

> The BBC in its transmissions to Hungary and to the world during these historic days has tried to represent faithfully the admiration and sympathy of the whole British people for the suffering, the victories and the courage of the Hungarian nation. In the knowledge that Hungarians have written a glorious chapter in the history of Europe, we hope that the result will be for the Hungarian people peace based on justice and moderation, and we rejoice that the Free Hungarian Radio [Budapest Radio], in the midst of the struggle, accepted and declared to the world the supremacy of truth.[61]

This lament for the Hungarian uprising was followed at 04.19 GMT on 4 November by the haunting and desperate voice of Imre Nagy in what was to be his last communication: 'In the early hours of this morning Soviet troops launched an attack against our capital with the obvious intention of overthrowing the lawful democratic Hungarian Government. Our troops are fighting. The Government is in its place. I am informing the people of the country and world public opinion of this.'[62] It was rebroadcast by the BBC across Europe and the world in English and vernacular output. Thereafter, increasingly frantic messages were transmitted by Free Hungarian Radio. For example, just before 05.00 GMT the Defence Minister, Pal Maleter, and the Chief of the General Staff, Istvan Kovacs – both of whom had by this time been captured by the Russians – were ordered to return to their posts. Ten minutes later, Nagy's message of 3 November to the Secretary-General of the United Nations, Dag Hammerskjold, was repeated in Hungarian, English and French. After another hour, in Hungarian and Russian, a desperate plea was made to the advancing Soviet troops: 'Attention! Attention! Important announcement! The Hungarian Government appeals to the officers and men of the Soviet Army not to shoot. Let us avoid bloodshed. The Russians are our friends and will remain our friends.' Then at 07.10, after a further appeal for help by the Association of Hungarian Writers followed by music, the radio signal was discontinued and Free Hungarian Radio fell silent for the last time.[63]

The subsequent recrudescence of Soviet authority over Hungarian affairs and the passage of power to a new regime could be audibly observed in the hours that came. At dawn on 4 November 1956, Ferenc Munnich, who with Janos Kadar had absconded to Moscow a few days earlier, was heard broadcasting on a Soviet wavelength from Szolnok, a town east of Budapest and field headquarters of the Soviet Military Command. He announced the establishment of the new Hungarian Revolutionary Worker-Peasant Government to be led by Janos Kadar as Prime Minister. An hour later, Kadar broadcast details of his political programme, explaining why it had been necessary to ask the Soviet Army Command to 'smash the sinister forces of reaction'.[64] Meanwhile, at 10.00 BBC Monitoring caught a fragment of speech on the Budapest Radio wavelength that, after the hiatus, now regained the idiom of authoritarian rule: 'Counter-revolutionary elements have found their way back into the movement . . .'[65] The BBC Hungarian Section's analysis of that morning's events led it to conclude that Budapest Radio was 'now believed to be in Soviet hands',[66] and at 21.00 Budapest Radio itself returned to the airwaves with music from an emergency programme put out by Moscow Radio followed, after five minutes, by a rebroadcast of Kadar's appeal to the nation.[67] Budapest Radio was once again the mouthpiece of the Soviet-backed Hungarian authorities with a return to normal service indicated by the reading out of an order by the Commander of Soviet troops in which it was noted, with ominous certainty, that 'the complete liquidation of the counter-revolutionaries is under way'.[68]

Reflecting this new reality, BBC output sought to emphasize that while unable to resist Soviet might, the indomitable revolutionary will of the Hungarians had survived and was very much in evidence. To this effect, the BBC's Diplomatic Correspondent argued that 'while the events in Hungary may well be a Russian victory, they are a defeat for Communism', with Martin Esslin noting that the people of Hungary 'may have been repressed by an unprecedented weight of armour', but their 'spirit remains unbroken'.[69] Running alongside such sentiment was the judicious application of satire. Leslie Fry had been quick to report the emergence of numerous spoof notices circulating Budapest that revealed the dark humour of Hungary after the revolution. 'Wanted', announced one, 'A Hungarian Prime Minister. Qualifications, a criminal record and Russian nationality. Character and backbone unnecessary.'[70] Another warned Hungarians that 'ten million counter-revolutionaries are at large in the country', approximately equivalent to the population of Hungary.[71] The value of these was immediately realized in Bush House where the Assistant Director of External Broadcasting, Tangye Lean, was prompted to ask Gregory Macdonald whether it was possible to 'keep these in play throughout our output, e.g. by keeping them in front of the eyes of commentators on Hungary' as they were 'the kind of thing that sticks deeply in the mind'.[72]

The BBC's Maurice Latey, in a commentary broadcast on the day Soviet troops re-entered Budapest, spoke for many when he articulated the sense of anger and futility which attended those observing and listening from a distance to events in Hungary: 'And now must we stand by impotent and guilty watching the destruction of the Hungarian nation which won that victory? I think the feeling must be one of shame at this.'[73] Radio had been there at the start of the revolution and also broadcast its last breath. In beaming the story of the uprising into homes around the world it engaged a global audience in the personal and political lives of those behind the Iron Curtain and engendered a visceral sense of Cold War in action. But as with other programmes to Central and Eastern Europe, how should the influence and impact of international broadcasters be assessed in such circumstances? In what ways did radio matter during the Hungarian uprising?

Audience and influence

Understanding the size and nature of its audience in Hungary was a considerable challenge for the BBC. In 1946 a Hungarian survey of 1,200 radio owners in Budapest found that over 90 per cent listened to the BBC in Hungarian indicating, perhaps, the significance of the wartime legacy to overseas broadcasting. Since then, evidence had been hard to come by and largely anecdotal, based on Legation reports and dissident stories of listening. The advent of jamming between 1948 and 1952 further increased the tentative nature of any assessment, but the scraps of evidence that did emerge suggested that the western radios maintained a significant profile in the region. For example, a survey in neighbouring Poland carried out before the Poznan riots found that 80 per cent of listeners tuned to western broadcasters,[74] while a RFE report based on 238 Hungarian interviews in May 1956 noted that 'there is considerable evidence that the BBC outranks all other western stations in prestige and authority with the better educated sector of the audience'.[75] The great escape and mass exodus of over 200,000 Hungarians during and after the uprising – about two per cent of the entire population – therefore provided an unparalleled opportunity to examine listening habits behind the Iron Curtain in some detail.[76] What emerged was a powerful, if imprecise appreciation of the remarkable extent to which the western radios appeared to have penetrated, despite jamming, the domestic lives of listeners.[77]

Based on a number of studies conducted in the wake of the uprising for the BBC, the United States Information Agency (USIA) which oversaw the VOA, and RFE, what became immediately apparent was the sheer scale of those tuning in to the West. Of those canvassed, between 83 and 97 per cent identified themselves as listeners.[78] Among western broadcasters RFE was the most popular with, according to one USIA study, 96 per cent of those receiving foreign broadcasts admitting to listening to RFE in the last year. VOA and the BBC scored 82 and 67 per cent respectively in this analysis,[79] reflecting a possible correlation between broadcasting hours and their positive appreciation: RFE transmitted 19 hours of programmes a day in Hungarian, VOA approximately five hours and the BBC two hours daily.[80] By contrast, on the measure of trust the BBC was considered the most reliable in the largest of the post-uprising surveys with 91 per cent, followed by VOA on 85 per cent and RFE on 69 per cent.[81] Therefore, despite its relatively short broadcasting schedule, Bush House had built up an enviable reputation for credibility among listeners in Hungary leading even RFE to note that 'among many more critical members of the audience in Hungary, news is accepted as true only if confirmed by the BBC'.[82]

The challenge to internal media sources was not limited to these three stations. Jamming permitting, audiences within Hungary had access to a relatively wide range of external broadcasters, suggesting a rather more complex interrelationship between international and domestic media consumption than might at first appear to be the case. For the determined listener, services were also available from Radio Vatican, Radio Madrid, Radio Paris, Radio Vienna, RIAS (Radio in the American Sector, Berlin) and the American Forces Network, among others. Evidence of cross-listening signified not just the considerable penetration of overseas media into Hungarian domestic life, but the extent to which, as the BBC pointed out, 'broadcasting to Hungary has been essentially a combined operation by a range of western broadcasters who share the audience and also dilute no doubt the jamming attempts of the communists'.[83] Within this collective effort, news output was considered as the most valuable corrective against regime media, followed by political commentaries and music programmes. In this early Cold War period, accompanied by challenging reception conditions, news and current affairs provided an audience for entertainment programming, not the other way round. But perhaps one of the most striking findings was the revelation that of those questioned by USIA (an admittedly self-selecting and not necessarily representative diasporic group) only 4 per cent had faith in regime media while 80 per cent said they relied on foreign radio for news of what was happening inside Hungary before the uprising.[84] Even if only indicative, it illuminates the degree to which international broadcasting had become an established and active participant in the political and cultural life of many Hungarians. For the BBC there was a wider lesson to be drawn:

> If the Cold War is a battle of ideas in which the West is trying to put across accurate information to Communist countries and attempting to get that information accepted in the face of Communist distortions, then there is abundant evidence from Hungarian listeners that the West is winning this aspect of the Cold War and is doing so through the microphone.[85]

The Hungarian uprising had arguably shown the western radios at their most potent. Even jamming, an audible reminder of state surveillance and the spectre of authority in the 'private sphere of the secret listener', as the Hungarian historian István Rév has characterized it, evidently failed to prevent the establishment of a widespread listenership.[86] And yet it was questions over the presumed influence of international radio in Hungary which became a *cause célèbre* of Cold War broadcasting and provoked a crisis of confidence among western broadcasters as to what constituted legitimate aims in the radio arms race. The principal allegations made against foreign broadcasters by the Hungarian leadership after the uprising (RFE in particular) were that they played an 'essential role in the ideological preparation and practical direction of the counter-revolution, in provoking the armed struggle, in the non-observance of the cease-fire, and in arousing the mass hysteria which led to the lynching of innocent men and women ... [and] ... for the bloodshed between Hungarians'.[87] In effect, their output had incited Hungarian listeners to a point of revolution and, once underway, had encouraged their continued resistance against Soviet forces. The radios were also criticized for undermining Imre Nagy and therefore weakening his position as a credible leader able to manage the crisis in the eyes of Moscow, and for being the source of much of the virulent anti-Soviet sentiment expressed in Hungary. Above all, however, it was alleged that these broadcasters had raised unreasonable expectations that the West would intervene, diplomatically and militarily, to help the Hungarians in their struggle for freedom. The combined indictment was that the radios had instigated, encouraged and prolonged the uprising and as a consequence, were partly responsible for the deaths of many the Hungarians (as well as Soviet troops) who fell in pursuit of an unrealizable objective.

President Eisenhower subsequently summed up the geopolitical realities of intervention when he described Hungary 'as inaccessible as Tibet'.[88] Yet, among very many of those who left Hungary during the uprising (96 per cent in the USIA study) there was an expectation that the West would provide aid during the revolution.[89] In fact, half of all those surveyed thought that the 'American broadcasts gave the impression that the US was willing to fight if necessary to save Hungary'.[90] This was a highly damaging indictment of international radio and a highly exploitable one for Soviet propaganda. Perhaps unsurprisingly for such a notorious incident in the Cold War battle of the airwaves, these charges have been the topic of substantial examination and re-examination as evidence and additional sources have been revealed and uncovered.[91] This has focused in particular on the activities of RFE which was the most emboldened and forthright of the radio stations engaged in the collective western broadcast offensive over the Iron Curtain. If VOA spoke for the American government and its political and diplomatic ambitions, the BBC External Services, paid for by government but editorially independent, spoke in the British national interest. Meanwhile RFE, which since its inception in 1950 was principally funded by the CIA, was more explicitly identified in this period with the idea and language of 'liberation'. As the development of US policy towards Europe became more nuanced through the 1950s evincing alternative and competing strategies, those in charge of RFE, Charles Gati argues, 'undoubtedly *listened* to all of Washington's signals, but *heard* only those it wanted to hear – the calls for confrontation'.[92]

Reflecting the requirement made of it to broadcast 'news coverage and commentary from the US policy viewpoint', VOA adopted a cautious editorial approach during the uprising, deciding to self-censor and 'omit material, although verified, which might have an incendiary effect on the Hungarian audiences such as stories concerning Soviet atrocities'.[93] A softer line had also been advocated in September 1956 by RFE Policy Advisor in Munich, William Griffith, when he argued in a guidance memorandum that RFE's aim should be to prolong and extend the 'thaw' observed as a result of the Twentieth Congress of the CPSU in February even if that meant liberation under Communist rule.[94] Translating such guidance into practice, however, proved to be especially difficult for an organization marked by internal bureaucratic conflict and a breakdown of editorial controls at its Munich broadcast centre.[95] While the Voice of Free Hungary (the name of RFE's Hungarian language service) reported, for example, Eisenhower's cautious US television broadcast on 31 October 1956 emphasizing that America was not looking to make 'military allies' in Eastern Europe, its wider programme palette suggested a rather different set of broadcasting aims and objectives.

Contemporary public criticism of RFE was kept to a minimum with both the Council of Europe and the West German government clearing the broadcaster of serious wrongdoing.[96] Similarly, a CIA report concluded that 'Radio Free Europe neither incited the Hungarian people to revolution nor promised outside military intervention.'[97] Beyond the realm of public scrutiny and institutional biases, however, more candid assessments of RFE's editorial approach illuminate a rather different picture. In his appraisal for the American President in the immediate aftermath of the uprising the Director of the CIA, Allen Dulles, explained that 'RFE broadcasts went somewhat beyond specific guidelines in identifying itself with Hungarian patriot aims, and in offering certain tactical advice.'[98] This was in tune with the report subsequently put together by William Griffith which stands as the most detailed and explicit assessment of VFH output during the uprising. Out of 308 programmes reviewed he found that four had violated policy with three offering tactical military advice and one implying western help, while a further sixteen reflected 'distortions of policy or serious failure to employ constructive techniques of policy application'.[99] According to Griffith, the Hungarian programme editor, Gyula Borsanyi, under the pseudonym of Colonel Bell, instructed listeners in partisan warfare and implied foreign assistance if the fighting could be prolonged.[100] On 30 October his colleague, Gyula Litterati, educated listeners on the use of Molotov cocktails in anti-tank warfare, while the day before Katlin Hunyadi explained that Americans and Hungarians in Cleveland, Ohio, were volunteering to go to Hungary to fight.[101] Griffith concluded that broadcasts were 'overexcited', contained 'too much rhetoric, too much emotionalism', lacked 'humility and subtlety' and had a 'distinct émigré tone'.[102]

Griffith believed it was an RFE broadcast on the 4 November that provoked specific expectations of assistance from the West. In a programme entitled *Short World Press Review*, Zoltan Thury quoted a report from the London *Observer* newspaper, written before that morning's military activity, by its Washington Correspondent. It suggested that if the Hungarians could hold out for another three or four days (until the US elections were over) 'the pressure upon the government of the United States to send military help to the freedom fighters will become irresistible'. Combining a potent mixture of speculation and aspiration, Thury continued: 'The reports from London, Paris, the United States and other Western reports show that the world's reaction to the Hungarian events surpasses every imagination. In the Western capitals a practical manifestation of Western sympathy is expected at any hour.'[103] Predictably, such practical manifestations never appeared, but for those who had listened to these encouraging broadcasts during the uprising such sobering realities were not avowed.

There remains, however, another, highly revealing, review of RFE's output that until now has received little if no coverage in the literature on Cold War broadcasting. Although not directly concerned with the Hungarian uprising, this confidential report, written in January 1956, is remarkable for two reasons. First, in its analysis on the objectivity of RFE news output the report prefigures many of the problems experienced during the uprising. Secondly, the review was conducted by the BBC's Head of Central European Services, Gregory Macdonald, and as such reflects many of the governing principles inherent in BBC practice. Commissioned by the Director of the Munich station, Richard Condon, and his deputy, Allan Michie, this was Macdonald's fourth in a series of reviews undertaken since the American broadcaster started operating in 1950. Such was the sensitivity of the report that Macdonald was careful to warn IRD, with whom he liaised, that 'I have been very cagey about it in Bush House, so will you please treat it as *confidential*.'[104]

Macdonald began his analysis with two basic assumptions: 'News is the foundation of radio operation upon which programmes are built' and on which 'the credibility of the station depends'; a 'distinction must be preserved between News and Comment – between the reporting of facts and developments on the one hand and the analysis or interpretation of facts'. Despite being impressed by the 'energy' and 'idealism' of staff in Munich, Macdonald detected profound problems in the running of RFE and concluded that broadcasts had, in fact, 'too marked a tendency in them to be persuasive or polemical' – a verdict that chimed with attitudes in Whitehall.[105] Unlike the BBC, which prepared its news and most of its other programme material centrally for retranslation at the language section level, RFE's Central News Desk was 'confined to intake and supply for the Regional News Desks, with a minimum of editorial control'. Macdonald found little evidence of 'any mechanism to ensure that the various News Desks really do interpret the same news in the same way'. Individual producers set the editorial tone according to individual agendas. It was a dangerously permissive system. This lack of common output standards across RFE led Macdonald to note that 'Under a system where the raw material flows through almost unprocessed to five different editorial centres there are bound to be daily examples of the misapprehension or omission of important stories, and of the inclusion of stories not fully verified.'[106]

Just as important was Macdonald's analysis of the cultural differences between RFE and the BBC. 'The American mind', he argued, 'politically and historically, is "dedicated to a proposition", so that news can be discussed in terms of trends and linked with future vindication'. Conversely, the English and by extension the BBC 'do not believe in "causes" (except in wartime) or in absolute principles, but wait for the vindication of truth out of conflict and contradiction'. To emphasize his point, Macdonald turned to RFE's *Special Guidance Notice No.20 'On Objective Truth'* which exemplified this peculiar dialectic: 'We believe that only the truth can win us credibility with our listeners. We have faith in our cause. We believe it must triumph in the end.' It is perhaps not surprising, therefore, that Macdonald identified a 'tendency in RFE to regard News as a trend towards the future, so that stories indicate (sometimes predict) what is about to happen rather than what has happened'.[107] Macdonald perceived in RFE an editorial outlook that sought to condition the truth in terms of the political, historical and emotional convictions of both the institution and its broadcasters which was very different from his understanding of the BBC tradition where 'News is what has happened, set if necessary against a background of past happenings so that proportion is achieved'.[108]

The dangers inherent in the polemic and prophetic tendencies identified by Macdonald were recognized in the report of the United Nations' Special

Committee on the Problem of Hungary where it advised that 'the greatest restraint and circumspection are called for in international broadcasting'. While refuting the substance of Hungarian and Soviet accusations against the western broadcast effort, the committee noted that 'certain broadcasts by Radio Free Europe helped to create an impression that support might be forthcoming for the Hungarians'.[109] Nevertheless, the committee made it clear that what had occurred in Hungary was 'a spontaneous national uprising, caused by longstanding grievances', not the work of external actors.[110] Convened in January 1957, the committee was charged with providing 'the fullest and best available information regarding the situation created by the intervention of the Union of Soviet Socialist Republics, through its use of armed force and other means, in the internal affairs of Hungary'.[111] Relying heavily on the BBC Monitoring Service's Summary of World Broadcasts and the American FBIS' Daily Reports for its evidential spine its Report, published in June 1957, painted a picture of life in Hungary devoid of human rights and free speech.[112] The Hungarian government was 'maintained by the weapon of terror, wielded by the AVH or political police' and supported by 'a complex network of agents and informers permeating the whole of Hungarian society'. Moreover, the power of Moscow over the country meant 'an alien influence existed in all walks of life'.[113] For the BBC the report was an extremely valuable and, crucially, independent source of critical analysis of life behind the Iron Curtain which provided a rich vein of material to get its broadcasting teeth into. For 24 hours from noon on the publication date of 20 June the BBC European Services (in English and vernacular languages) were instructed to 'devote the maximum possible time to the UN Committee's report' in news output adding that 'comments, talks and press reviews will be used entirely for the purpose of quoting from, explaining and commenting upon the report'. In addition, 'services to Iron Curtain countries will devote their entire transmission periods to this subject until Saturday [22 June], with the primary task of making as much as possible of the text of the report known to the audience which will not receive it through its own radio and press services'. Thereafter, it was intended that the Report would provide programme material, 'particularly for the services to countries behind the Iron Curtain, for many months to come'.[114]

This, then, was the final function performed by radio in the Hungarian uprising: the continuing effort by western broadcasters, as part of the Cold War battle of the airwaves, to keep the memory of it alive as an exemplar of Soviet illegitimacy in Central and Eastern Europe. It also adds to the numerous roles played by the BBC and other international broadcasters in the course of the Hungarian uprising. As an emergency service reporting on the revolution and global reaction to it, the existing habit of Hungarian listeners to rely on external media sources for news of events both inside and outside Hungary became even more significant and pronounced. As did the importance of radio as the mouthpiece and unofficial record of the uprising, from the studios of Budapest Radio to those noting down every word, tone and inflection of its output at the BBC Monitoring Service at Caversham, a vital part of the Corporation's overall journalistic machinery. An important source of information about fast-moving events, BBC broadcasts in Hungarian and about Hungary were greatly aided by the continuous feed Bush House received from the British Legation in Budapest via the Foreign Office and its impressive Diplomatic Wireless Service. This was significant too in terms of the contribution the BBC made in managing expectations, particularly in terms of the possibility of western intervention in Hungary, and in mediating geostrategic tensions as a diplomatically sensitive source of information for consumption in Budapest, Moscow, Washington and London. It nevertheless took full advantage of the uprising to underline and develop its well-rehearsed critical narrative on Soviet domination of Central and Eastern Europe while identifying BBC output with the culture and aspirations of indigenous national identity. At the same time, and regardless of their personal politics and allegiances, there was an understanding among broadcasters at the BBC that programmes carried with them a moral as well as editorial responsibility. Broadcasting on 26 October 1956, Maurice Latey stated clearly that listeners should not expect intervention from the west 'because that would mean war . . . we here on the sidelines cannot encourage one man to shed his blood since we ourselves can take no part'.[115]

The BBC coverage of the Hungarian uprising was a source of pride for both the BBC and the British government that funded its overseas services. The machinery of broadcasting had worked relatively well alongside the diplomatic machinery of government and there had been a general accord of opinion on the approach to be taken. The Foreign Office's Paul Grey subsequently praised the BBC for 'following a cautious policy in its broadcasts to the satellites'.[116] Nevertheless, there is no doubt with whom the sympathies of the BBC lay in Hungary. While attitudes in Bush House towards Nagy and his various and hastily arranged administrations was equivocal and, in some instances, openly hostile, the fight of the Hungarian people for freedom against their Soviet-backed oppressors was a common theme in output that went right the way back to the imposition of a one-party system in Hungary. The uprising only magnified the importance and pertinence of this message. At both a corporate and individual level a set of values hostile to the Soviet Union that were shaped by the course of the Cold War, British government attitudes and the experiences of the BBC's broadcasters, were projected from Bush House and no less so during the Hungarian uprising. As Tarjan succinctly put it in January 1957, 'It was our job to follow the uprising not to lead it, but at the same time it was not for us to set limits to the aims of the Hungarian uprising, and certainly not to underbid them from London in their fight for freedom and national independence.'[117]

10

Suez

The virtually unanimous condemnation of the Soviet Union's repressive intervention in Central Europe contrasted starkly with the acute divisions of opinion within both British society and the wider international community concerning the United Kingdom's policy towards Egypt following that country's nationalization of the Suez Canal in July 1956. In reflecting this state of affairs in its domestic and overseas broadcasts, the BBC consequently found itself in direct confrontation with the British government over what was considered appropriate to broadcast from the perspective of the national interest. The result, in broadcasting terms, was the defining post-war argument between the government and the BBC, which shaped future relations between the two. When the Director-General, Sir Ian Jacob, was summoned to the Foreign Office (FO) on the eve of British military engagement on the Suez Canal it appeared to be an argument the BBC was about to lose.

At that meeting on 25 October 1956 with the Foreign Office Minister of State, Anthony Nutting, Jacob, accompanied by Tangye Lean, was informed that the government 'had been giving thought over a long time to the external services, which in recent months had not, in their view, given value for money spent on them'. On the basis of a Cabinet discussion the previous day it was intended that £1 million, around 20 per cent of the money spent on broadcasting overseas, would be cut from the External Services budget. As a result, Nutting told Jacob, the majority of services to Western Europe would be abolished along with some for Africa and India. If this did not provide the required savings, further cuts in services to Latin America and economies in the General Overseas Services would be considered.[1] Meanwhile, in order to 'advise the BBC on the content and direction of the oversea programmes' and thereby enforce a measure of governmental editorial control, a Foreign Office liaison officer with a desk in Bush House would be imposed on the broadcaster.[2] Furious at the sudden presentation of these proposals without prior consultation, Jacob argued forcefully that these measures 'would have the effect of destroying a large and integral part of the Corporation's organisation built up to carry out work on behalf of the Government'. Nevertheless, as Jacob was forced to concede, the government had the right 'to terminate prescription of services' and at this moment of crisis, it also appeared to have the necessary appetite to do it.[3]

At the start of what was one of the most significant fortnights in international relations since the Second World War – with Britain, Israel and France colluding in a Parisian suburb to engineer a war against Egypt while blood was being spilt on the streets of Budapest – senior management at the BBC suddenly had to come to terms with a first order challenge to its editorial independence and the future of its overseas services. To really appreciate the scale and nature of the argument between the BBC and the government, it is necessary to understand not just the proximate, but also the underlying causes that brought it about. Anyone who overheard the tense and bad-tempered exchange between the Director-General and the Minister of State that day would have been struck by the similarities between Nutting's proposals and the recommendations of the Drogheda Committee which, until then, had not been implemented. In this respect, the Suez crisis was the spark that lit a pyre of governing resentments under Bush House that had been long under construction.

Earlier, in February 1956, Nutting had proposed a re-calibration of overseas broadcasting and tasked Paul Grey, who was responsible for it, to 'look once more into the question of the BBC' which, at £5.14 million represented nearly 44 per cent of the overall information services budget.[4] As Peter Partner has put it, 'this request seems to have released a small landslide in Foreign Office thinking about the BBC'.[5] The subsequent review by Grey on the 'BBC External Services', completed in April with the drafting assistance of the head of IPD, Cosmo Stewart, began a paper trail that led directly to Nutting's meeting with Jacob on 25 October.

Grey thought it 'questionable whether the BBC contribute greatly either to publicity overseas or to our anti-communist work', except in 'broadcasts to the iron curtain'. Moreover, the 'conditions under which the BBC acquired its influence . . . during the war no longer exist this side of the curtain'. By way of contrast, the areas of contemporary strategic interest where direct sound broadcasting remained effective were considered to be the Middle and Far East and Central and Eastern Europe.[6] These conclusions, echoing those of the Drogheda Committee, promised an estimated reduction of 188 hours from the overall weekly transmission time of 554 hours. In particular, Grey proposed the abolition of the language services to countries in Europe outside the iron curtain; reorganization of the German Service with East Germany as the principal target; retention and possible increase of English by Radio to Europe; the abolition of the Latin-American Services; retention and possible extension to Middle Eastern, South-East Asian, and Far Eastern Services; greater expenditure on sound and television transcriptions and exchanges. There remained, however, the tricky question of public reaction to these proposals. On this point Grey thought the abolition of a large part of the overseas services 'would cause a certain storm in Parliament and the Press'. Nevertheless, if the government 'based their view on the Drogheda Report and announced at the same time that they would provide money for activities in other directions' the period of criticism might be 'shortlived'.[7] Ivone Kirtpatrick agreed, noting that 'the protests will be loud and angry'.[8] So too did Nutting, who added, with political astuteness, that 'I have always wanted this kind of redeployment. But it can only be sold in Parliament if it is a redeployment.'[9]

The subsequent Cabinet paper and debate on 5 July 1956 resulted in the establishment of a Committee on Overseas Broadcasting (GEN 542) to 'examine the scale and distribution of expenditure on oversea broadcasting'.[10] Its chairman was the Parliamentary Under-Secretary of State for Foreign Affairs, Douglas Dodds-Parker – an ex-SOE hand with a well-developed appreciation of the darker arts of overseas publicity. Only two months earlier, he had indicated his personal feelings about the BBC in response to the Corporation's film on Khrushchev and Bulganin's visit to the United Kingdom in April. In a letter to Paul Grey he fumed at this 'disgraceful occurrence', continuing that 'Many people, far beyond the confines of the Tory Party, believe that there are sinister, extreme left, influences in the BBC who since the war have slanted news, etc, against HM Government's long-term interests.'[11] However, it was not until 11 July that the BBC was consulted on Whitehall plans for the redevelopment of the External Services. In a conversation with Jacob, Foreign Secretary Selwyn Lloyd acknowledged the 'mutual lack of confidence between Government circles and the British Broadcasting Corporation' and the need for a 'frank discussion' on overseas broadcasting. Jacob's pithy response was to argue that 'the BBC since the war had been faced with an annual financial freeze. The orange was now just about dry.' Lloyd for his part countered by suggesting 'that the BBC was too respectable' and should be prepared to be more 'aggressive'.[12] If this meeting had been designed to build bridges, it seems to have created as many anxieties as it sought to resolve.

Just before GEN 542 submitted its Interim Report to the Prime Minister, very much on the lines of Grey's April paper, the Egyptian President, Colonel Abdel Gamal Nasser nationalized the Suez Canal and within an instant the calculus of Whitehall policy making was changed. The report had proposed the abolition of the French, Italian, Portuguese, Swedish, Danish, Norwegian and Dutch services with further consideration given to those in Spanish, Finnish and Greek, and a reduction in the scale of the General Overseas Service. The intellectual journey to this point had, on the morning of 26 July, more to do with the unresolved outcome of the Drogheda recommendations than anything else. When news came through that evening of the dramatic turn of events in Egypt, all previous business between the BBC and the government immediately came to be seen through this new and threatening prism. This is the point at which the strategic reassessment of the overseas services of the BBC became fused with the problem of Britain's evaporating influence in the Middle East and the government's desperate attempt to rectify this by all means possible. The result was to assign to the mission of the External Services' reorganization a zeal for punitive reform that owed far more to the inability of Britain to retain a credible purchase in the Middle East in an age of emerging Arab nationalism than it did to a well-thought out and implementable programme for change in overseas information policy and the BBC's place within that framework.

Broadcasting to the Middle East

Although the atmospherics of the relationship between Bush House and Whitehall in 1956 were heavily charged with the effects of long-term discord over the distribution and funding of overseas services, it was already apparent by the beginning of the year that developments in the Middle East were to be a major preoccupation for the government and broadcaster alike in the months ahead. As the Director of External Broadcasting, J. B. Clark, noted in the spring of 1956, when surveying the 'Political Scene' for the BBC Board of Governors, 'the focus of international political interest has not been on Europe . . . but on the Middle and Far East'.[13] Meanwhile, British concerns over its ebbing influence in the region, punctuated by the Egyptian military coup in 1952 and subsequent seizure of power by Colonel Nasser, cultivated deep-rooted political and military anxieties about the threat this posed to Britain's key strategic interest in the region – the Suez Canal. Notwithstanding the October 1954 Anglo-Egyptian Treaty, which extended the international status of the Canal Zone to 1961, as the last British troops left the Canal in 1956, senior ministers were acutely aware of the 'vicious circle', as a Defence Committee paper put it, 'in which a reduction in our ability to influence events leads to a loss of prestige . . . [that] . . . in turn creates both the incentive and the opportunity for countries hostile to us to take action harmful to our interests'.[14]

Radio and particularly international broadcasting had not only followed the shifts in the post-war struggle for influence in the Middle East, but was an essential adjunct to regional political and diplomatic ambitions. As with broadcasting through the Iron Curtain, radio was a means of communicating competing regional visions with an unparalleled immediacy that made it a key component in the escalating diplomatic battle for control in the area. In this regard, Egypt's well-developed domestic and international broadcasting operation represented a highly significant and potentially damaging threat to British interests. Launched on 4 July 1953 to promote Arab nationalism and attack its opponents, the Voice of the Arabs (VOTA) was the Arabic-language service for the Middle East from Cairo Radio.[15] It soon commanded the attention of the British government as the emblem of a 'virulent and highly effective Egyptian propaganda campaign against the Western powers, and particularly the United Kingdom'.[16] By the beginning of 1956, Egyptian broadcast services had a reach that covered the whole of the Middle East, North, Central and Eastern Africa and were audible in Western Africa. As the British Joint Intelligence Committee (JIC) prophetically noted of the Egyptian government in July 1956, just days before Nasser used this formidable network to announce to the world the nationalization of the Suez Canal, 'Cairo Radio is probably the most effective single propaganda medium at its disposal.'[17]

British authorities, meanwhile, were developing several strategies to enhance the prominence and credibility of UK policy in this increasingly competitive propaganda war. The British radio station in Aden and, more significantly, the Sharq-al-Adna Arabic-language station broadcasting from Cyprus – a nominally commercially music-based operation which was controlled by the British government – were highly valuable resources for transmitting Whitehall's point of view. In addition, plans were also in place for the establishment of 'a chain of low-powered VHF stations in the Persian Gulf', including Kuwait, which would complement the material produced at a 'proposed covertly controlled Arab Production Centre of transcripts'.[18] These in turn would be supported by a build-up of clandestine, or 'black', broadcasting stations capable of beaming propaganda into the region, primarily from facilities in Cyprus.[19] However, the formative nature of these plans severely limited the British government's range of broadcast options in the Middle East, as was the case with Radio Baghdad, the centrepiece of the 1955 Baghdad Pact's communication strategy, which was still not operational by the time of the Suez crisis. As a consequence, Whitehall found itself primarily reliant on the BBC's services to the Middle East as the most effective means of presenting the British case to an Arabic audience.

Any analysis of the BBC Arabic Service in the run up to the Suez crisis would be hard pushed to find any great cleavages between broadcast output and British policy. Within the 28 hours of programmes broadcast a week in Arabic, in addition to English language services, ample opportunity was found to reflect government policy and British concerns.[20] Programmes such as *Mirror of the West*, *Topic of Today*, *British Thought and the British Way of Life* and the popular audience correspondence-based *Political Questions and Answers* allowed the Arabic Service to transmit comparative, expositional and projection-of-Britain material in some detail. As J. B. Clark noted of developments in the Arab world, including Jordan's decision not to join the Baghdad Pact and the sudden dismissal of the British General Glubb as head of the Jordanian military, the Arab Legion, 'Listeners to the Arabic Service were left in no doubt of the British reaction to these events.'[21]

A prime example of this was the BBC/British government response to Nasser's decision in October 1955 to accept the Soviet Union's offer of arms, under cover from the Czechoslovak authorities. There was an undoubted synergy between Whitehall's response to the arms deal with the consequent threat of Soviet penetration in the region and Bush House's by now well-established Cold War rhetoric. Such was the closeness of the fit that IRD regularly sent BBC talks scripts such as 'Communist Economic Offensive in Egypt' by Alfred Zauberman and 'The Colonialism of Anti-Colonialists', 'Khrushchev the Colonialist' and 'The USSR and Islam' all by Walter Kolarz, to the Regional Information Office in Beirut to be translated and transcribed for dissemination in the Middle East.[22] The arms deal provided the opportunity to attack Soviet regional intentions as well as Nasser personally for having invited this threat to Arab independence. Accordingly, all overseas services, according to Clark, 'continued to hammer away at the theme of "Soviet Imperialism"' into the summer of 1956 as a response to both this development and the persistent Soviet 'diatribes' against the western colonial powers and Britain in particular.[23] The BBC was also at pains to emphasize the positive achievements of the British Commonwealth, drawing comparisons between 'the Russian record of oppression and the British record of education for independence'.[24] For example, the BBC's Eastern Services produced a series of talks by Sir Ivor Jennings for the Arabic Service 'on the development of self-government in British Colonies and Dependencies' which was echoed in talks by Patrick Gordon Walker in the Pakistan Service comparing this with the fate of the Central Asian republics in Soviet Russia.[25]

Whitehall's 'Sovietisation' of the Middle Eastern propaganda war certainly had its advantages – one line of attack for two strategic threats – and easily fitted into tried and tested Cold War publicity strategies. However, the argot of anti-communist rhetoric, Rawnsley persuasively argues, was a rather ineffective vehicle for projecting British influence in the Middle East.[26] The need for closer attention to be paid in Whitehall to Britain's specific publicity requirements in the Middle East was reflected in the April 1956 decision to give the Head of IRD, Jack Rennie, 'a special brief to counter Egyptian propaganda'. On the surface this might have indicated more of the same from the head of a department that, since 1948, had been concerned with anti-communist publicity. But, as a Foreign Office note from May makes clear, IRD had been 'given a new charter to include anti-subversive work in general in the field of propaganda and publicity, and, as an immediate objective, this work in the Middle East will, in IRD, take priority over anti-Communism'.[27] It is important to appreciate, in this respect, the very large degree to which British publicity in the Middle East by 1956 was conditioned by and responding to the hostile propaganda coming from Cairo Radio. As Anthony Nutting recalled in print a decade later, when programmes 'boomed forth from the "Voice of the Arabs" radio transmitter in Cairo, the British Government desperately tried to tighten its grip upon those countries where its writ still ran'.[28] The fear of Egyptian radio's influence prompted members of the Whitehall Committee on Overseas Broadcasting to describe Britain as being 'engaged on what amounted to a "radio war"' in the region.[29] As a consequence, BBC services were encouraged to join the battle with an extra half-hour of broadcasting time in the evening from 5 August, while plans were advanced for an Arabic transcription service (to supply radio stations in the Arab world) and the beaming in, at the Colonial Office's request, of Arabic, Hindu and Urdu services to East Africa.[30] These belated attempts to improve the reach of the BBC in the Middle East nonetheless concealed a history of parsimonious resourcing that went back to before the Second World War.

In his May 1956 paper on the 'External Services of the BBC', an attempt to pre-empt current government thinking on broadcasting, Ian Jacob noted that 'For a generation successive British governments have shown reluctance to finance propaganda services in Arabic corresponding to the size of the problem and the virulence of our competitors.' The most damaging cost of this prevarication, he argued, was that the 'BBC's case for a medium wave relay has been shelved for nearly twenty years on grounds of economy.' In a media environment that had become dominated by listening on medium wave, something embraced and enhanced by Cairo Radio, BBC Arabic and other regional services that transmitted predominantly on shortwave simply did not have the reach and audibility to compete on equal terms. What Jacob advocated was the installation of a medium-wave transmitter on Cyprus at a capital cost of £250,000.[31] On this, there was an accord of outlook with the FO, in keeping with the recommendations of the Drogheda committee. But the persistent refusal of the Treasury to countenance the release of funds necessary to achieve it led Tangye Lean to conclude that there was 'no prospect of our being able to carry out the extension of the Arabic Service'.[32] Indeed, by June 1956, and with the Treasury looking for an overall saving of £100 million from the public purse, the Chancellor, Harold Macmillan, proposed to the Cabinet the slashing of expenditure on the External Services by £1 million.[33] A review into British broadcasting in the Middle East commissioned by Eden in May nevertheless recommended that the BBC's Arabic Service should be broadcast on medium wave.[34] Whitehall quickly followed suit and in July the powerful Policy Review Committee, chaired by the Prime Minister, invited the Foreign Secretary to arrange for a medium-wave relay station to get underway in the Middle East.[35]

On the eve of the nationalization of the Suez Canal there existed two critical debates in Whitehall over the External Services of the BBC, one which brought to a head years of unresolved tensions about the funding and distribution of the overseas broadcasting effort and another which focused on the political and diplomatic preoccupations of the time. The unifying theme between the two was the sense that BBC services to both Western Europe and the Middle East had become ineffective. From Drogheda onwards Whitehall considered the former as superfluous because its output did not contribute to the government's overseas publicity objectives there.[36] By contrast services to the Middle East were ineffective, not because the job they did was undervalued, but because they did not have the reach and impact necessary to maximize their usefulness to government. As the Committee on Overseas Broadcasting, GEN 542, pointed out on 12 July 1956, the objectives of overseas broadcasting were not the same around the world: 'the emphasis in Europe was on culture, but in the Middle East we were engaged on what amounted to a propaganda war'.[37] With the Treasury unwilling to provide the financial resources to fund both it was an obvious political decision which would survive. In this way the fate of the overall distribution of the BBC's External Services became fused with the course of events in the Middle East.

Controlling tendency

The growing conviction within government that something should be done about the BBC's External Services found expression in an improved appetite for more centralized direction over output. On 25 July, the Policy Review Committee asked Selwyn Lloyd 'to consider by what means the Government could best secure a larger measure of control over the context of broadcasts to the Middle East and Far East'.[38] A blueprint for reorganization had already been established by Paul Grey in his April paper on the 'BBC External Services' and was now advanced in Douglas Dodds-Parker's Committee on Overseas Broadcasting. Meeting just hours after the Policy Review Committee it was suggested the 'possibilities were either to arrange with the BBC that its broadcasts should be used as an instrument of Government policy, or to make use of a different organization and reduce Government expenditure on BBC overseas broadcasts'. This was perhaps an example of rhetoric exceeding realism, but it was nonetheless an indication of the extent to which the political debate in government was by now willing to contemplate radical solutions with respect to the BBC. Practical considerations were brought to bear, however, and it was pointed out that 'to use overseas broadcasting as a means of disseminating what would be known to be United Kingdom propaganda was open to serious objections, which might outweigh the advantages of abandoning a wholly impartial approach'.[39] This view was echoed by Grey who felt that 'it would be strongly resisted by the BBC as destroying their present independence and thereby damaging their reputation abroad; and H.M.G. themselves might find that there would be disagreeable consequences, including responsibility, both in Parliament and abroad, for every word broadcast'.[40]

Substantial obstacles to government seizure of control for overseas broadcasting were also contained in the 1946 *Broadcasting Policy* White Paper which stated 'that the Corporation should remain independent in the preparation of programmes for overseas audiences'. Nevertheless, the government retained the right to provide guidance and various liaison arrangements had been devised over the years to satisfy this impulse. For example, there was daily contact between the heads of the BBC language services and the regional desks of the Foreign Office, while special information was passed through the BBC's Diplomatic Correspondent. 'Aside' and guidance telegrams specifically for Bush House consumption were sent by British Missions abroad in addition to telegrams on the Foreign Office and Whitehall distribution (below 'SECRET' grading) which were circulated to selected External Services personnel. Specifically to assist broadcasting over the Iron Curtain the Foreign Office maintained 'a special desk which gives the BBC virtually an hour-to-hour service of information and comment'. Yet, in the climate of July 1956, existing mechanisms of influence appeared inadequate for the job the government wanted done. However, to effect such radical change would, as Grey cautiously noted, require rewriting the Licence and Agreement if not the BBC's Charter itself.[41]

GEN 542's Interim Report, delivered to the Prime Minister on 2 August 1956, assumed 'the BBC continues to be the agent used by the Government for general external broadcasting'. However, the Corporation's overseas output was 'quite out of balance with political requirements'. Broadcasting to Western Europe accounted for about one-third of the total cost of the External Services while 'expenditure on services to the Middle East and the Far East combined is less than one-tenth', with not much more than that spent on services over the Iron Curtain.[42] It was little wonder, then, that the Committee concluded that in the case of Western Europe 'Direct broadcasting is, in our view, now a relatively uneconomic means of making our influence felt'.[43] Ian Jacob, meanwhile, maintained that an increase in funding, not a cost-cutting exercise, was the only viable route to build up a global service with sufficient means to deliver genuine value for money for the British government. The perceived inadequacies of overseas broadcasting were the product of historic under-resourcing by government, not a reason for further diminishing it: 'For lack of a comparatively insignificant fraction of national expenditure, a valuable aid to the British international position and an institution of world-wide fame, is being eaten away year by year, with a corresponding loss of sympathy and understanding throughout the world'.[44]

When Jacob met Kirkpatrick on 28 August 1956, in what Asa Briggs describes as an unpleasant, even threatening, interview, he was told that ministers 'were increasingly dissatisfied with the BBC'. There were 'two powerful schools of thought, one of which was disposed to favour governmental control in the overseas services and the other, the curtailment of the £5 million grant in aid to the BBC and its expenditure in other propaganda enterprises'.[45] The second of these, combined with the style Kirkpatrick chose to deliver the ultimatum, echoed his rhetoric of ten years earlier when as a member of the Official Committee on GIS (which helped frame the post-war settlement of the BBC External Services) he left none of his colleagues in doubt as to his understanding of the future scope for government action:

> It was not intended that the Government should accept any formal responsibility for the conduct of the overseas services, but finance would be provided on the basis of an approved programme, and the Government would be fully entitled to bring pressure to bear on the BBC in order that the service should accord with the aims of Government policy. The ultimate sanction would be a financial one.[46]

A decade on, and now Permanent Under-Secretary at the Foreign Office, he was in a position to assert his conviction of what it meant to broadcast in the national interest. This was political warfare of a domestic sort and an old hand like Kirkpatrick seemed to relish this opportunity to engage in a new radio war. As he later noted, 'Sir Ian Jacob looked stricken like a mother about to be deprived of her child.'[47]

Figure 9 Ivone Kirkpatrick, Controller, BBC European Services, February 1943

A diplomatist and Head of Chancery in Berlin, 1933–38, Kirkpatrick joined the Ministry of Information in 1940 before becoming Controller of BBC European Services in 1941 under the auspices of the Political Warfare Executive. After the war he was appointed Assistant Under-Secretary in the FO responsible for information work rising to the position of Permanent Under-Secretary, 1953–57.

It was ironic that at the point when Suez became an all-consuming crisis in Whitehall, 26 July 1956, relations between the BBC and the government could not have been, literally, any closer. That evening Jacob attended a dinner hosted by the Prime Minister at No.10 Downing Street, marking the official end of the state visit of King Faisal of Iraq and his Prime Minister, Nuri Said.[48] Among others in attendance were the Foreign Secretary, Selwyn Lloyd and the Leader of the Opposition, Hugh Gaitskell. As news arrived during the evening of Nasser's nationalization of the Suez Canal Company, those present were united in shock by Nasser's audacious and highly successful propaganda coup. By the autumn, however, relations among the BBC, government and opposition would be remarkable for their disunity and, at times, their outright hostility reflecting a general disintegration of consensus in British political and public life over what should be done about Suez. Eden's announcement in the House of Commons on 2 August, the eve of the summer recess, that 'certain precautionary measures of a military nature' were underway was immediately followed with a speech by Gaitskell comparing Nasser's actions to those of Mussolini and Hitler in the years before the last war.[49] However, a day later in a private letter to Eden, Gaitskell made it clear that the Labour Party could only accept 'forceful resistance' by Britain under United Nations auspices.[50] This was the beginning of a cleavage in opinion that would become wider and more public in the coming weeks. Meanwhile, after the initial flash of public and press support in favour of taking a firm line with Nasser, there were concerns in government that it might all too quickly evaporate, thereby undermining long-term planning.[51]

What the government wanted was to maintain the momentum of anti-Nasser sentiment and there was a clear expectation that the BBC should acquiesce. For its part, the Corporation felt obliged to reflect 'the conflicting views about British policy which had begun to be voiced after the House of Commons debate'. It was to this end that on 15 August, the eve of the London Conference of Maritime Nations – convened to deal with the canal dispute with Egypt – the BBC replaced a broadcast entitled *Dancing by the Sea* from Brighton on the domestic Light Programme with a *Special Survey of the Suez Canal Crisis*.[52] This 'round-up of opinion' lasted 25 minutes and contained a short contribution from Major Salah Salem, editor of *Al Shaab* and former Egyptian Minister of National Guidance, giving an Egyptian perspective on the Suez crisis.[53] Coming at the same time as the BBC's initial refusal to allow the visiting Australian Prime Minister, Sir Robert Menzies, to broadcast in support of the government's stance towards Egypt – an important part of Eden's public relations campaign – the giving-over of airtime, no matter how little, to Egyptian representations at such a delicate moment confirmed in Eden and others around him suspicions that the BBC was against them.[54] Were those responsible for this at the BBC, wondered Eden, 'enemies or just socialists'?[55] On 17 August Jacob was summoned back from holidaying at his Suffolk house and in a frosty interview with Eden was informed that if the BBC failed in its duty to 'educate' the country as to the 'seriousness of the situation', a Foreign Office official would be posted to the BBC for 'liaison' purposes.[56] And as the Suez crisis deepened, political disgust with both the BBC's home and overseas services threatened to eclipse the work the Corporation was in fact doing, under challenging circumstances, to support the government line abroad.

Great care had been taken in the External Services to ensure that the British government's case was heard around the world, particularly in the Middle East, and that the themes pursued in output reflected Whitehall's publicity strategies. Eden's domestic television broadcast concerning the crisis on 8 August had been simultaneously transmitted by the General Overseas Service and given in full on the Arabic Service. Such was Bush House's desire to cement in the minds of listeners the government's message, that the Arabic translation of Selwyn Lloyd's ministerial broadcast two days before the London Conference started transmission even before he had finished speaking in English.[57] On the first day of the London Conference, 16 August, Guy Wint in *Topic of Today* on the Arabic Service argued that Nasser was damaging regional development by 'scaring away those who are most anxious to promote international cooperation'.[58] The Conference itself was very closely followed by the BBC in all services with two commentators specially assigned to cover proceedings for the Arabic Service, transmitting reports at very short notice from a studio at Carlton House Terrace. Special importance was also attached to broadcasting translations of important speeches in full, as was the case with statements by Lloyd and the American Secretary of State, John Foster Dulles, 'as it was rightly anticipated that only distorted versions of the speeches would be available to newspaper readers in Egypt and other parts of the Arab world'.[59]

Bush House was a willing partner in giving voice to the public themes expressed by politicians and statesmen as the crisis developed: Eden arguing that Nasser 'is not a man who can be trusted to keep an agreement'; Lloyd describing Nasser as military dictator who 'maintains himself in power by methods so well known to us from what happened in certain countries in the inter-war years'.[60] Nasser's pan-Arabic imperialist ambitions and the dangers of communism in the Middle East through Egypt's links with the Soviet Union were covered in detail in the BBC's Arabic output as were other Foreign Office targets such as the 'futility of Nasser's economic plans' and the 'intricacies of the Canal organization and the danger of running it without experienced pilots'.[61] In this sense, the relationship with Whitehall was close and even Douglas Dodds-Parker 'expressed appreciation of the vigorous line which has been taken' by the BBC.[62] Yet despite this obvious dovetailing of government aims with External Services output the outstanding characteristic of the relationship between the two was a growing sense of attrition. Against the reality of the substantial effort being made by the BBC to accommodate government attitudes in its programming, the perception in Whitehall was of a broadcaster failing to fulfil its duty to support national, that is government, overseas policy.

The return of Parliament on 12 September heralded 'two difficult days', as Eden put it, of debate on Suez during which Gaitskell condemned the military preparations being made and pushed the government to refer the matter to the United Nations. Demonstrations in London also demanded 'No War Over Suez'.[63] The following day Ian Jacob sought the advice of the Board of Governors on this 'unusual situation for the BBC', where 'for the first time for many years there was a foreign policy issue of great gravity on which there was a sharp division on party lines'. Their reply, 'that the BBC should do nothing to underline the existence of party division and disunity at a time of crisis' was as political as it was unrealistic.[64] For those actually making programmes such as *Topic of Today* and writing broadcast reviews of the British press it was impossible to conceal, except by deliberate censorship, the divisions evident within British society.

When the subject of 'Oversea Broadcasting' resurfaced at the Cabinet on 26 September the Prime Minister's continued dissatisfaction with the conduct of the overseas services led Eden to order that 'the whole basis of existing arrangements should be reviewed'.[65] In doing so he gave executive authority to those in Whitehall, who sought to rewrite the post-war constitutional settlement for overseas broadcasting, resulting in the biggest challenge to its editorial independence that the BBC had ever faced. The first meeting of the Ministerial Committee on Oversea Broadcasting, GEN 554, on 9 October and chaired by the Lord Privy Seal, R.A. Butler, took as its starting point the question of 'whether the Government should have greater control than at present over the content of overseas broadcasts by the BBC, even perhaps to the extent of assuming full responsibility for the content and operation of overseas broadcasting services'.[66] Once again, the sheer impracticality of this was quickly apprehended. As the Postmaster-General, Charles (later Lord) Hill, pointed out, while it was incumbent upon the Corporation to consult and collaborate with government departments 'the final content of those programmes was dependent on the BBC's own interpretation of the national interest'.[67] In the face of such a genuine obstacle the general mood of the committee appeared far more equivocal than might otherwise have been expected. Even Alan Lennox-Boyd, Colonial Secretary and one of Bush House's more vocal critics that summer, felt that 'while the BBC's External Services handling of topics was sometime inept . . . it is necessary to bear in mind the very large volume of programmes put out by the BBC in which the British point of view was constantly kept before overseas audiences'.[68] It was left to Ivone Kirkpatrick, who had been specially invited to this first meeting, to succinctly sum up the present difficulty: 'In short, there was no logical half-way house between no control over the BBC and total control.'[69]

If total control was out of the question, in terms of both the Corporation's continued credibility and the government's liability for overseas broadcasting, another mechanism was needed for exercising influence over Bush House. At this point, Kirkpatrick made a decisive intervention. The 'best course', he suggested,

> might be for the Government to advise the BBC that, while they recognised it to be inherent in the BBC's constitution that it could not undertake propaganda activities, the Government regarded the expenditure of some £5 millions a year on overseas broadcasting out of a total expenditure of some £8 millions on overseas information services as a whole as being disproportionate.[70]

Consequently, the government would in future 'no longer contemplate devoting so large a proportion to the external services of the BBC as at present constituted'. This approach would, he thought, 'administer a psychological shock to the BBC and might bring the Corporation to consider more seriously than hitherto the problem of reconciling its independence under the Charter with the need to conduct its external services in the national interest'.[71] The government's right to prescribe the services it wanted the BBC to broadcast overseas at a cost it set was, as Kirkpatrick had predicted, the soft underbelly of the External Services' editorial independence. At its second meeting on 18 October, GEN 554 agreed in principle to recommend to the Cabinet 'a saving of at least £1 million in expenditure on existing BBC External Services, and that language broadcasts to all European countries (other than the Soviet Union and its satellites), Latin America, South Africa, India and Pakistan should be abolished to the extent necessary to secure such a saving'. Nevertheless, 'subject to the creation of closer liaison between the FO and the BBC, the Corporation should continue to be the vehicle for overseas broadcasting'.[72]

The wish for 'closer liaison' provided the opportunity to propose the appointment of a liaison officer who would oversee 'the whole range of the external services though he would, to begin with, devote special consideration to their presentation of the news on the Middle East'.[73] Kirkpatrick likewise felt that in framing its output in the national interest the 'Corporation would derive considerable help in this direction from the appointment of a competent liaison officer from the Foreign Office.'[74] Not since the dissolution of the PWE and the end of wartime broadcasting measures had the government attempted to influence the BBC's editorial line from within. The Suez crisis provided both the cover and, for those convinced of the all-consuming importance of toppling Nasser, the necessary conflict to insist on a derogation of the constitutional safeguards designed to prevent official control over overseas output.

With Jacob's long-planned visit to the Commonwealth Broadcasters' Conference in Australia imminent it was decided that 'it would be useful if the Committee's provisional conclusions could be disclosed to him before his departure'. Accordingly, on the same day that Britain secretly signed a pact with the French and Israelis in the Parisian suburb of Sèvres to engineer a war in the Middle East to overthrow Nasser, 24 October 1956, the Cabinet gave authority for a meeting with Jacob to inform him of the following:

(i) The Government grant of about £5 millions in respect of the BBC's external services would be reduced by at least £1 million, mainly by the elimination of the European-language services.
(ii) This saving would be devoted, in part, to an intensification of the BBC's services to the Middle East and South East Asia.
(iii) Some part of the saving might also be used to increase the effectiveness of our information services by other means over which the Government would retain more direct control – for example, the production of television material, for use wholly overseas, by the COI.
(iv) The Government would not seek to impose any direct control over the BBC's external services, but they would require the appointment of a Foreign Office liaison officer to advise the BBC on the content of the overseas programmes.[75]

After a decade of peacetime broadcasting and careful negotiation with Whitehall over broadcast objectives and outcomes the BBC External Services now found themselves on an unavoidable collision course with the British government.

The firing line

On 25 October, Anthony Nutting, along with Dodds-Parker and Cosmo Stewart, met with Jacob and Lean. He proceeded to outline the government's demand that the BBC make a saving of £1 million in the Grant-in-Aid of the External Services and, in pursuit of 'closer and more formal liaison', agree to the appointment of a Foreign Service Liaison Officer.[76] At Jacob's request Dodds-Parker drafted a letter to the BBC containing the provisions laid out by Nutting in order that 'the existing pattern of the external services of the BBC might be redirected so as to be rendered more effective and to accord more closely with the policy objectives abroad of the Government'.[77] However, in the time between the initial writing of this letter and its delivery to Broadcasting House the following day there occurred what Briggs has described as a 'twist of fortune' that even now is hard to explain satisfactorily.[78] With Jacob due to fly out of the United Kingdom on the afternoon of Friday, 26 October a subsequent meeting between Jacob accompanied by the BBC's Chairman, Sir Alexander Cadogan, and the Lord Privy Seal, R. A. Butler with Dodds-Parker was hastily arranged for that morning. The letter was then revised by the Cabinet Office official Burke Trend (who would later become Cabinet Secretary) along the lines of this second meeting. When the letter arrived at the BBC a few hours later, importantly still in a draft form, it contained the original suggested cuts in many of the language services and improvements in others to the Middle East and South East Asia, but the amount to be saved in the External Service budget had been radically reduced by half to £500,000.[79]

The reason for this change is still not entirely clear. Was it the ferocity of Jacob's response to Nutting's proposals that weakened the resolve of Butler the following day? Was it as the consequence of an intervention by the BBC's Chairman who, as the wartime Permanent Under-Secretary at the Foreign Office, had access to Eden and other ministers and senior officials in Whitehall? Or was it just evidence of the confused, uncertain and increasingly unhinged state of affairs in government at the time? For BBC management and Governors there was little time to reflect on these motivational nuances as critical judgements of strategy had to be devised post-haste. The chosen solution, and perhaps the only realistic one available, was to delay.

The manner and timing of the government's proposals, the lack of prior consultation, the apparent flexibility on the core budgetary requirement and the sheer administrative, logistical and technical impracticality of implementing these changes without a substantial period of preparation struck those involved at the BBC as highly peculiar, and was quickly interpreted as a means to exert immediate and considerable influence over output regardless of the genuine reorganizational aims these proposals otherwise reflected. However, while Jacob's trip to Australia imposed a deadline of sorts on the BBC's initial response, it was also something that could be, and was, used to the Corporation's advantage. The letter had requested, probably in response to Jacob's criticisms about the lack of consultation, an informal response from the BBC 'so that we can take account of the Corporation's views'.[80] As Jacob departed across the Atlantic that evening his Secretary, Miss Torry, called the FO to say that the BBC had 'no comment' to make on the draft and 'supposed that the BBC would now be getting the letter in final form'.[81] Meanwhile, behind the scenes and under the executive authority of Sir Norman Bottomley, the Corporation's newly installed Assistant Director-General (a former Deputy Chief of the Air Staff and air officer commanding-in-chief, Bomber Command), a formal riposte to these proposals was being prepared.[82] The BBC was, in effect, calling the government's bluff and, as it turned out, successfully so. On hearing of the BBC's response, Dodds-Parker, aware of the 'Cabinet hoops to be gone through' before any action against the BBC could be taken, assumed 'that the next step will be the circulation of the draft to the Overseas Broadcasting Committee'.[83] Events, however, intervened and Butler's committee would not meet again until 12 December by which time both the BBC's and the government's negotiating positions would be radically altered. Meanwhile, on the afternoon of Monday, 29 October, Israeli paratroopers landed east of the Mitla Pass in Egypt, 45 miles from the town of Suez. The following day in accordance with the Sèvres agreement, Britain and France issued ultimatums to both Egypt and Israel to 'halt all acts of war' and withdraw 10 miles from the Canal, with the extra stipulation for the Egyptians that they 'accept temporary occupation of key positions on the Canal by the Anglo-French forces'.[84] Following Egypt's expected failure to comply, allied Anglo-French bombing of Egyptian airfields began on 31 October and five days later British and French paratroopers landed at Port Said at the northern end of the Suez Canal.

While the desire to exert greater control over the External Services had been the motor behind government planning on this issue through the summer of 1956, these new circumstances concentrated minds in Whitehall on the need for the BBC, home and overseas, to broadcast with a sense of national duty under wartime conditions. Accordingly, Bottomley and Harman Grisewood, who as Chief Assistant to the Director-General was on the front line between the BBC and No.10 during Suez, were invited to a meeting at the Ministry of Defence after Jacob's departure.[85] Here, according to Grisewood, they were told of the imminent military operations and informed of the government's intention, though not possible to enact immediately, to revive wartime broadcasting measures which would involve an elaborate system of censorship and direction.[86] They were, in effect, being asked to reconsider the BBC's editorial attitude on the basis of Britain being a country at war. This was at odds not only with the direct experience of many in the BBC who could vividly remember the broadcasting requirements and meaning of war, but with public and parliamentary opinion and the government's own rationale for military operations in the Middle East as a police action. As J. B. Clark pointed out at the end of November, the widening gap in Parliament on policy had been difficult but manageable for the External Services 'because policy had not yet turned into considered intervention. The difficulties became acute when military operations were involved because Party conflict, instead of settling down, flared still higher.'[87] Rather than acquiesce to the government's line, the BBC's response to domestic division and international condemnation of British action, particularly by America and the Soviet Union, was to administer the kind of heightened sense of impartiality the FO had been so critical of in the past. As the BBC's 1956–57 *Annual Report and Accounts* pointed out in retrospect,

> At no time since broadcasting began had there been such a lack of agreement in Parliament and in the country on a major matter of foreign policy. Never previously, therefore, had the BBC's tradition of objective reporting in its external as in its home programmes led it to show to the world a large part of the nation deeply critical of the Government of the day on a matter of vital national concern.[88]

It was to counter just this type of editorial balance that the proposal of a Foreign Office Liaison Officer had been made. On 31 October Paul Grey telephoned the Acting Director-General, Norman Bottomley, seeking the BBC's approval for an immediate appointment on an experimental basis. As he put it, 'the FO wished to know what the BBC was saying in its External Services and the BBC ought to know what the FO was saying and thinking'. After consulting Cadogan, Bottomley rang back to say that 'the BBC was willing to fall in with the

Government's suggestion' on the basis of the terms of reference laid out in the Dodds-Parker draft letter. Accordingly, the Corporation received an important assurance that the

> appointment would not, of course, be intended to derogate in any way from the existing degree of independence of the BBC and from their own responsibility for the programmes which they transmit. Its purpose would be to improve the arrangements for consultation between the Corporation and the prescribing Government Departments, and it would supplement, not replace, the existing arrangements for the transmission of information from these departments to the Corporation.[89]

The Foreign Office's diplomatic choice as Liaison Officer, Lanham Titchener, seemed ideally qualified for this delicate task being someone who, as an ex-SOE man, understood the exigencies of political warfare and, as a former BBC television producer, appreciated the technical and editorial requirements of broadcasting.[90] However, at the end of October 1956 he was stationed in Tehran and did not arrive at Bush House until 12 November, well after the Suez crisis had turned into a disaster for the British government. In his stead, on 1 November Duncan Wilson, who would later become British Ambassador to Moscow, arrived at Bush House.[91] His work in that first 24 hours perfectly exemplified the essential problem of relations between the BBC and the government in this critical period and helps explain the *de facto* stalemate reached between the two. It also demonstrated the impossibility of achieving the 'effective' liaison that the Dodds-Parker letter had called for.

Conscious of the suspicion and resentment with which staff at Bush House would have greeted his arrival, Wilson was upbeat when he volunteered his assessment of a talk by Maurice Latey called *Government and Critics*, the External Services' main comment piece on 1 November. As J. B. Clark later reported, Wilson thought the programme, which explained that the British government was forced to act because of the predictable delays in action by the United Nations, was 'not only a brilliant piece of work, but the best justification until then which had been made of the Government's action' and was a theme subsequently taken up by the Prime Minister in his broadcast on 3 November.[92] Yet at the same time Wilson was charged with complaining to Clark about the coverage given in the previous day's press review of a *Manchester Guardian* leader which accused the British and French governments of 'an act of folly without justification in any terms but brief expediency'.[93] In this way, Wilson gave voice to the conflicting demands the government was making of the External Services at the start of the military phase of the Suez crisis. On the one hand, Bush House ably demonstrated the value to Whitehall of having independent and professional broadcasters make sense of Britain's actions for overseas listeners. On the other, broadcasting as an adjunct to Britain's military campaign required central direction and the stamping out of contrary and competing views. The one was incompatible with the other, a fact which had repeatedly dawned on ministers and officials in their deliberations earlier in the year and had resulted in the ultimatum put to the BBC on 25 and 26 October. In this sense, the imposition of a liaison officer was the manifestation of an unresolved problem, not the solution to it.

While news remained the truly independent core of the External Services operation, and the fly in the broadcast ointment as far as the government was concerned, there was a well-developed appreciation in the External Services of the need, under the rubric of the national interest, to also project an understanding of the motivations that lay behind British government policy and action. In this, Clark felt 'the BBC's critics were obscuring the difference between news and comment, for while the news could not be otherwise than objective and impartial, in comment it was possible to put the British case for action forcefully and effectively'.[94] By 'British case', Clark evidently meant the government's and as Peter Partner has put it: 'There does not seem to be much evidence that the Arabic Service did anything but loyally try to present the British government's policies in the best light it could during the Suez crisis.'[95] In achieving this balance a liaison officer might have had some clear benefit, aiding the flows of information at a critical time, had it not been for the fact that Wilson and then Titchener were charged with the highly political task of influencing output to suit government wishes. In this, however, they were undermined by their relatively toothless terms of reference. So, while Wilson made suggestions 'on the undesirability of news items ranging from the views of the Opposition to communiqués issued from GHQ in Cyprus on the bombing of military installations in Egypt', editorial judgements, albeit conditioned by the cumulative effect of immense government pressure, remained with the BBC.[96] Accordingly, while the government agitated for broadcasts overseas, either by omission or commission, to reflect the government's line, Bush House remained adamant that, as laid out in the 1946 White Paper on *Broadcasting Policy*, the 'treatment of an item in an Overseas news bulletin must not differ in any material respect from its treatment in a current news bulletin for domestic listeners'.[97] As the former Director-General, Sir William Haley had pointed out earlier in the year:

> It has been the primary conception of British broadcasting ever since it decided to speak to peoples beyond its borders, that it would pour through the world hour by hour, day by day, and year by year an unending, undeviating, irrigating flow of truthful news given as objectively and as impartially as British professional men and women could make it. The BBC does not attempt to have one story for its own people and another for the rest of the world.[98]

This was to cause particular problems in relation to the English-language General Overseas Service which, to the great frustration of the FO as Grey ruefully noted in a memo to Kirkpatrick, 'escapes our influence almost entirely'.[99] Reporting to the Cabinet, the Minister of Defence laid out the concerns of the Allied Commander-in-Chief, General Keightley, with regard to troop morale 'in view of the conflicting statements on the wireless and in the Press about the value of operations'.[100] Programmes detailing press comment and public opinion at home lay at the heart of this disquiet, particularly the news talks featuring the speeches by Eden and Gaitskell broadcast on 3rd and 4th November, respectively. In these, Eden attempted to invoke the image of war leader and spoke of the solemn duty that lay in front of the country. Gaitskell, by contrast, effectively appealed to the nation in general and disillusioned Conservative MPs in particular to force Eden's resignation. As General Keightley later remarked in his perceptive and influential review of the military operations, 'His Majesty's Opposition "rocked the landing craft" in the early stages' and, in the eyes of the government, the BBC helped them do it.[101]

It was the government's own psychological warfare plans, however, and not the BBC's reporting of events, which was to prove the Achilles heel of Britain's communication strategy during the Suez crisis. In this tactical field of operations, as Keightley pointed out, 'the Egyptians had it all their own way'.[102] Emblematic of this failure to win the 'psy-war' were the shortcomings of the Voice of Britain radio station, the United Kingdom's mouthpiece in the Middle East from the start of the military phase of the crisis. Brought into being on 31 October 1956, the Voice of Britain (VOB) was the focus of the United Kingdom's psychological warfare operation and was intended to break the will of the Egyptian government and its people and prevent them from resisting the allied military intervention. However, in its planning, implementation and subsequent execution, VOB was a bungled, ineffective and ultimately counterproductive error of judgement. Formerly the Near East Arab Broadcasting Station (NEABS), it had been established during the Second World War by the British and was run by the FO in conjunction with the Secret Intelligence Service. Relaunched in 1948/49 and disguised as a commercial station, known popularly as Sharq-al-Adna, its headquarters were moved from Lebanon to Limassol in Cyprus where it broadcast entertainment programmes, mainly music, in an attempt to align itself with regional sentiment. Indeed, the FO had requested that the BBC nominate candidates from its own Arabic staff to 'act as "stooge" directors of the Company' – an offer the BBC felt obliged to decline.[103] The major changes in the sequencing and planning of Anglo-French military operations (codenamed 'Musketeer (Revise)') necessitated by the signing of the Sèvres Protocol in October and the rapid mobilization to enact its provisions meant that that by the time VOB was hastily pressed into operation it had neither the capacity nor the expertise to broadcast effectively.

Arabic staff at Sharq-al-Adna refused to broadcast and walked out when it became apparent what the station's new role would be. Such was the anger of its Director, Ralph Poston, at both the manner of the takeover and the damage to the government's reputation in the Middle East that he thought would follow, not only did he refuse to broadcast, but had to be held under house arrest until he could be safely sent home.[104] The result was a disaster for the centre-piece of Britain's psychological warfare campaign during Suez. The Voice of Britain was poorly planned, chronically under-resourced and without merit. Its output consisted of entertainment records broadcast from Cyprus, news and talks by the FO in London, in addition to the warnings and threats to the people of Egypt emanating from the Allied High Command.[105] And from 7 November (as well as one transmission on 2 November), relays of the BBC's Arabic Service.[106] The blatant and damaging use, by the British government, of broadcasting to subdue and intimidate listeners in the Middle East had immediate consequences for the BBC. Already understaffed, four of the Arabic Service's expatriate staff resigned at the start of hostilities – one-third of its workforce.[107] The activities of VOB eroded confidence in the independence of the BBC by association as well as diverting critical technical resources earmarked for the Corporation. Earlier in the summer, the government's Policy Review Committee had agreed to fund a medium-wave transmitter for BBC output to the Middle East with the announcement of the decision to requisition the Sharq-al-Adna transmitter for this purpose scheduled for 20 October.[108] Just days before the Sèvres agreement was signed, the announcement was postponed, according to the BBC Board of

Management minutes, because of 'a hitch in Whitehall'.[109] Whether preparing the ground for the outcome of the meetings in Sèvres or not, the result was that at the eleventh hour the BBC's 20-year pursuit of a medium-wave transmitter in the region was again put on hold.

Neither the BBC, nor the government's attempt at political warfare and fear-mongering, gave the British authorities what they really wanted during Suez. Official and political incompetence could not hide the vast chasm that had opened up between the government's objectives and the means with which to achieve them. With widespread global misgivings at the action taken by Britain, a subsequent run on sterling with an irate America blocking access to Britain's International Monetary Fund account, a humiliating climb down was all that was left for the government. As a result, with British troops having advanced just over 20 miles down the Suez Canal from Port Said, Eden announced a ceasefire in the House of Commons at 6 o'clock on 6 November, effective from midnight that night.

The irony, in broadcasting terms, was that for all the criticism fired at them from Whitehall during the crisis, the BBC External Services remained the most effective and credible platform from which to promote British government interests and the wider national interest in the Middle East and beyond. This mission and the leverage it gave the Corporation in dealings with Whitehall were not lost on the BBC. It was also appreciated with considerable rapidity among those who so recently had been willing to dispense with the constitutional niceties of the government's relationship with the BBC and the earlier hostile tone noticeably softened. Even the harshest of critics, such as the Colonial Secretary, Alan Lennox-Boyd, were eager to view the future of Bush House in a new light. In a paper prepared for the Overseas Broadcasting Committee at the end of November, once ministers had had time to digest the events of the previous weeks, he argued that it was 'only when we have made up our minds what a broadcasting operation can do that we can fairly measure the performance of the BBC External Services'.[110] Accordingly, the government was forced to rethink, in the light of very recent experience, its attitude towards overseas broadcasting requirements. The Suez crisis had been a hiatus, albeit a terribly destructive one on all fronts, but with Eden's resignation on 9 January 1957 the balance of the broadcasting relationship with government took on more measured tones. The governing desire for a strategic reorganization within Bush House that had predated Suez remained, but was now put on a more consultative and orthodox footing. The 'bad dream' of Suez, as Jacob put it, was finally over.[111]

End of an era

At its most acute the Suez crisis exposed different appreciations of what it meant to broadcast in the national interest and the corporate obligations resting on the BBC. In both its domestic and overseas services, the government demanded, at a time of war, the Corporation's adherence to its specific publicity requirements. The BBC, meanwhile, argued that without a national consensus – and there was none at the time of Suez – it could not, in its 'news' output (as opposed to other genres of programming), solely and explicitly give preference to the claims of one element of British society, in this case the government, over the widespread and competing claims of others. To do so, it thought, would be to act against the national interest and undermine the credibility of the BBC. As Jacob had made clear in his paper for the FO on the 'The External Services of the BBC' at the end of May 1956:

> The BBC's standing abroad is a national asset comparable with the country's reputation for parliamentary institutions, a free press and a stable system of justice. . . . unlike other foreign broadcasting systems which have followed the tactical needs of the moment and earned a corresponding notoriety and lack of trust.[112]

In this analysis the BBC, and the External Services in particular, occupied a position of constitutional significance in the exercise of British influence overseas. While Whitehall may have imagined broadcasting abroad under Licence as an expression of governmental will, the BBC saw itself (and had done so for quite some time) as an institution whose very creed was a manifestation of the long-term national interest. As Jacob's predecessor as Director-General, William Haley, had noted when reflecting on the future needs of censorship in war, 'Something very vital to both the nation and the BBC would be damaged' if belief in the BBC's editorial independence were lost.[113]

Editorial independence was the public emblem of the BBC's virtue, but the Corporation's moral compass could not wholly discount the needs of the British government, especially when in crisis. Away from the microphone, and out of the public gaze, the BBC provided considerable assistance in the pursuit of covert government aims in the Middle East. Psychological warfare, as the Suez campaign had ably demonstrated, was a concept that appeared to many in Whitehall to have come of age, but which in practice fell well short of its intended objectives. Nevertheless, as military plans for Musketeer (Revise) progressed it became apparent that specific broadcast techniques would be at the forefront of the planned 'Psy-War' against Egypt.[114] But where should the military go for the kind of specialist training this required? The answer was Bush House where in September 1956, just as the government was gearing itself to take on the BBC over its perceived inadequacies, the BBC's Arabic and Greek services hosted a special course on 'radio communications with particular reference to psychological warfare' for 'twenty Military Officers (Secret Branch)'.[115]

At the same time, the BBC was engaged in the activities of a highly secretive part of the Whitehall machinery known as the Advisory Committee. Chaired by the Parliamentary Under-Secretary of State for Foreign Affairs, Douglas Dodds-Parker, it provided the link between the policy set in Eden's war cabinet, the Egypt Committee, and the plans made for psychological warfare operations in Egypt, which were to be implemented by the Information Coordination Executive (ICE) formed out of IRD for this purpose. The BBC was represented on the Advisory Committee from the summer of 1956 by the future Director-General, Hugh Carleton Greene, and then the Head of Eastern Services, Donald Stephenson, allowing the BBC to put its expertise at the disposal of the committee's highly covert objectives. This active participation in the government's Suez strategy stands at odds with the febrile and overtly negative tone of relations between the two at the time. It does, however, point to the Corporation's own extraordinary sense of constitutional 'duty' at a moment of national stress, through which an understanding of the wider context of the External Services activities should be read. It reveals an institutional sense of diplomatic, political and cultural guardianship towards the nation's long-term interests that had become an essential part of Bush House's outlook.

These 'silken cords', as much as anything in the turbulent weeks of October and November 1956, provided a seam of continuity in the relationship between Whitehall and the BBC. The picture on the more familiar battlegrounds of editorial policy and the External Services' organizational remit was, however, more fractured than it had ever been. Yet, just as with questions concerning Britain's post-Suez place in the world, so the new year heralded an opportunity for a 'new deal' between the government and the External Services. The person chosen to lead this initiative – and emblematic of the change in tone from aggression to constructive engagement – was an old broadcasting hand, the wartime 'radio doctor', Charles Hill. Postmaster-General during the Suez crisis, Hill was appointed Chancellor of the Duchy of Lancaster after Eden's resignation on 9 January 1957, with responsibility for Information Services in Harold Macmillan's new Cabinet. His style was a return to hard bargaining within a framework of collective negotiation. At a meeting between Jacob, Cadogan, Butler and Hill on 14 December 1956 it was decided that the Dodds-Parker letter of 26 October should no longer be considered as an ultimatum. Instead, it was 'agreed that the draft letter should serve as a basis of discussions between the BBC and the Government'.[116] The effect was to turn the clock back nearly a year and to take as their stating point the Drogheda-inspired agenda for reform drafted by Paul Grey in April 1956.

This is not to say that the antagonisms of 1956 were entirely forgotten. The external context in which government relations with the BBC played out may have changed, but many of the underlying tensions remained. This was particularly so in the case of the Russian Service where the battle between the Foreign Office and the External Services concerning the tone and vehemence of its output became a matter of public comment in June 1957 after the 'Pharos' column in the *Spectator* magazine argued that its inability to 'either represent Britain or offend totalitarian susceptibilities' made the Russian Service a 'notorious waster of time'.[117] This line was followed up in the magazine's letters pages by some prominent members of the British academic establishment who accused the Russian Service of 'moral compromise and appeasement'.[118] It has been suggested that this was part of a concerted campaign against the BBC that reflected the *modus operandi* of IRD in its use of academics and media outlets to disseminate and give credence to its claims.[119] While a definitive smoking gun remains elusive, so close were these printed charges to the language and concerns expounded by members of the Foreign Office's Information Policy and Information Research departments internally during the previous year that there exists a strong correlation between the two. The effect of this intervention was the establishment towards the end of 1957 of a 'Working Group' on Broadcasting to the Soviet Union comprising the BBC, IRD and the Foreign Office's Research Department.[120] Its conclusions formed the basis of a re-articulation of the principles and purpose of broadcasting in Russian that reflected, to a much greater degree, Foreign Office analysis and outlook. It was certainly convenient, for the future of Bush House's relations with Whitehall in the post-Suez context, that the figure most identified with the empathetic style of broadcasting criticized by the FO and the focus of its opprobrium, Anatol Goldberg, had, in the autumn of 1957, been quietly removed by the BBC from his post as head of the Russian Service and given a less politically damaging role as the External Service's senior regional commentator and the Russian Service's chief scriptwriter. This belated and somewhat qualified success for the FO in recalibrating the BBC's output in Russian was more than matched by the achievement of Hill's committee in redrawing the map of overseas broadcasting where others had failed. As recommended in the subsequent White Paper on *Overseas Information Service*, output to the Middle East and Far East was expanded at the expense of programmes to Europe: services in Portuguese, Dutch, Norwegian, Swedish and Danish were abolished while those in French, German, Italian and Spanish were greatly reduced.[121] The result was a global realignment of the BBC's multilingual broadcast remit that would remain essentially similar in character until the end of the Cold War.

Figure 10 Bush House, The Aldwych, London, April 1948

The home of the BBC European Services since 1941, by the mid-1950s it housed all of the BBC's language services.

Reflections

In analyses of the media, much is said about the nature and meaning of the interaction and dialogue between broadcasters and their audiences. For the Grant-in-Aid-funded BBC External Services this meant the British Foreign Office as much as it did listeners overseas. The deliberations of the Woolton Committee in 1944 and the discussions of Morrison's GEN 81 Committee, resulting in the July 1946 White Paper on *Broadcasting Policy*, represent the beginnings of this conversation in its post-war form. Over the next ten years, and as the vocabulary changed to reflect external pressures, key among them being the Cold War, and internal pressures, such as finance and governance, Whitehall and the BBC came to a negotiated appreciation of the tone necessary to allow that conversation to continue. Charles Hill's return to a consultative, yet critical engagement with the BBC in 1957 reflected this. The result was the settling of relations between the two into a kind of attritional consensus: a robust and often combative discourse which managed to keep in focus the political and fiscal requirements of government alongside the editorial and professional demands of the External Services.

Sir Robert Bruce-Lockhart, diplomat, former head of the PWE and regular contributor to the BBC's Czechoslovakian Service, noted in 1950 that the government's funding of the External Services meant that for 'the cost of a small cruiser you could secure the services of a battle fleet'.[1] The question that inevitably followed was who got to command this fleet of language services: the BBC which made the programmes or Whitehall who paid for them? The answer given by Morrison in 1946 was that the BBC would 'remain independent in the preparation of programmes for overseas audiences' albeit with a requirement to consult the government on output 'as will permit it to plan its programmes in the national interest'.[2] This was a fudge, albeit a politically necessary one, that provided the External Services with a constitution as opposed to a contract. The significance of this lay in the autonomy it gave the BBC to assert its interpretation of the purpose of broadcasting abroad based on professional expertise and the precedent of experience. It was only when the government tried to unilaterally impose its will, as it did during the Suez crisis, thereby rescinding this approach to managing outcomes that the relationship came under the serious threat.

The activities of Bush House were not entirely negotiated through the prism of policy versus practice. Finance was an equally significant determinant of the shape and direction of overseas broadcasting. From the outset, the gap between Grant-in-Aid income and rising BBC expenditure grew at a rapid rate. Austerity Britain provided the economic background against which decisions about broadcasting abroad had to be measured. Between 1947 and 1952, income had risen by 18 per cent while costs had grown by 50 per cent.[3] The problems resulting from this tension forced a cost-benefit analysis of the global remit of the External Services which led directly to the setting up of the Drogheda Committee. Ironically, the effect of this was to ensure that decisions on the core spending issues were put into abeyance for another three years. However, by 1956 the disparity between income and expenditure remained just as acute and with the added strain of the Suez crisis the delicate balance finally broke. The immediate result was the government's splenetic assault on Bush House and the biggest challenge to the BBC's independence to date. In the longer term, though, it led to Hill's far more considered and far more coherent White Paper on *Overseas Information Services*, a kind of second-chance Drogheda, and a settlement that rethought the strategic priorities for overseas broadcasting for a generation to come.

Yet, for all the domestic challenges, the External Services engagement with audiences overseas was the defining objective of both the government and the BBC. The post-war External Services, designed for a world at peace, had had little time to find a new voice before the Cold War enforced a change in the broadcast climate. It was to this end that Whitehall's new machinery of control, in respect of overseas broadcasting, was first used in an attempt to re-engineer the tone of Britain's voice abroad. And as Cold War tensions rose there was no more compelling goal than to try and influence attitudes behind the Iron Curtain. How, though, do you communicate with an imagined audience? The occupation of Central and Eastern Europe by Soviet-backed regimes in the years after the Second World War had severely limited the BBC's opportunities to access audiences and comprehend their broadcast requirements. The flood of letters received after the liberation of Europe, indicating the tastes, aspirations and preoccupations of audiences, rapidly evaporated under the glare of official censors. Those that did reach the BBC – perhaps posted on a trip overseas or through a chain of forwarding addresses – were avidly read in Bush House for evidence of the BBC's editorial affinity with listeners in the Soviet sphere of influence. Nevertheless, it was the case that the BBC's Cold War audiences could never be satisfactorily quantified in this period.

In the absence of reliable and regular sources of information about audience needs and conditions in reception countries, the External Services were required to piece together a mind's-eye picture of listeners and the political and social context in which they tuned into the BBC. Accordingly, this process of triangulation attempted to fit together a variety of sources: feedback from British Missions overseas, particularly in the 'Aside' series of telegrams; collaborative intelligence from other Western broadcasters such as RFE and VOA; anecdotal evidence from staff trips abroad, as with the visit to Russia in 1956; and the testimony of émigrés and dissidents, from Colonel Tokaev to the bedraggled masses leaving their homeland in the death throes of the Hungarian uprising.

At the core of this perpetual system of editorial calculation was the BBC's own staff and the nature of the work they did. The Corporation's open-source collection arm, the BBC Monitoring Service (in partnership with its American counterparts in the CIA), provided an unending stream of information from the world's media – a contextualized backstory for the BBC's own narration of events. But it was in the External Services itself, in the Talks and Features departments, the CRU, in the editorial selection of news, in its corridors and in the individual language sections, that the corporate understanding of audiences was translated into output. Despite a predominantly Anglo-Saxon management, Bush House's multinational and cosmopolitan character (a consequence of the displacement of vast numbers of people during the Second World War, supplemented by Cold War refugees) offered an insight into, and cultural affinity with audiences no longer visible behind the Iron Curtain. In addition, the journalistic endeavour of BBC staff – the digestion and production of news and the daily intellectual engagement with the lives of listeners – itself became an intuitive part of the critical assessment of what tone of voice, or variety of tones, was appropriate for these constantly re-imagined audiences.

Such judgements were not, however, made in isolation, and the political and diplomatic context of these decisions was an ever-present feature as the BBC's debates with the Foreign Office (FO) make very apparent. Indeed, at times the degree of integration between the two spheres, as with Jacob's membership of the Russia Committee and CIPC and, later, Greene and Stephenson's contribution to the Suez Advisory Committee, seems remarkable. Although demonstrating, especially in the case of certain individuals, the amphibian nature of post-war public service, these ties should not be taken as clear evidence of a shared outlook and communality of purpose, but rather as a binding together of expertise on both sides of the broadcast divide to produce a synergy of aims, often not without conflict, around the idea of the national interest. The collective editorial effort, in terms of communicating with the BBC's Cold War audiences, was a mixture of political and diplomatic drivers, broadcast professionalism, fiscal restrictions, sociological and behavioural guesswork, shared cultural identities and the received wisdoms of broadcasting under war conditions for listeners living under oppressive circumstances.

The result was the recasting of broadcasts to the satellite states designed to exploit listeners' sense of indigenous political and cultural tradition and history in order to emphasize the illegitimacy of their Soviet-sponsored governments. Or, in the case of the Soviet Union itself, to speak as a concerned friend and identify with listeners' aspirations while exposing and discrediting the methods of control used by their leaders. Nevertheless, the establishment of these Cold War broadcasting strategies (within a peacetime regulatory framework) was an inexact science, with the potential to engender considerable discord between the government and the BBC over their application. This, along with the tensions associated with financing the External Services, was the fault line on which relations between the two rested. At the same time, it was necessary to acknowledge the limits of this broadcast offensive. While radio was able to tear holes in the Iron Curtain (despite the best efforts of Soviet jammers), there was nothing the BBC, nor any of the other western broadcasters, could do in providing material support for listeners. This was ably and repeatedly demonstrated in Hungary, Czechoslovakia, Poland and East Germany. What could be achieved, however, was to create a sense of solidarity through the spoken word, a social contract formed in the ether between broadcaster and listener, based on the long-term policy, as the architect of the BBC's Cold War broadcasting machinery, Ian Jacob, adroitly described it, of 'acquiring a reputation for stable responsibility which precisely responds to the needs of Britain's international position'.[4]

Notes

Introduction

1 The National Archives of the United Kingdom (TNA); Public Record Office (PRO), Kew, London. CAB134/102, Committee on Colonial Information Policy, CI(50)21, 'The Overseas Services of the BBC', Memorandum by the BBC, 19 June 1950.
2 William Haley, 'The Next Five Years in Broadcasting', *BBC Yearbook 1948* (London: BBC, 1949), p. 7.
3 Asa Briggs, *The History of Broadcasting in the United Kingdom, Volume III: The War of Words, 1939-1945* (Oxford: Oxford University Press, 1995), p. 642.
4 Ibid., p. 74.
5 For the pre-war development of foreign language services see, Asa Briggs, *The History of Broadcasting in the United Kingdom, Volume II: The Golden Age of Wireless, 1927-1939* (Oxford: Oxford University Press, 1995), pp. 342, 368–80.
6 Briggs, *War of Words*, p. 18; 'Broadcasts to Europe', *BBC Yearbook 1945* (London: BBC, 1945), p. 109.
7 Haley, 'The Next Five Years', p. 11.
8 *Broadcasting Policy*, Cmd.6852 (London: HMSO, July 1946), para. 58.
9 On 1 November 1939, the BBC's Control Board (its executive management committee) dropped the designation "Empire Service" in favour of "Overseas Service".
10 192 million as of June 2013. BBC Media Centre, 'Record audience figures as quarter of a billion people tune into BBC global news services', 25 June 2013. Available at: http://www.bbc.co.uk/mediacentre/latestnews/2013/global-audience-estimate.html. Accessed 28 October 2013.
11 Philip Taylor, *Global Communications, International Affairs and the Media Since 1945* (London: Routledge, 1997), p. 4.
12 Nicholas Cull, 'Book Review of *War of the Black Heavens: The Battles of Western Broadcasting in the Cold War* by Michael Nelson'. *Historical Journal of Film Radio and Television*, 20(1), 2000, p. 136.
13 Kathleen Starck (ed.), *Between Fear and Freedom: Cultural Representations of the Cold War* (Newcastle upon Tyne: Cambridge Scholars Publishing, 2010), p. 3.
14 Giles Scott-Smith and Hans Krabbendam (eds), *The Cultural Cold War in Western Europe 1945-60* (London: Frank Cass, 2003), p. 3.

15 For example: James Smith, *British Writers and MI5 Surveillance* (Cambridge: Cambridge University Press, 2013); Marie Gillespie and Alban Webb (eds), *Diasporas and Diplomacy: Cosmopolitan Contact Zones at the BBC World Service, 1932-2012* (New York: Routledge, 2012); Peter Romijn, Giles Scott-Smith, and Joes Segal (eds), *Divided Dreamworlds?: The Cultural Cold War in East and West* (Amsterdam: Amsterdam University Press, 2012); Patrick Major and Rana Mitter (eds), *Across the Blocs: Cold War Cultural and Social History* (London: Frank Cass, 2004); Yale Richmond, *Cultural Exchange and the Cold War: Raising the Iron Curtain* (University Park: Pennsylvania State University Press, 2003); Frances Stoner Saunders, *Who Paid the Piper?: The CIA and the Cultural Cold War* (London: Granta Books, 1999); Walter Hixson, *Parting the Curtain: Propaganda, Culture and the Cold War 1945-61* (Basingstoke: Macmillan, 1997); Stephen Whitfield, *The Culture of the Cold War* (Baltimore: John Hopkins University Press, 1996).

16 Starck, *Between Fear and Freedom*, p. 3.

17 David Caute, *The Dancer Defects: The Struggle for Cultural Supremacy during the Cold War* (Oxford: Oxford University Press, 2003), p. 1; Jessica Gienow-Hecht and Mark Donfried (eds), *Searching for a Cultural Diplomacy* (Oxford: Berghahn, 2010), p. 15.

18 Caute, *The Dancer Defects*, p. 5.

19 For example: The "Waldegrave Initiative" leading to, *Open Government*, Cmd.2290 (London: HMSO, July 1993); *Code of Practice on Access to Government Information* (Cabinet Office: OPSS, April 1994); *Freedom of Information Act 2000* (London: TSO, 2000).

20 Anthony Adamthwaite, 'Nation Shall Speak Peace Unto Nation: The BBC's response to peace and defence issues, 1945-58'. *Contemporary Record*, 7(3), 1993, p. 557.

21 Hixson, *Parting the Curtain*, p. xii.

22 Nicholas Cull, '"Public Diplomacy" Before Gullion: The Evolution of a Phrase', *USC Center on Public Diplomacy*, undated. Available at: http://uscpublicdiplomacy.org/pdfs/gullion.pdf. Accessed 1 October 2013. For recent examinations of public and cultural diplomacy, particularly in the context of strategic communications and "soft power" see, for example: James Pamment, *New Public Diplomacy in the 21st Century: A Comparative Study of Policy and Practice* (Abingdon: Routledge, 2013); Jan Melissen, 'Public Diplomacy', in Andrew Cooper, Jorge Heine and Ramesh Thakur (eds), *The Oxford Handbook of Modern Diplomacy* (Oxford: Oxford University Press, 2013); Lord Carter of Coles, *Public Diplomacy Review*, December 2005. Available at: http://www.britishcouncil.org/home-carter-report. Accessed 1 October 2013; Jan Melissen (ed.), *The New Public Diplomacy: Soft Power in International Relations* (Basingstoke: Palgrave Macmillan, 2005); Joseph Nye, *Soft Power: The Means to Success in World Politics* (New York: Public Affairs, 2004); Manuela Aguilar, *Cultural Diplomacy and Foreign Policy: German-American Relations, 1955-1968* (New York: Peter Lang, 1996).

23 Edward Tangye Lean, *Voices in the Darkness: The Story of the European Radio War* (London: Secker & Warburg, 1943); John Tusa, *A World in Your Ear: Reflections on Changes* (London: Broadside, 1992). See also, George Urban, *The Nineteen Days: A Broadcaster's Account of the Hungarian Revolution* (London: Heinemann, 1957); Harman Grisewood, *One Thing at a Time: An Autobiography* (London: Hutchinson, 1968); Thomas Barman, *Diplomatic Correspondent* (London: Hamish Hamilton, 1968); Hugh Carleton Greene, *The Third Floor Front: A View of Broadcasting in the Sixties* (London: Bodley Head, 1969); Peter Johnson, 'Working as the BBC's German Service representative and news correspondent in West Berlin, 1965-1970', in Charmain Brinson and Richard Dove (eds), *"Stimme der Wahrheit": German-language broadcasting by the BBC*, Yearbook of the Research Centre for German and Austrian Exile Studies, 5 (Amsterdam: Rodopi, 2003), pp. 207–19.

24 Charles Hill, *Both Sides of the Hill* (London: Heinemann, 1964); Hill, later Baron Hill of Luton, broadcast on the BBC during the Second World War as the 'Radio Doctor' and later served as Postmaster-General and Chancellor of the Duchy of Lancaster with responsibility for information services. He was subsequently Chairman of both the Independent Television Authority and the BBC. Robert Marett, *Through the Back Door: An Inside View of Britain's Overseas Information Services* (London: Pergamon, 1968). See also, Christopher Mayhew, *A War of Words: A Cold War Witness* (London: I.B. Taurus, 1998).

25 See, for example, Martin Esslin, 'The Listener in Occupied Europe and Behind the Iron Curtain', *London Calling*, 10 December 1953; Ian Jacob, 'The BBC as a national and international force', address to the 8th Annual Conference of the Institute of Public Relations, 18 May 1957; J. B. Clark, 'The BBC's External Services'. *International Affairs*, 35(2), 1959, pp. 170–80; Maurice Latey, 'Broadcasting to the USSR and Eastern Europe', *BBC Lunchtime Lectures 3rd Series* (London: BBC, 1964); Gerard Mansell, 'Why External Broadcasting?: A lecture', *BBC Lunchtime Lectures, 10th Series* (London: BBC, 1975); BBC External Services Publicity Unit, *Voice for the World: 50 years of Broadcasting to the World, 1932-1982* (London: BBC, 1982).

26 Gerard Mansell, *Let Truth be Told: 50 years of BBC External Broadcasting* (London: Weidenfeld and Nicolson, 1982). For a concise history of the BBC's Arabic Service see, Peter Partner, *Arab Voices: The BBC Arabic Service, 1938-1988* (London: BBC, 1988).

27 John Black, *Organising the Propaganda Instrument: The British Experience* (The Hague: Martinus Nijhoff, 1975).

28 Great Britain, Foreign and Commonwealth Office, *IRD: Origins and Establishment of the Foreign Office Information Research Department, 1946-48*, Library and Records Department (London: Foreign and Commonwealth Office, 1995).

29 See, for example, Lyn Smith, 'Covert British Propaganda: The Information Research Department, 1947-77'. *Millenium*, 9(1), 1980, pp. 67–83; Richard Fletcher,

'British Propaganda since World War Two – A Case Study'. *Media, Culture and Society*, 4(2), 1982, pp. 97–109; Scott Lucas and C. J. Morris, 'A very British crusade: The Information Research Department and the beginning of the Cold War', in Richard Aldrich (ed.), *British Intelligence, Strategy and the Cold War, 1945-51* (London: Routledge, 1992), pp. 85–110.

30 Hugh Wilford, 'The Information Research Department: Britain's secret Cold War weapon revealed'. *Review of International Studies*, 24(3), 1998, pp. 353–69. In contrast to this well-documented article, Paul Lashmar and James Oliver's book, *Britain's Secret Propaganda War*, also published in 1998, fails to take advantage of the archival releases and raises as many questions as it seeks to answer. Paul Lashmar and James Oliver, *Britain's Secret Propaganda War, 1948-1977* (Stroud: Sutton Publishing, 1998).

31 Files relating to the post-war activities of the Intelligence Agencies remain closed.

32 Andrew Defty, *Britain, America and Anti-Communist Propaganda 1945-53: The Information Research Department* (London: Routledge, 2004); James Vaughan, *The Failure of American and British Propaganda in the Arab Middle East, 1945-1957: Unconquerable Minds* (Basingstoke: Palgrave Macmillan, 2005); John Jenks, *British Propaganda and News Media in the Cold War* (Edinburgh: Edinburgh University Press, 2006); Lowell Schwartz, *Political Warfare Against the Kremlin: US and British Propaganda at the Beginning of the Cold War* (Basingstoke: Palgrave Macmillan, 2009). See also, Gary Rawnsley (ed.), *Cold War Propaganda in the 1950s* (Basingstoke: Macmillan, 1999); Tony Shaw, 'The Information Research Department of the British Foreign Office and the Korean War, 1950-1953'. *Journal of Contemporary History*, 34(2), 1999, pp. 263–81; James Vaughan, 'Propaganda by Proxy? Britain, America and Arab radio broadcasting, 1953-1957'. *Historical Journal of Film, Radio and Television*, 22(2), 2002, pp. 157–72; Andrew Defty, '"Close and Continuous Liaison": British Anti-Communist Propaganda and Cooperation with the United States, 1950-51'. *Intelligence and National Security*, 17(4), 2002, pp. 100–30; Richard Aldrich, 'Putting Culture into the Cold War: The Cultural Relations Department (CRD) and British Covert Information Warfare'. *Intelligence and National Security*, 18(2), 2003, pp. 109–33; James Vaughan, '"Cloak Without Dagger": How the Information Research Department Fought Britain's Cold War in the Middle East, 1948-1956'. *Cold War History*, 4(3), 2004, pp. 56–84; James Vaughan, '"A Certain Idea of Britain": British Cultural Diplomacy in the Middle East, 1945-57'. *Contemporary British History*, 19(2), 2005, pp. 151–68.

33 Tony Shaw, *Eden, Suez and the Mass Media: Propaganda and Persuasion during the Suez Crisis* (London: I.B. Taurus, 1996); Linda Risso (ed.), 'Radio Wars: Broadcasting During the Cold War'. Special issue of *Cold War History*, 13(2), 2013. See also, Tony Shaw, 'Government manipulation of the press during the 1956 Suez

crisis'. *Contemporary Record*, 8, 1994, pp. 274–88; Tony Shaw, 'Eden and the BBC during the Suez Crisis: A Myth Re-examined'. *Twentieth Century British History*, 6(3), 1995, pp. 320–43; Tony Shaw, 'Cardigan's last fling: Sir Alexander Cadogan, Chairman of the Board of Governors of the BBC'. *Contemporary British History*, 13(2), 1999, pp. 126–45.

34 Gary Rawnsley, *Radio Diplomacy and Propaganda: The BBC and VOA in International Politics, 1956-64* (Basingstoke: Macmillan, 1996). See also, Gary Rawnsley, 'Cold War Radio in Crisis: The BBC Overseas Services, the Suez Crisis and the Hungarian Uprising'. *Historical Journal of Film, Radio and Television*, 16(2), 1996, pp. 197–219; Gary Rawnsley, 'Overt and Covert: The Voice of Britain and Black Radio Broadcasting in the Suez Crisis, 1956'. *Intelligence and National Security*, 11, 1996, pp. 497–522.

35 TNA: PRO, CAB134/102, CI(50)26, 'Working Party for the Colonial Information Policy Committee', 11 July 1950.

Chapter 1

1 PWE's sponsoring Departments were the Foreign Office (policy) and the MOI (administration). On the organization and operation of PWE see, David Garnett, *The Secret History of PWE: The Political Warfare Executive 1939-1945* (London: St Ermin's Press, 2002). On the initial relations between the BBC and PWE see, in particular, pp. 75–95.

2 Bush House was first occupied by the BBC European Services in January 1941.

3 WAC, R1/80/1, G15, Untitled Report on the Reorganisation of the BBC, Robert Foot and William Haley, 14 February 1944.

4 Asa Briggs, *The History of Broadcasting in the United Kingdom, Volume III: The War of Words, 1939-1945* (Oxford: Oxford University Press, 1995), p. 161.

5 Asa Briggs, *The History of Broadcasting in the United Kingdom, Volume IV: Sound and Vision, 1945-55* (Oxford: Oxford University Press, 1995), p. 27.

6 *Social Insurance and Allied Services*, Cmd.6404, November 1942, para. 8. The Second Battle of El Alamein was fought between 23 October and 11 November 1942. Soviet forces at Stalingrad mounted a counteroffensive a week later on 19 November 1942 with the surrender of the German Sixth Army, accompanied by part of the Fourth Panzer Army and allied units, coming on 2 February 1943.

7 BBC Written Archive Centre (WAC), Caversham, Berkshire, R1/79/2, G64, Note by Foot, 12 October 1943.

8 WAC, R1/80/1, G15, Untitled Report on the Reorganisation of the BBC, Robert Foot and William Haley, 14 February 1944.

9 The BBC's overseas services had been funded through a parliamentary grant-in-aid since World War Two. As a result of the British government's 2010 Comprehensive Spending Review, from April 2014 the World Service will be funded through the Licence Fee.
10 Briggs, *Sound and Vision*, p. 30.
11 TNA: PRO CAB76/16, CP(45)293, 'Broadcasting Policy: Report by the Lord President of the Council, The Minister of Information, the Postmaster-General and the Minister of State', 20 November 1945. The original members of the committee were Lord Woolton, Minister of Reconstruction (Chair); Clement Attlee, Lord President of the Council; Brendan Bracken, Minister of Information; Harry Crookshank, Postmaster-General; and a representative of the Foreign Office.
12 'General Overseas Service', *BBC Yearbook 1947* (London: BBC, 1947), p. 96.
13 TNA: PRO, CAB76/16, B(44)7, 'The Future of Broadcasting', 12 July 1944.
14 Ibid., B(44) 1st Meeting, 15 May 1944.
15 WAC, R1/80/2, G51, 'Broadcasting to Europe', 12 October 1944.
16 Ibid. For comparison see, TNA: PRO, CAB76/16, B(44)7, 'The Future of Broadcasting', 12 July 1944.
17 Ibid.
18 Ibid.
19 Ibid. This was later amended to just English, French and German.
20 TNA: PRO, CAB76/16, B(45) 3rd Meeting, 'Broadcasting Committee', 24 April 1944.
21 WAC, R1/80/2, G51, 12 October 1944.
22 GEN 81 consisted of Morrison (Chair), the Minister of Information, E. J. Williams, the Postmaster-General, the Earl of Listowel and Philip Noel-Baker, a Minister of State at the Foreign Office.
23 WAC, R34/408/2, Note of General Liaison Meeting held in the Council Chamber, Broadcasting House, 23 November 1945.
24 TNA: PRO, CAB128/2, CM(45)64(1), 'Broadcasting; Future Policy', 20 December 1945.
25 The initial path through Parliament was a far from easy one. Prime Minister Clement Attlee's announcement to the House of Commons that there would not be an independent inquiry into the future of the BBC prior to a new Charter, as there had been in 1936 (Ullswater Committee), sparked anger and protest, particularly from the Conservative benches. In the House of Lords, a proposal for an independent inquiry was tabled by Lord Brabazon, while in the Commons Winston Churchill attracted 211 signatures to his motion for a Joint Select Committee to consider the issue. The Labour government acceded to a reduced Charter period of 5 years with the possibility of an inquiry. The result was the

1949 Broadcasting Committee chaired by Lord Beveridge. Hansard, Fifth Series, *House of Commons Debates*, vol.419, col.953, 19 February 1946; Ibid., vol.425, col.1063, 16 July 1946; TNA: PRO, CAB128/5, CM(46)62(5), 'Broadcasting', 27 June 1946.

26 WAC, R1/82/3, G68, 'The Principles and Purpose of the BBC's External Services', 30 October 1946.

27 TNA: PRO, CAB76/16, CP(45)293, 20 November 1945.

28 *Broadcasting Policy*, Cmd.6852, HMSO, July 1946, para. 59.

29 WAC, R1/82/3, G68.

30 Ibid.

31 Ibid.

32 The dissolution of MOI had been recommended in August 1944 by the War Cabinet's Machinery of Government Committee and confirmed by Cabinet in December 1945 after being considered in the GEN 85 committee.

33 TNA: PRO, CAB128/2, CM(45)60(6), 'Government Publicity Services', 6 December 1945.

34 TNA: PRO, CAB129/7, CP(46)54, 'Government Information Services', 12 February 1946.

35 TNA: PRO, CAB129/10, CP(46)241, 'Broadcasting Policy', para. 19, 21 June 1946.

36 Before the war, 'Questions on matters of high policy affecting the BBC' were addressed to the Prime Minister. TNA: PRO, CAB129/7, CP(46)54, 'Government Information Services', 12 February 1946.

37 TNA: PRO, CAB129/2, CP(45)168, 'The Future of British Publicity to Foreign Countries', 13 September 1945.

38 TNA: PRO, CAB134/306, GIS(46)8, 'Ministerial Responsibility for the BBC', 8 February 1946.

39 *Broadcasting: Copy of the Licence and Agreement*, Cmd.6975, HMSO, December 1946, para's. 4(3) and 4(4).

40 TNA: PRO, CAB76/16, B(44)3, 'General Questions Affecting the British Broadcasting Corporation', 5 June 1944.

41 Briggs, *Sound and Vision*, p. 465.

42 *Broadcasting Policy*, Cmd.6852, HMSO, July 1946, para. 60.

43 'Statement of Policy for the European Service', 29 July 1946. As quoted in, Briggs, *Sound and Vision*, pp. 142–3.

44 WAC, R1/82/3, G68, 30 October 1946.

45 TNA: PRO, CAB76/16, B(44)3, 5 June 1944.

46 WAC, R1/83/1, G29, 'Proposed Principles to Govern Capital Settlement with the Treasury', 10 April 1947.

47 WAC, R1/80/2, G51, 12 October 1944.

48 TNA: PRO, CAB76/16, CP(45)293, 20 November 1945.

49 WAC, R1/80/2, G51, 12 October 1944.
50 TNA: PRO, CAB76/16, CP(45)293, 20 November 1945; TNA: PRO, CAB128/2, CM(45)64(1), 20 December 1945.
51 Ibid.
52 WAC, R1/80/2, G51, 12 October 1944.
53 TNA: PRO, CAB134/306, GIS(46) 4th Meeting, 28 February 1946.
54 Ibid.
55 *House of Commons Paper* 158, First Report from the Select Committee on Estimates, Session 1945–46, 'The British Broadcasting Corporation', 26 June 1946, p. vii. A similar proposal had been rejected by the GIS Official Committee: TNA: PRO, CAB134/306, GIS(46) 4th Meeting, 28 February 1946.
56 WAC, R1/82/2, G52, 'The Select Committee on Estimates' Report', 10 July 1946.
57 WAC, R1/82/2, G52, 10 July 1946.
58 WAC, R1/82/3, G67, 'Financial Control under the New Charter', 24 October 1946.
59 WAC, R1/14, Board of Governors meeting, 'Financial Control Under New Charter', 31 October 1946.
60 Ibid., 'Director-General's Report', 14 November 1946.
61 Hansard, Fifth Series, *House of Commons Debates*, vol.425, col.1087, 16 July 1946.
62 Ibid., col.1088, 16 July 1946.
63 WAC, R1/82/3, G68, 30 October 1946.

Chapter 2

1 TNA: PRO, CAB134/544, OI(O)(46)10, 'Projection of Britain', 6 June 1946.
2 This paper was based on one prepared by the MOI prior to its demise. See, TNA: PRO, CAB134/544, OI(O)(46)8, 'Projection of Britain – World Common Themes', 29 May 1946.
3 TNA: PRO, CAB134/543, OI(46)7, 'Projection of Britain Overseas', 24 July 1946. Annex: 'Projection of Britain'.
4 Ibid., OI(47)3, 'Publicity on the British Commonwealth and Empire', 9 April 1947; Ibid., OI(47) 1st Meeting, 'Publicity on the British Commonwealth and Empire', 19 May 1947. Two months later, the Dominions Office merged with the India and Burma Office to form the Commonwealth Relations Office.
5 WAC, R1/12, Board of Governors meeting, 'European Service Direction', 21 March 1946. It was by his middle name, Ian, that he was more commonly known; Ibid., 'European Service Direction', 3 April 1946.
6 General Sir Charles Richardson, *From Churchill's Secret Circle to the BBC: The Biography of Lieutenant General Sir Ian Jacob GBE CB DL* (Oxford: Brassey's, 1991), p. 218.

7 John Colville, *The Fringes of Power, Downing Street Diaries 1939-1955, Volume One: September 1939–September 1941* (Sevenoaks: Sceptre, 1986), p. 560.
8 TNA: PRO, CAB66/67, CP(45)59, 'Standing Ministerial Committees of the Cabinet', 3 July 1945.
9 Ibid.; TNA: PRO, CAB21/823, 'Cabinet Committees: Composition, terms of reference and organisation', 1945.
10 Richardson, *Churchill's Secret Circle*, p. 218.
11 Colville, *Fringes of Power*, p. 561. See also, Garnett, *Secret History of PWE*, pp. 87–8; Briggs, *War of the Words*, p. 23.
12 Briggs, *War of Words*, p. 34.
13 TNA: PRO, CAB134/306, GIS(46) 4th Meeting, 28 February 1946.
14 WAC, R1/12, Board of Governors meeting, 'Controllership, European Services Division', 30 March 1944.
15 Ann Lane, 'Kirkpatrick, Sir Ivone Augustine (1897-1964)', in H. Matthew and Brian Harrison (eds), *Oxford Dictionary of National Biography* (Oxford: Oxford University Press, 2004), pp. 807–9.
16 WAC, R1/12, Board of Governors meeting, 'Director-General's Report', 7 September 1944.
17 Briggs, *Sound and Vision*, p. 141.
18 He was awarded a Knighthood in the 1946 Birthday Honours List.
19 Briggs, *Sound and Vision*, p. 142.
20 Ibid.
21 Major-General Sir Ian Jacob, 'The European Service Holds The Mirror Up To British Opinion', by the Controller of the European Service, *BBC Yearbook 1947* (London: BBC, 1947), p. 16.
22 Briggs, *Sound and Vision*, p. 142.
23 Ibid.
24 Simon of Wythenshawe, Lord. *The BBC from Within* (London: Victor Gollanz, 1953), p. 154.
25 WAC, R1/82/3, G68, 30 October 1946.
26 Ibid.
27 Ibid. The MEID would also have been known to many as the Middle East Publicity Department.
28 WAC, R34/399, 'Liaison with Foreign Office, etc.', C(OS) to Robertson and FESD, 27 February 1947.
29 WAC, R1/82/3, G68, 30 October 1946.
30 TNA: PRO, CAB134/545, OI(O)(47)4, 'Board of Trade Information Services to Overseas Countries', 28 January 1947.
31 Ibid., OI(O)(47), 1st Meeting of the Official Committee on Overseas Information Services Committee, 29 January 1947; WAC, R1/82/3, G68, 30 October 1946.

32 Ibid.
33 WAC, R34/399, 'Meeting at Middle East Publicity Department, Foreign Office', 8 August 1946; Ibid., 'Relations with Foreign Office', 19 November 1946.
34 Ibid., 'Meeting at Middle East Publicity Department, Foreign Office', 8 August 1946.
35 Ibid., 'Meeting at Middle East Publicity Department, Foreign Office', 10 August 1946; Ibid., 'Relations with Foreign Office', 20 November 1946.
36 Ibid., 'Relations with Foreign Office', 19 November 1946.
37 Ibid., '"Inspired" News Items from the FO', NENE to DES, 26 March 1947.
38 Ibid.
39 Ibid., 'News Items from the FO', DES to NENE 1 April 1947.
40 Ibid.

Chapter 3

1 TNA: PRO, CAB129/6, CP(46)7, 'Publicity Services in South-Eastern Europe', 4 January 1946.
2 TNA: PRO, CAB129/22, CP(47)313, 'Extinction of Human Rights in Eastern Europe', 24 November 1947.
3 Ibid.
4 Briggs, *War of the Words*, p. 209.
5 Ann Applebaum, *Iron Curtain: The Crushing of Eastern Europe 1944-56* (London: Allen Lane, 2012), p. xxxiv; Alan Bullock, *Ernest Bevin: Foreign Secretary, 1945-1951* (London: Heinemann, 1983), pp. 525–6.
6 In addition to his regular broadcasts in the European, and particularly Czechoslovak, Services of the BBC during the war, Robert Bruce Lockhart had been the British representative to the Czechoslovakian government in exile in 1940 and from 1941 Deputy Under-Secretary of State in charge of the PWE.
7 Briggs, *Sound and Vision*, p. 466.
8 Ibid., p. 524.
9 'Overseas: Broadcasts to Europe', *BBC Yearbook 1949* (London: BBC, 1949), p. 101.
10 The National Archives, Kew, Middlesex (TNA), CAB81/132, JIC(46)1(0), 'Russia's Strategic Interests and Intentions', 1 March 1946.
11 Ibid.
12 Foreign and Commonwealth Office, *IRD: Origins and Establishment of the Foreign Office Information Research Department 1946-48* (London: Foreign and Commonwealth Office Library and Records Department, 1995), p. 2.
13 Ibid.

14 Ibid.; Andrew Defty, *Britain, America and Anti-Communist Propaganda 1945-53: The Information Research Department* (London: Routledge, 2004), p. 38.
15 TNA: PRO, FO371/66371, N9345, Russia Committee meeting, 31 July 1947.
16 The original members of the Cominform were: Soviet Union, Bulgaria, Czechoslovakia, France, Hungary, Italy, Poland, Romania and Yugoslavia.
17 TNA: PRO, CAB129/23, CP(48)6, 'The First Aim of British Foreign Policy', 4 January 1948.
18 TNA: PRO, CAB129/23, CP(48)8, 'Future Foreign Publicity Policy', 4 January 1948.
19 FCO, *IRD*, p. 4.
20 Mayhew, *A War of Words*, p. 18.
21 Ibid., p. 19.
22 Mayhew met with Sargent, Kirkpatrick and Warner on 18 November 1947.
23 Mayhew, *A War of Words*, p. 21.
24 The IPD was established in April 1946 to co-ordinate overseas publicity within the FO after the demise of the MOI. Its six regional departments covered America, Eastern Europe, Far East, Latin America, Middle East, and Western Europe. Kirkpatrick had been promoted to Deputy Under-Secretary overseeing policy administration for Western Europe.
25 The Memoranda were: CP(47)313, 'Extinction of Human Rights in Eastern Europe', 24 November 1947; CP(48)6, 'The First Aim of British Foreign Policy', 4 January 1948; CP(48)7, 'Review of Soviet Policy', 5 January 1948; CP(48)8, 'Future Foreign Publicity Policy', 4 January 1948. See, TNA: PRO, CAB129/22 & 23.
26 TNA: PRO, CAB129/23, CP(48)8, 4 January 1948.
27 Ibid. Christopher Mayhew, then Under Secretary of State at the Foreign Office, attributes these comments to the Minister of Health Aneurin Bevan. See, Christopher Mayhew and Lyn Smith (eds), *A War of Words: A Cold War Witness* (London: I.B. Tauris, 1998), p. 22.
28 TNA: PRO, FO953/701, Note by Warner, 6 June 1950.
29 TNA: PRO, CAB128/12, CM(48)2(5), 'Foreign Policy In Europe', 8 January 1948.
30 TNA: PRO, CAB129/23, CP(48)8, 4 January 1948.
31 Mayhew, *A War of Words*, p. 22; FCO, *IRD*, p. 7. For a detailed history of the early years of IRD see, Andrew Defty, *Britain, America and Anti-Communist Propaganda 1945-53* (Abingdon: Routledge, 2004).
32 FCO, *IRD*, p. 6. The Secret Vote is the budget set aside by government for the Intelligence Services.
33 TNA: PRO, CAB128/12, CM(48) 19th Conclusions, 'Foreign Policy In Europe', 5 March 1948; FCO, *IRD*, p. 9; Mayhew, *A War of Words*, p. 23.
34 TNA: PRO, CAB129/23, CP(48)8, 4 January 1948.

35 Michael Nelson, *War of the Black Heavens* (London: Brassey's, 1997), p. 14; FCO, *IRD*, p. 6.
36 'Overseas: Broadcasts to Europe', *BBC Yearbook 1949* (London: BBC, 1949), p. 101.
37 Applebaum, *Iron Curtain*, pp. xxvii–xxviii.
38 WAC, R1/80/2, G51, 'Broadcasting to Europe', 12 October 1944; TNA: PRO, FO953/228, PE1318/55/967, 'Comments on the BBC Bulgarian Broadcasts from May 4th - May 18th 1948', British Legation, Sofia, to Ernest Bevin, 18 June 1948.
39 WAC, E2/329, Warner to Jacob, 19 March 1948.
40 Ibid., 'Note on the European Service of the BBC', Jacob to Warner, 19 March 1948.
41 TNA: PRO, FO953/227, 'BBC Central and East European Services', 9 March 1948.
42 Ibid., 'Central and East European Services', 2 March 1948.
43 The nature of output was different, however, for the General Overseas Services in English which at that time ran throughout the day and some of the larger individual language services such as French and German.
44 A colourful account of the problems that led to the failure of these attempts can be found in, Kim Philby, *My Silent War: The Autobiography of a Spy* (London: Arrow, 2003), pp. 153–9.
45 WAC, E2/209/5, European Service: Output Reports, 3 January 1946–17 April 1949. See, for example, Output Report numbers 7, 9 and 11 for details of broadcasts to these countries.
46 WAC, E2/327/1, H.C.Eur.S to Lean, 'Foreign Office Questionnaire', 24 April 1948. Programme Organiser was the BBC title for heads of distinct language services.
47 TNA: PRO, CAB130/37, GEN 231/1, 'Anti-Communist Publicity', 30 April 1948.
48 WAC, E2/328, 'Telegram No.289', 17 April 948. A final report on this review was compiled in August 1948.
49 TNA: PRO, FO953/229A, PE2030/55/967, Warner to Mayhew, 11 August 1948.
50 WAC, E2/328, Sterndale-Bennett to Bevin, 18 June 1948.
51 TNA: PRO, FO953/228, PE1318/55/967, Note by Storey, 1 July 1948.
52 Ibid., PE1460/55/967, 'The BBC's broadcasts to Eastern European countries', Memorandum by Bowen, 11 August 1948.
53 WAC, E2/328, 'Embassy Criticisms of the European Service', Lean, 17 September 1948.
54 Ibid.
55 TNA: PRO, FO953/228, PE1460/55/967, Memorandum by Bowen, 11 August 1948.
56 Warner was additionally Chair of the Overseas Information Services Official Committee.
57 WAC, E2/325/1, Jacob to Warner, 26 April 1948.
58 WAC, E2/328, Warner to Jacob, 4 September 1948.
59 TNA: PRO, FO953/229A, PE2030/55/967, Bowen to Gainer, 19 October 1948.

60 Ibid.
61 *Broadcasting Policy*, Cmd.6852, HMSO, July 1946, para. 59.
62 WAC, E2/328, 'Telegram No.289', 17 April 1948.
63 TNA: PRO, FO953/228, PE1460/55/967, Memorandum by Bowen, 11 August 1948. Emphasis in the original.
64 WAC, E40/252/1, George Barnes to DOS, undated.
65 Ibid.
66 Ibid., Jacob to DSW, 5 October 1948.
67 Haley, who had edited the *Manchester Evening News* before joining the BBC, left the Corporation in 1952 to edit *The Times*. As Director-General, he was the BBC's Editor-in-Chief and constitutionally responsible for its news output.
68 WAC, E40/252/1, Haley to DOS, 1 October 1948.
69 Ibid., Jacob to Heads of the Overseas Services, 6 October 1948.
70 Ibid.; WAC, E2/208, 'The Task of the Overseas Services of the BBC', Note by the Director of Overseas Services, 4 October 1948.
71 Ibid.
72 Ibid.
73 TNA: PRO, FO953/543, PE233/1/967, Warner to Mayhew, 5 January 1949. In this context the phrase 'Eastern Europe' also covered Central European territories.
74 Ibid.
75 Ibid., Memorandum by Ruthven-Murray, 4 January 1949; In September 1949, the Regional Information Departments, except for the German Information Department, were replaced by a Regional Adviser 'to advise Information Policy Department, Information Services Department. . . . Information Research Department and Cultural Relations Department on regional aspects of their work, and for that purpose to maintain continuous contact with the appropriate political departments. They will also continue . . . the duties of the Regional Departments as regards contact with visiting journalists, &c., and liaison with the Regional Directors of the BBC Overseas Services'. Ruthven-Murray became regional Adviser for Eastern Europe. See, WACE2/327/1, Circular No.0108, 'Regional Information Departments', Ernest Bevin, 12 September 1949.
76 WAC, E2/120/3, 'Critical Notes No.25', 5 May 1949. Critical Notes were critiques of the 'Output Report' summaries sent to Jacob and the relevant Service Director as the basis of discussions on the output of a particular service. See, WAC, E40/251/1, 'European Services Directive No.3'.
77 Ibid.
78 WAC, E2/327/1, Murray to Lean, 1 January 1949. In January 1951, Gretton (A.H.E.Eur.S) noted that 'with the exception of "Life in the Roumanian Peoples Republic", which went out in Swedish and Turkish, I do not think any of these

have been broadcast outside the Roumanian Service. . . . I think it answers Murray's point, that they have certainly not been generally broadcast'. See, WAC, E2/327/2, Gretton to C.Eur.S., 11 January 1951.

79 WAC, E2/208, 'The Task of the Overseas Services of the BBC', Note by the Director of Overseas Services, 4 October 1948.

80 WAC, E40/251/1, 'European Services Directive No.12', 1 January 1948.

81 WAC, R1/84/5, G103/48, Report by Director of Overseas Services, 4 November 1948.

82 TNA: PRO, FO371/71687, N11882/765/G38, Russia Committee: Minutes of a Meeting held on 28 October 1948.

83 WAC, R1/84/5, G103/48, 4 November 1948.

84 WAC, E2/206/8, 'Output', D.O.S. to C.Eur.S., 24 November 1948; WAC, E2/325/1, Jacob to Dudley, 14 October 1948.

85 Major-General Sir Ian Jacob, 'The European Service Holds The Mirror Up to British Opinion', *BBC Yearbook 1947* (London: BBC, 1947), p. 16.

Chapter 4

1 Briggs, *The History of Broadcasting in the United Kingdom, Volume V: Competition* (Oxford: Oxford University Press, 1995), p. 701.

2 WAC, E3/24, Appendix to the European Service Review of the Year: 'Listening to the BBC in Europe', March 1949.

3 WAC, E3/24, European Service Directive No.8 'Intelligence', 8 February 1947.

4 WAC, E3/24, Appendix to the European Service Review of the Year: 'Listening to the BBC in Europe', March 1949.

5 WAC, E3/279/1, 'Hostility to Western Broadcasts', undated memorandum.

6 WAC, E2/208, Controller's Circular No.1, 'Political Information Section', 16 August 1946.

7 Ibid.

8 WAC, E2/327/2, J. B. Clark to Speaight, 14 March 1950.

9 WAC, E2/327/2, Miss Baker to C.Eur.S., 27 April and 26 June 1951.

10 WAC, E2/327/1, Peake, Belgrade to Attlee, 12 January 1948.

11 Ibid., Sterndale-Bennett, Sofia to Bevin, 23 January 1948.

12 In a letter to Jacob on 20 May 1948, Warner noted that 'by an oversight we have not replied to Peake's suggestion in Paragraph 12 of his despatch [of 12 January 1948] that he should send us special telegrams on any events which seem to him to require mention or comment in your Service and it is for that reason I suppose that he has not started doing so. We are now asking him to begin'.

It is unclear whether other Missions had started to do this earlier in the year or only at this point. See, WAC, E2/324/2, Warner to Jacob, 20 May 1948; TNA: PRO, FO953/543, PE233/1/967, Comments on the BBC broadcasts to the Iron Curtain countries.

13 It came as somewhat of a surprise to Warner when Jacob informed him in September 1948 that only the Diplomatic Correspondents saw the ASIDE telegrams. They were subsequently added to the telegrams passed to Lean. See, TNA: PRO, FO953/228, PE1773/55/967, Note by Warner, 3 September 1948.

14 WAC, E2/327, Mitchell to D.O.S., 24 November 1948.

15 Ibid.

16 Ibid. It was still possible, in special circumstances, for certain staff to view the contents of Foreign Office telegrams and secured documentation from other sources in the Political Information Section on approval from Jacob or Lean.

17 TNA: PRO, FO953/229A, PE2030/55/967, Bowen to Gainer, Warsaw (also sent to Budapest, Bucharest, Belgrade, Sofia and Prague), 19 October 1948.

18 WAC, E1/1268, Lean to Malcolm, 18 June 1951; Malcolm to Lean, 26 June 1951.

19 TNA: PRO, FO953/229A, Note by Bowen, 15 November 1948.

20 WAC, E2/329, Warner to Jacob (written by Bowen in Warner's absence), 2 March 1949.

21 Briggs, *Sound and Vision*, p. 136.

22 Despite the Foreign Office decision not to broadcast to Russia during the war, there had been a series of 15-minute weekly newsletters broadcast between 7 October 1942 and 26 May 1943. See, Briggs, *War of Words*, p. 362.

23 Briggs, *War of Words*, p. 167.

24 Julian Hale, *Radio Power: Propaganda and International Broadcasting* (London: Elek, 1975), p. 52.

25 See, TNA: PRO, FO371/56885, N6092/5169/G38, Russia Committee meeting, 7 May 1946.

26 WAC, R1/14, Board of Governors meeting, 'Controller (European Services) Report', 14 November 1946.

27 WAC, R1/82/4, Ga2, 'BBC Broadcasts in Russian', 6 November 1946.

28 Ibid.

29 WAC, E2/209/5, 'Output Report No.6', 1 April 1947.

30 'The European Service: The East European Service; Russia', *BBC Yearbook 1947* (London: BBC, 1947), p. 123.

31 WAC, E2/209/5, 'Output Report No.6', 1 April 1947.

32 WAC, R1/82/1, G39, 'Russian Broadcasts', 7 May 1946.

33 WAC, E3/285/1, 'Listening Behind the Iron Curtain: USSR, 1947–1955'.

34 Ibid.

35 WAC, E2/209/5, 'Output Report No.11', 27 August 1947.

36 TNA: PRO, FO371/56886, N13979/5169/G38, Russia Committee meeting, 24 October 1946.
37 WAC, E3/285/1, 'Listening Behind the Iron Curtain: USSR, 1947–1955'.
38 Ibid.
39 WAC, R1/82/4, Ga2, 'BBC Broadcasts in Russian', 6 November 1946.
40 WAC, R1/15, Board of Governors meeting, 'Controller (European Services) Report', 26 June 1947.
41 WAC, E2/328, Moscow Embassy to Grey, 13 July 1948; WAC, E2/120/3, 'Output Report No.27', 3 August 1949.
42 TNA: PRO, FO953/544, PE1197/1/967, Note by Ian Grey, 7 April 1949.
43 WAC, E2/120/2, 'Output Report No.19', 25 August 1948.
44 For an account of Tokaev's opposition to Stalin's Russia see, Grigori Tokaev, *Comrade X*, translated by Alec Brown (London: Harvill Press, 1956).
45 WAC, E2/327/2, 'Foreign Office to East European Missions', 9 June 1950.
46 TNA: PRO, CAB159/6, JIC(Germany)(49)18 Final, 'Encouragement of Deserters', 11 March 1949.
47 TNA: PRO, FO953/545, PE1401/1/967, Note by Hankey, 18 March 1949.
48 WAC, E2/329, 'Broadcast by Kerensky on Displaced Persons and Labour Camps', 26 November 1949.
49 WAC, E2/329, Peterson, Moscow, to Bevin, 26 January 1949.
50 TNA: PRO, FO953/543, PE233/1/967, Mayhew to Warner, 11 January 1949.
51 WAC, E2/329, Greene to DOS, 22 March 1949.
52 WAC, E2/329, Warner to Jacob, 2 March 1949.
53 Ibid.
54 Ibid., Peterson, Moscow, to Bevin, 26 January 1949.
55 Ibid., Greene to DOS, 22 March 1949. Emphasis in the original.
56 Ibid.
57 Ibid.
58 TNA: PRO, FO953/545, PE1401/1/967, Note by Bowen, 17 March 1949.
59 WAC, E2/120/3, 'Critical Notes No.27', 2 September 1949.
60 Hugh Carleton Greene, *The Third Floor: A View of Broadcasting in the Sixties* (London: Bodley Head, 1969), p. 29.
61 WAC, E2/329, Jacob to Warner, 27 April 1949.
62 WAC, E2/120/3, 'Output Report No.27', 3 August 1949.
63 Ibid., 'Critical Notes No.27', 2 September 1949.
64 TNA: PRO, CAB134/99, CI(49)8(1), 'Trends of Communist Propaganda: Russian Jamming', 24 May 1949. Original emphasis.
65 WAC, R1/85/6, G117, undated.
66 TNA: PRO, CAB134/101, CI(49)72, 'BBC Broadcasts in Russian', 9 September 1949.

67 Ibid.
68 Ibid.
69 WAC, E2/608/1, European Services Meeting, 'Jamming', 29 July 1949. A crash start is where a programme begins on a particular frequency without being preceded by test transmissions; WAC, E3/285/1, 'Listening Behind the Iron Curtain: USSR, 1947–1955'.
70 WAC, E40/259/1, Report by H.E.Eur.S., 4 January 1950.
71 Ibid., Lean to DOS, 4 January 1950.
72 Ibid., Report by H.E.Eur.S., 4 January 1950.
73 TNA: PRO, FO953/701, Embassy, Moscow to IPD, 24 February 1950.
74 WAC, R1/87/1, G8, 'Report by the Director of Overseas Services', 10 January 1951.
75 WAC, E3/285/1, 'Listening Behind the Iron Curtain: USSR, 1947–1955'.
76 WAC, R1/86/1, G30, 'Report by the Deputy Director of Overseas Services', 7 February 1950.
77 WAC, E3/285/1, 'Listening Behind the Iron Curtain: USSR, 1947–1955'.
78 WAC, R1/86/4, G107, 'Report by the Director of Overseas Services', 20 June 1950.
79 WAC, E2/120/5, 'Output Report No.40', 22 May 1951.
80 WAC, E2/120/5, 'Critical Notes No.40', 1 June 1951.
81 Ibid., Graham to Ransome, 1 June 1951.
82 Ibid., 'Output Report No.40', 22 May 1951; 'Critical Notes No.40', 1 June 1951.
83 WAC, E40/259/1, Malcolm to Jacob, 17 August 1951.
84 Ibid., Jacob to Nicholls, 1 October 1951.
85 WAC, E2/119/1, Venables to C.Eur.S., 24 August 1951.
86 Ibid., Graham to C.Eur.S., 31 August 1951.
87 Ibid., Venables to C.Eur.S., 24 August 1951.
88 Ibid., Jacob to Nicholls, 1 October 1951.
89 TNA: PRO, CAB131/9, DO(50)34, 'Defence and Global Strategy', 1 May 1950.
90 TNA: PRO, CAB134/549, OIS(51)5, 'Overseas Publicity', 16 July 1951.
91 TNA: PRO, FO953/229A, PE2030/55/967, Bowen to Gainer, 19 October 1948.
92 WAC, E2/208, 'The Task of the Overseas Services of the BBC', 4 October 1948.
93 Ibid.
94 Ibid.
95 WAC, E40/251/1, European Services Directive No.3: 'Output Report', 3 October 1946; WAC, E2/120/4, 'Output Report No.29', 23 December 1949.
96 TNA: PRO, FO953/229A, PE2222/55/967, Note by Bowen, 25 October 1948; TNA: PRO, FO953/545, PE1401/1/967 'Comments on criticisms by Lord Vansittart in the House of Lords about BBC Services to Eastern Europe', 17 March 1949.
97 WAC, E2/327/2, Foreign Office to East European Missions, 9 June 1950.
98 WAC, E40/251/1, 'European Services Directive No.20', 29 June 1948.
99 Ibid.

100 Ann Lane, 'Coming to Terms with Tito: Britain and Yugoslavia, 1945–49', in Richard Aldrich and Michael Hopkins (eds), *Intelligence, Defence and Diplomacy: British Policy in the Post-War World* (London: Frank Cass, 1994), p. 12; Fitzroy Maclean, *Eastern Approaches* (London: Jonathan Cape, 1949).
101 TNA: PRO, FO953/229A, PE2779/55/967, Peake to Bowen, 11 December 1948.
102 Ibid.
103 TNA: PRO, FO953/229A, PE2222/55/967, Note by Bowen, 25 October 1948.
104 TNA: PRO, FO953/543, PE233/1/967, Memorandum by Ruthven-Murray, 4 January 1949.
105 WAC, E2/324/2, Warner to Jacob, 12 January 1949.
106 Ibid.
107 Ibid.
108 Ibid., Warner to Jacob, 7 February 1949.
109 Ibid., Telegram No.40, Peake to Warner, 21 January 1949.
110 Ibid., Telegram from Warner to Belgrade, 5 February 1949.
111 Mark Selverstone, *Constructing the Monolith: The United States, Great Britain, and International Communism, 1945-1950* (London: Harvard University Press, 2009), pp. 116–19.
112 WAC, E2/120/5, 'Output Report No.41', 6 July 1951.
113 TNA: PRO, FO371/77624, N10086/1052/38G, Russia Committee meeting, 22 November 1949.
114 TNA: PRO, FO953/547, Wallinger to Bevin, 24 August 1949.
115 WAC, E40/259/1, Warner to Jacob, 17 March 1950.
116 WAC, E2/120/4, 'Output Report No.29', 23 December 1949.
117 Ibid., 'Critical Notes', 6 January 1950. The BBC programme was called *Life of Stalin*. Isaac Deutscher moved to Britain from his native Poland, where he had been expelled from the Polish Communist Party, just before the Second World War. He subsequently worked for *The Observer* and *The Economist* as an expert on Soviet and European affairs. Isaac Deutscher, *Stalin: A Political Biography* (London: Oxford University Press, 1949).
118 Ibid.
119 WAC, E2/120/4, 'Output Report No.29', 23 December 1949.
120 Ibid.
121 The instruction was sent out on 3 May 1949. See, TNA: PRO, FO953/545, PE1374/1/967, Greene to Bowen, 22 April 1949.
122 TNA: PRO, FO953/547, Wallinger to Bevin, 24 August 1949.
123 Ibid.
124 TNA: PRO, FO371/77624, N8665/1052/38G, Russia Committee meeting, 27 September 1949. For comparative details on the American 'Campaign of Truth' see, Defty, *Anti-Communist Propaganda*, pp. 139–43.

125 WAC, E2/327/2, Jacob to Warner, 21 June 1950.
126 WAC, E2/120/4, 'Output Report No.32', 20 April 1950.
127 WAC, E2/327/2, Foreign Office to East European Missions, 9 June 1950.
128 TNA: PRO, FO953/544, EEID to Information Officer, Belgrade, 9 April 1949.
129 Ibid.
130 WAC, E2/325/2, Murray to Jacob, 28 August 1950. At the end of 1948 Kolarz, along with the Hungarian born author Arthur Koestler, had been recruited by Murray to prepare a report for a Working Party of the CIPC on the 'Use of Words in Propaganda' which was approved by ministers in March 1949. See, TNA: PRO, CAB134/98, CI(48)6(4), 'The Use of Words in Propaganda', 17 December 1948.
131 Ibid.
132 Ibid.
133 Ibid., Tangye Lean to Ralph Murray, 2 October 1950.
134 WAC, E3/285/1, 'Listening Behind the Iron Curtain: USSR, 1947–1955'.
135 TNA: PRO, CAB134/102, CI(50)4(4), 'Overseas Broadcasting: Europe; Jamming', 20 June 1950.
136 WAC, E2/119/1, Greene to H.C.Eur.S., 20 July 1950.
137 WAC, R20/53, 'Report of the Independent Committee of Enquiry into the Overseas Information Services', 27 July 1953, p. 73.
138 WAC, E2/120/5, 'Critical Notes on the Russian, Rumanian, Bulgarian and Albanian Services', 1 June 1951.
139 Ibid., 'Output Report No.40', 22 May 1951; 'Critical Notes', 1 June 1951.

Chapter 5

1 Briggs, *The History of Broadcasting in the United Kingdom, Volume IV: Sound and Vision, 1945-55* (Oxford: Oxford University Press, 1995), p. 480. In 1948 the weekly number of hours broadcast was: BBC = 650; USSR and satellites = 440; VOA = 240. By 1951 the totals were: BBC = 550; USSR and satellites = 1,050; VOA = 320 (+320 in repeats).
2 An initial report on 'Russian Jamming' by J. B. Clarke stated that jamming began on Sunday, 24 April. All subsequent reports of the start of jamming, however, gave the date of commencement as 25 April. See, WAC, E2/119/1, DDOS to DOS, 29 April 1949. The jamming initially began on short-wave, but was later extended to medium-wave transmissions. See, WAC, E2/119/1, 'Russian Jamming', 23 May 1951.
3 WAC, R1/85/3, G73, 'Report by the Director of Overseas Services', 1 June 1949.
4 TNA: PRO, CAB130/37, GEN 231/2, 'Liaison between the Foreign Office and Chiefs of Staff: Collaboration with the United States', 31 March 1948.

5 TNA: PRO, FO371/71687, Russia Committee meeting, 1 April 1948.
6 WAC, E2/119/1, DDOS to DOS, 29 April 1949.
7 WAC, R1/85/3, G73, 1 June 1949.
8 Ibid.
9 WAC, E2/119/1, Clark to Carter, 19 May 1949.
10 WAC, E2/119/1, US Embassy, Moscow to State Department, in Harrison, Moscow, to Speaight, 24 May 1949.
11 Ibid., Speaight to Harrison, 7 June 1949.
12 Ibid., Harrison, Moscow to Speaight, 24 May 1949.
13 For example, in October 1946 the Board of Governors had considered a proposal to offer the use of two transmitters to the Americans for relaying broadcasts to Russia and in January 1948 the US State Department approached the BBC as to what facilities could be made available for VOA broadcasts to Europe and the Middle East. WAC, R1/14, Board of Governors meeting, 'Director-General's Report', 17 October 1946; WAC, R2/45/1, BM8, 'Availability for relay over BBC facilities of VOUSA programme', 14 January 1948.
14 WAC, R2/1, Board of Management meeting, 'America Calling Europe', 19 January 1948.
15 Woofferton was also known as OSE10. The Shropshire and Herefordshire border actually runs through the site bisecting the aerial field.
16 The programmes were 'picked up at the Tatsfield receiving station and fed by line to Bush House, there to be mixed with local announcements and passed to the transmitters at Woofferton'. See, Edward Pawley, *BBC Engineering, 1922-1972* (London: BBC, 1972), p. 348.
17 WAC, E2/119/1, 'Russian Jamming', 23 May 1951. Post-war Russian jamming had started in 1946 when short-wave transmissions from Madrid became a target. By April 1949 it was thought by the BBC that Russian broadcasts from Yugoslavia, Greece and Persia were also being jammed. See, WAC, E3/285/1, 'Listening Behind the Iron Curtain: USSR, 1947–1955'.
18 TNA: PRO, CAB130/37, GEN 231/1st Meeting, 'Overseas Services of the BBC', 11 May 1948.
19 WAC, R1/85/3, G73, 1 June 1949.
20 WAC, E2/324/2, DOS to McLean, 13 June 1949. The first two transmissions were fully synchronised while the evening broadcast was only partly synchronised due to technical difficulties – the VOA programme ran from 21.00 to 21.30 GMT. See, WAC, R1/85/6, G117, 'Report by the Director of Overseas Services', undated.
21 Ibid.
22 WAC, E2/608/1, European Services Meeting, 'Jamming', 29 July 1949.
23 WAC, R1/85/6, G117, undated.

24 WAC, E3/285/1, 'Listening Behind the Iron Curtain: USSR, 1947–1955'.

25 WAC, R1/85/8, G150, 'Report of the Director of the Overseas Services', 17 November 1949. Using the recently devalued rate of conversion of $2.80 to £1, this equates to £3,928,571.

26 The Grant-in-Aid amount issued to the BBC External Services for 1949/50 was £4,365,000. See, Briggs, *Sound and Vision*, p. 476.

27 WAC, R2/46/8, 'Voice of America', Note by DOS, undated.

28 WAC, R1/85/8, G150, 17 November 1949.

29 On 1 September 1949 a medium-wave transmitter in Munich began to relay VOA broadcasts to Russia for 6 hours a day. See, E3/285/1, 'Listening Behind the Iron Curtain: USSR, 1947–1955'. By November 1949 the Americans had also completed the erection of a medium-wave transmitter at Salonika aimed at broadcasting to the Balkans and Turkey. See, WAC, R1/85/8, G150, 17 November 1949.

30 WAC, R2/46/8, 'Voice of America', Note by DOS, undated.

31 WAC, R2/2, Board of Management meeting, 'The Voice of America', 24 October 1949; WAC, R1/17, 'Voice of America', 26 October 1949.

32 WAC, E2/119/1, US Embassy, Moscow, to State Department, 24 May 1949.

33 WAC, E2/324/2, Speaight to Jacob, 7 October 1949.

34 Ibid., Carter to Browne, 21 August 1950.

35 Ibid., Carter to Jacob, 23 August 1950.

36 Ibid., Carter to Browne, 21 August 1950.

37 By June 1938 news bulletins in English were monitored from Paris, Berlin, Rome Prague, New York, Pittsburg and Tokyo on a rota basis. Asa Briggs, *The History of Broadcasting in the United Kingdom, Volume II: The Golden Age of Wireless, 1927-1932* (Oxford: Oxford University Press, 1995), p. 373.

38 Asa Briggs, *The History of Broadcasting in the United Kingdom, Volume II: The Golden Age of Wireless, 1927-1932* (Oxford: Oxford University Press, 1995), p. 373.

39 Hillelson went on to become, in October 1941, Director of the BBC's Near East Services. Asa Briggs, *The History of Broadcasting in the United Kingdom, Volume III: The War of Words, 1939-1945* (Oxford: Oxford University Press, 1995), p. 257.

40 Olive Renier and Vladimir Rubinstein, *Assigned to Listen: The Evesham Experience, 1939-43* (London: BBC External Services, 1986), p. 14. By June 1938 selected news bulletins in English were also being monitored via Tatsfield from Paris, Berlin, Rome, Prague, New York, Pittsburg and Tokyo. Briggs, *The War of the Words*, p. 170n.

41 Ibid.

42 Briggs, *The History of Broadcasting in the United Kingdom, Volume II: The Golden Age of Wireless, 1927-1939* (Oxford: Oxford University Press, 1995), p. 604.
43 Ibid.
44 Briggs, *The War of Words*, p. 171.
45 Renier and Rubinstein define the structure of the Monitoring Service in terms of four branches – M Unit, Information Bureau, Editorial and Y Unit. The BBC Board of Governors, however, define the organization in three parts – Reception Unit, Information Bureau and the Editorial Unit. The later distinction is used here. Renier and Rubinstein, *Assigned to Listen*, pp. 69–70; WAC, R1/82/1, G34/46, 'Monitoring Service', Note by the BBC, 5 April 1946.
46 300,000 of these were in English. Briggs, *The War of Words*, pp. 40 and 172.
47 WAC, R1/82/1, G34/46.
48 Briggs, *The War of Words*, p. 254.
49 WAC, R1/82/1, G34/46.
50 Briggs, *The War of Words*, p. 40.
51 Ibid., p. 172.
52 WAC, R1/82/1, G34/46.
53 Ibid.
54 Briggs, *The War of Words*, p. 254.
55 See, for example, TNA: PRO, CAB134/99, CI(49)3(1), 'Trends of Russian Propaganda', 17 February 1949. It was at this meeting that it was decided to change the title to 'Trends in Communist Propaganda'.
56 Briggs, *The War of Words*, p. 329.
57 Crowsley Park was soon established as the main reception centre for Monitoring, connected to Caversham by land lines. 'The Monitoring Service', *BBC Yearbook 1947* (London: BBC, 1948), p. 101. For the controversy surrounding the move and its part in the retirement of the Director-General and the resignations of the Director of the Monitoring Service and the Chief Monitoring Supervisor see, Briggs, *The War of Words*, pp. 329–33; Renier and Rubinstein, *Assigned to Listen*, pp. 118–23.
58 Briggs, *Sound and Vision*, p. 159.
59 WAC, R1/81, G24/45, 'Report to Postmaster-General, 1st April – 31st March 1945', 7 August 1945. This was the draft version of that year's Annual Report.
60 WAC, R1/14, Board of Governors Meeting, Minute 320. 'Controller (Overseas Services) Report', 12 December 1946; 'The Monitoring Service', *BBC Yearbook 1948* (London: BBC, 1949), p. 144.
61 Ibid.
62 WAC, R1/85/2, G42, 'Report by Director of Overseas Services: January 21st to March 23rd, 1949', March 1949; WAC, R2/46/6, BM 95, 'British Broadcasting Corporation: Annual Report 1948-49'. At this time transmissions were monitored

from: Ankara, Athens, Belgrade, Berlin, Brussels, Bucharest, Budapest, Buenos Aires, Cairo, Chungking, Copenhagen, Delhi, Helsinki, Hilversum, Lisbon, Madrid, Melbourne, Montreal, Moscow, Oslo, Paris, Prague, Rome, Rio de Janeiro, Sofia, Stockholm, Teheran, Tokyo, Vatican, Vienna and Warsaw. 'The Monitoring Service', *BBC Yearbook 1948* (London: BBC, 1949), p. 114.

63 'The Monitoring Service', *BBC Yearbook 1947* (London: BBC, 1948), p. 103.

64 WAC, R1/82/1, G34/46.

65 Renier and Rubinstein, *Assigned to Listen*, p. 138. 'The despatch of a few Americans to work with the BBC Monitoring Service and provide a flow of information to Washington via the US Embassy had been suggested by Robert Sherwood of the Office for Coordination of Information in Washington as early as September 1941, but had not materialised until just after the US entry into the war'.

66 WAC, R1/82/1, G34/46.

67 WAC, R1/85/1, G5, 'Report by Director of Overseas Services: November 12th 1948 to January 20th 1949', 12 January 1949. The Foreign Broadcast Intelligence Service, after absorbing the work of OWI, was transferred in December 1945 to the US War Department (Military Intelligence Division) before coming under the auspices of the Central Intelligence Group in August 1946. On 1 November 1946 the Foreign Broadcast Intelligence Service was abolished and succeeded by the Foreign Broadcast Information Service. From January 1947 its name changed to the Foreign Broadcast Information Branch before reconstituting as the Foreign Broadcast Information Service (FBIS) as part of the Central Intelligence Agency following the passing of the National Security Act.

68 Ibid.

69 WAC, R1/82/1, G34/46.

70 WAC, R1/15, Board of Governors Meeting, Minute 204. 'Controller (Overseas Services) Report', 24 July 1947.

71 Richard Aldrich, *The Hidden Hand: Britain, America and Cold War Secret Intelligence*, John Murray, 2002, p. 567.

72 WAC, R1/85/1, G5, 'Report by Director of Overseas Services: November 12th 1948 to January 20th 1949', 12 January 1949.

73 TNA: PRO, HW80/4, 'British-US Communication Intelligence Agreement', 1946.

74 'The Monitoring Service', *BBC Yearbook 1947*, p. 103.

75 WAC, R1/85/1, G5.

76 Ibid., Annex. 'Monitoring Service of the United States: viz. the Foreign Broadcast Information Branch of the Central Intelligence Agency', Note by Mr M. Frost, December 1948.

77 Ibid.

78 WAC, R1/85/1, G5, Annex.

79 WAC, R2/45/1, BM10, 'The Future of Crowsley Park', Note by DOS, 26 January 1948.
80 WAC, R1/85/1, G5.
81 Ibid.
82 Ibid., Annex.
83 WAC, R1/85/1, G5. Towards the end of 1949 it was initially estimated that the capital cost of the move to Crowsley would be £170,000 and the project would be under way by the end of 1952. WAC, R2/46/9, BM156, 'Capital Expenditure for Three Years 1950-52', 30 November 1949.

Chapter 6

1 *Annual Report and Accounts for the Year 1950-51*, British Broadcasting Corporation, September 1951, pp. 104–5.
2 *Annual Report and Accounts of the British Broadcasting Corporation 1956-57*, Cmd.267, October 1957, pp. 142–3.
3 *Annual Report and Accounts, 1950-51*, pp. 106–7.
4 *Annual Report and Accounts of the British Broadcasting Corporation for the year 1952-53*, Cmd.8928, September 1953, p. 34.
5 Programme hours ranged between 21 and 24 hours a day in this period depending on the funding available through the grant-in-aid.
6 *Annual Report and Accounts, 1952-53*, p. 36.
7 *Annual Report and Accounts, 1950-51*, p. 45.
8 *Annual Report and Accounts of the British Broadcasting Corporation, 1955-56*, Cmd.9803, July 1956, p. 56.
9 *Annual Report and Accounts, 1953-54*, p. 50.
10 WAC, E2/120/3, 'Output Report No.23', undated, 1949.
11 Ibid., 'Critical Notes No. 26'.
12 *Annual Report and Accounts, 1956-57*, p. 18.
13 WAC, E2//608/1, European Service Meeting, 11 February 1949, 17 March 1950, 4 August 1950; *Annual Report and Accounts*, 1950–51, p. 43.
14 WAC, E2//608/1, European Service Meeting, 23 June 1950, 4 August 1950.
15 Ibid., 8 December 1950. Goldberg had been 'moved from the Russian Section to East European Direction, as his output was now used by and written for the wider audience'. Ibid., 7 September 1950.
16 Ibid., 12 January 1951.
17 *Annual Report and Accounts*, 1955–56, p. 52.
18 TNA: PRO, CAB129/23, CP(48)8, 'Future Foreign Publicity Policy', Memorandum by the Secretary of State for Foreign Affairs, 4 January 1948.

19 Ibid. In January 1948 it was intended by Bevin that this plan should be supported by the material resources, real and potential, supplied by Marshall Aid and the European colonial dependencies.
20 WAC, E2/329, Warner to Jacob, 19 March 1948.
21 Ibid., 'Note on the European Service of the BBC', with covering note from DOS to Warner, 19 March 1948.
22 Ibid.
23 WAC, R2/45/2, BM45, 'Broadcasting and European Recovery', Note by DOS, undated. Discussed by the Board of Management on 19 April 1948 – see, WAC, R2/1, Board of Management Meeting, Minute 111. 'Broadcasting and European Recovery', 19 April 1948.
24 Ibid.
25 WAC, R2/1, Board of Management Meeting, Minute 111. 'Broadcasting and European Recovery', 19 April 1948.
26 WAC, E2/585/1, Marriott to DDOS, 'Anglo-Benelux Broadcasts – Dutch Proposal', 9 March 1948.
27 Ibid., Tangye Lean to DOS, 'A New Programme', 17 March 1948.
28 WAC, E2/585/1, 'Western Union', paper by H.Eur.Prod., undated.
29 Their discussion was based on WAC, R2/45/2, BM 45, 'Broadcasting and European recovery' Note by DOS, undated. This paper by Jacob was very substantially based on Camacho's paper on 'Western Union'.
30 WAC, E2/585/1, memorandum on 'Cooperative European Programme', 24 April 1948.
31 Ibid., 'Notes on the First Meeting of the Working Party on "Spiritual" aspects of Western Union'.
32 WAC, Board of Management Meeting, Minute 140. 'Co-operative European Programme', 31 May 1948.
33 WAC, E2.585/1, 'Minutes of First Meeting of Committee on Cooperative European Programme', 4 May 1948.
34 WAC, E2.585/1, 'Draft Minutes of the Working Party on Spiritual Aspects of Western Union', 7 May 1948.
35 Ibid., WAC, Tangye Lean to DOS, 'A New Programme', 17 March 1948.
36 TNA: PRO, CAB129/29, CP(48)193, 'European Recovery Programme Information Policy', Note by the Prime Minister, 30 July 1948.
37 Ibid.
38 WAC, E2.585/1, 'Summary of a Meeting to Discuss the Proposals for European Recovery Progress Report', 29 April 1948.
39 WAC, R2/45/1, BM 107, 'Exchange Programmes', Note by DOS, 7 December 1948. These figures were compiled by Marriott.
40 WAC, BM 51, 'Exchange of Programmes', Note by DOS, 11 May 1948.

41 WAC, R2/1, Board of Management Meeting, Minute 139. 'Exchange Programmes', 31 May 1948.

42 WAC, E2/585/1, 'Draft Minutes of Working Party on Spiritual Aspects of Western Union', 7 May 1948.

43 WAC, E2/608/1, European Services Meeting, Minute 16. 'Working Party on Spiritual Union', 28 May 1948.

44 WAC, BM 51, 'Exchange of Programmes', Note by DOS, 11 May 1948.

45 Ibid.

46 Ibid.

47 WAC, Board of Management Meeting, Minute 139. 'Exchange Programmes', 31 May 1948.

48 WAC, R2/45/4, BM 107, 'Exchange Programmes', Note by DOS, 7 December 1948; WAC, R2/1, Board of Management Meeting, Minute 273. 'Exchange Programmes', 13 December 1948; WAC, R2/46/3, BM 28, 'Exchange of Programmes', Note by DOS, 10 February 1949.

49 WAC, WAC, E2/585/1, Summary of Meeting to Discuss the Proposals for European Recovery Progress Report, 19 April 1948; WAC, BM 55, 'Cooperative European Programmes', 24 May 1948.

50 WAC, BM 55, 'Cooperative European Programmes', 24 May 1948.

51 WAC, R2/45/3, BM 67, Report on the Conference of the Broadcasting Organisations of Belgium, France, Great Britain, Luxembourg and The Netherlands, 2 July 1948.

52 Ibid. The order of talks was to be: The Netherlands, Luxembourg, Great Britain, France, and Belgium.

53 Ibid.

54 WAC, R2/47/3, BM 49, 'Western European Cooperative Broadcasting', Note by Director of the Spoken Word, 30 March 1950.

55 WAC, R2/47/4, BM 69, 'Western Union Broadcasting – Brussels Meeting', Note by Director of the Spoken Word, 10 May 1950.

56 WAC, R2/46/5, BM 57, 'Western Union Broadcasts', Note by DSW, 7 April 1949.

57 Ibid.

58 Ibid.

59 Ibid.: WAC, Board of Management Meeting, Minute 102. 'Western Union Broadcasts', 11 April 1949.

60 WAC, BM 71, 'Western European Broadcasting Conference, Paris, April 1949', Report by DSW, 5 May 1949.

61 WAC, R2/46/9, BM A12, 'Western Union Conference: Luxembourg, 17th–19th October 1949', Report by DSW, 25 October 1949.

62 Ibid.

63 WAC, R2/47/3, BM 49, 'Western European Cooperative Broadcasting', Note by Director of the Spoken Word, 30 March 1950.

Chapter 7

1 See, for example, Alec Cairncross, *Years of Recovery: British Economic Policy 1945-51* (London: Methuen, 1985), pp. 17–46.
2 TNA: PRO, CAB134/545, OI(O)(47)12, 'Working Party on Estimates for BBC Overseas Services and other Services Performed for Government Departments', 16 April 1947. The Government departments attending this meeting were all 'Prescribing Departments' as laid out under clause 4(5) of the BBC Licence. The other Prescribing Departments at this time were the India Office, Burma Office and the Control Office for Germany and Austria.
3 WAC, R1/84/2, G23, Report by Director of Overseas Services, 11 March 1948.
4 WAC, R2/46/5, BM83, 'Draft Finance Section of the Annual Report of the BBC 1948-49', 27 May 1949.
5 WAC, R1/84/1, G2, Report by the Director of Overseas Services, 1 January 1948; Ibid. Daily programme hours came down from 64 to 52. Transmitter hours were reduced from 400 to 300.
6 Ibid. *Voz de Londres* (*This is London*) was the BBC's regional publication containing schedules and features.
7 David Reynolds, *Britannia Overruled: British Policy & World Power in the 20th Century* (London: Longman, 1991), p. 179.
8 John Young, *Cold War Europe: A Political History* (London: Arnold, 1991), p. 17.
9 TNA: PRO, CAB129/29, CP(48)199, 'Cost of Information Services', Memorandum by the Chancellor of the Exchequer, 4 August 1948.
10 TNA: PRO, CAB128/13, CM(48)66(4), 'Government Information Services', 25 October 1948.
11 TNA: PRO, CAB130/37, GEN 231/2nd Meeting, Minute 1, 'Colonial Propaganda', 22 July 1948; TNA: PRO, CAB134/98, CI(48)1, Committee on Colonial Information Policy, Note by the Acting Secretary of the Cabinet, 12 August 1948.
12 TNA: PRO, CAB130/37, GEN 231/4, 'Anti-Soviet and Pro-British Colonial Propaganda', Note by the Secretary, 16 June 1948.
13 TNA: PRO, CAB21/2499, Bevin to Noel-Baker, 22 September 1948. The Parliamentary Under-Secretary of State for Commonwealth Relations, Patrick Gordon-Walker, was the Chairman of the CIPC.
14 TNA: PRO, CAB21/2499, Colonial Information Policy Committee: Constitution and Terms of Reference, 23 November 1948. The misnomer of CIPC was kept to mask its anti-Communist publicity function. See, Ibid., Norman Brook to Prime Minister, 9 August 1949.
15 TNA: PRO, CAB128/13, CM(48)66(4), 25 October 1948. This conclusion came in for harsh criticism by the Cabinet Secretary, Norman Brook, who informed Cripps that 'it would be a mistake to ask this particular Committee to undertake the different job of auditing expenditure on overseas publicity' as it was 'inappropriate

that the Parliamentary Under-Secretaries of the Overseas Departments, which are the major users of overseas information services, should sit in judgment on the cost of these services'. He went on to say that the Prime Minister 'would prefer that the job of auditing expenditure on overseas publicity should be undertaken separately, either by an intensification of normal Treasury checks or by some separate Committee on the lines of that which has been appointed to review expenditure on information services at home'. See, TNA: PRO, CAB21/2499, Brook to Cripps, 22 November 1948.

16 TNA: PRO, CAB128/13, CM(48)66(4), 25 October 1948.

17 TNA: PRO, CAB134/98, CI(48)5(1), 'Composition and Terms of Reference of the Committee', 29 November 1948.

18 This was later reduced to £250,000. TNA: PRO, CAB134/99, CI(49) 15th Meeting, 'Three-Year Plan for the Expansion of Publicity Services in the Commonwealth Countries and the Colonies', 17 November 1949.

19 WAC, R2/2, 'Points for Report', Board of Management meeting, 24 January 1949.

20 WAC, R1/85/2, G42, 'Report by Director of Overseas Services', March 1949.

21 WAC, R1/85/6, G119, 'Report on Finance: Quarter Ended 30th June', 31 August 1949.

22 WAC, R2/2, Board of Management meeting, 'Devaluation', 19 September 1949.

23 The Canadian Office was described to the Board of Governors by Jacob as 'small and cheap, and yet very valuable'. WAC, R1/85/8, G150, 'Report by the Director of the Overseas Services', 17 November 1949; WAC, R2/2, Special Meeting of the Board of Management, 'Devaluation', 28 September 1949.

24 WAC, R1/85/8, G150, 17 November 1949.

25 Ibid.

26 TNA: PRO, CAB134/99, CI(49) 15th Meeting, 'Three-Year Plan', 17 November 1949.

27 Ibid.

28 Ibid., CI(49)17(2), 'Revised Three-Year Plan for the Overseas Information Services', 20 December 1949.

29 In fact, the BBC had received a government assurance that the Singapore project would not be the subject of cuts a week before the meeting and the standstill was withdrawn. WAC, R2/2, 'Points for Report', Board of Management meeting, 12 December 1949.

30 TNA: PRO, CAB130/37, GEN 231/7, 'Colonial Information Policy Committee: Revised Three-Year Plan for the Overseas Information Services', Note by the Committee, 12 December 1949.

31 Ibid., GEN 231/3rd Meeting, 'The Three-Year Plan for Overseas Publicity', 19 December 1949.

32 Ibid.

33 WAC, R1/86/3, G69, 'Report by the Director of Overseas Services', undated.

34 TNA: PRO, CAB134/460, IS(51)2, 'Overseas Information Expenditure', Memorandum by the Chancellor of the Exchequer, 7 February 1951.
35 Ibid.; WAC, R1/86/7, G177, 'Grant-in-Aid Estimates for 1950/1 (Revised) and 1951/2', Note by Director of Overseas Services, 17 November 1950.
36 WAC, R1/86/6, G160, 'Report by the Director of Overseas Services', 19 October 1950.
37 TNA: PRO, CAB134/102, CI(50)21, 'The Overseas Services of the BBC', Memorandum by the BBC, 19 June 1950. Jacob made it clear at the CIPC meeting that the memorandum 'represented at the moment his purely personal views and had not been approved by the Board of Governors'. See, Ibid., CI(50)4(4), 'Overseas Broadcasting: General Jacob's Memorandum', 20 June 1950.
38 Ibid., CI(50)32, 'The Case for an Increase in Overseas Information Expenditure', Memorandum by the Working Party, 21 July 1950.
39 Ibid., CI(50)5(2), 'Overseas Information Expenditure', 26 July 1950.
40 Ibid., CI(50)37, 'The Case for a New Approach to Overseas Information Expenditure', Memorandum by the Foreign Secretary, 19 September 1950.
41 Ibid., CI(50)7(1), 'Overseas Information Expenditure', 21 November 1950.
42 Ibid., CI(50)45, 'Overseas Information Expenditure', Note by Parliamentary Under-Secretary of State for Foreign Affairs, 23 November 1950.
43 WAC, R1/87/1, G8, 'Report by the Director of Overseas Services', 10 January 1951.
44 TNA: PRO, CAB134/460, IS(51)2, 'Overseas Information Expenditure', Memorandum by the Chancellor of the Exchequer, 7 February 1951; IS(51)3, 'Overseas Information Expenditure', Joint Memorandum by the Secretary of State for the Colonies, the Parliamentary Under-Secretary of State for Foreign Affairs and the Parliamentary Under-Secretary of State for Commonwealth Relations, 8 February 1951.
45 TNA: PRO, DEFE4/38, COS(50)200(9), 'Overseas Services of the BBC', 8 December 1950.
46 Ibid., IS(51)4, 'Overseas Information Services', Memorandum by the Minister of Defence, 8 February 1951.
47 TNA: PRO, DEFE4/39, COS(52)22(2), 'Annex: Overseas Services of the BBC', Note by the War Office, 31 January 1951. In appealing to their geostrategic sensibilities it was pointed out that all midday transmissions to Europe would be cancelled, as would entire services in Belgian, Portuguese, Austrian, Danish, Luxembourg, Maltese, Cypriot, Afrikaans, Tamil, Bengali, Mahratti and Singhalese, while German broadcasts would be limited to 2 hours a day and Arabic and Spanish broadcasts to one and a half.
48 WAC, R1/87/1, G8, 10 January 1951.
49 TNA: PRO, CAB134/460, IS(51)2, 7 February 1951.
50 Ibid., IS(51)1(2), 'Overseas Information Expenditure', 12 February 1951.

51 TNA: PRO, CAB129/44, CP(51)53, 'Expenditure on Overseas Information Services, 1951-52', 22 February 1951.
52 Ibid., CP(51)59, 'Overseas Information Expenditure', Memorandum by the Chancellor of the Exchequer, 28 February 1951.
53 TNA: PRO, CAB134/102, CI(50)1(11), 'Further Revision of the Three-Year Plan for the Overseas Information Services', 11 January 1950.
54 TNA: PRO, CAB134/460, IS(51)1(2), 'Overseas Information Expenditure', 12 February 1951.
55 TNA: PRO, CAB128/19, CP(51)23(2), 'Overseas Information Services', 2 April 1951.
56 WAC, R2/48/6, BMA8, 'A BBC Calendar for 1951', undated; WAC, R2/48/2, BM41, 'Staff Reductions in the External Services', Note by DOS, 30 March 1951.
57 Briggs, *Sound and Vision*, p. 476.
58 Ibid.
59 Hansard, Fifth Series, *House of Commons Debates*, vol.484, col.1269, 21 February 1951.
60 Mansell, *Let Truth be Told*, p. 223.
61 WAC, R1/88/1, G13, 'Report by the Director of Overseas Services', 6 February 1952.
62 Mansell, *Let Truth be Told*, p. 224.
63 *Annual Report and Accounts of the British Broadcasting Corporation for the year 1951-52*, Cmd.8660 (London: HMSO, September 1952), pp. 47–8.
64 WAC, R1/88/1, G13, 6 February 1952.
65 Hansard, Fifth Series, *House of Commons Debates*, vol.498, col.1716, 2 April 1952.
66 WAC, R20/53, 'Report of the Independent Committee of Enquiry into the Overseas Information Services', 27 July 1953, p. 5.
67 Hansard, Fifth Series, *House of Commons Debates*, vol.504, cols.1486–8, 30 July 1952.
68 WAC, R20/53, 'Report of the Independent Committee of Enquiry into the Overseas Information Services', 27 July 1953, p. 3. Other members of the committee were: J. L. Heyworth, Victor Feather, Mary Stocks, J. W. Platt, Donald McLachlan and Gervas Huxley. Sir Robert Bruce Lockhart had also been originally appointed but retired in November 1952 due to ill health.
69 Ibid., p. 6.
70 Ibid., p. 9.
71 On returning as Prime Minister in 1951 Churchill combined this role with that of Secretary of State for Defence, as he had done during the war. It was in this capacity that he had requested that Jacob return to his staff. By the time of Jacob's arrival A. V. Alexander had replaced Churchill as Minister of Defence. Haley announced his move to the editorship of *The Times* in June 1952 with Sir Basil Nicholls appointed Acting Director-General until Jacob's return.
72 WAC, R1/89/2, G32, 'Report by the Director of External Broadcasting', 25 February 1953; WAC, R1/88/6, G110, 'Report by the Director of External Broadcasting', 3 December 1952.

73 WAC, R1/89/3, G64, 'Report by the Director of External Services', 31 May 1953.
74 The BBC was given sight of the original report. However, it was nearly another year before a 'Summary' of the report, heavily redacted, was published: *Summary of the Report of the Independent Committee of Enquiry into the Overseas Information Services*, Cmd.9138 (London: HMSO, April 1954).
75 WAC, R1/88/6, G110, 3 December 1952.
76 WAC, R20/53, 'Report of the Independent Committee of Enquiry into the Overseas Information Services', 27 July 1953, p. 3.
77 WAC, R1/89/4, G89, 'Report by the Director of External Broadcasting', undated.
78 Ibid., G94, 'Comments on the Report of the Drogheda Committee', 29 September 1953.
79 Ibid.
80 *Summary of the Report of the Independent Committee of Enquiry into the Overseas Information Services*, Cmd.9138 (London: HMSO, April 1954).
81 Hansard, Fifth Series, *House of Commons Debates*, vol.532, cols.847–8, 8 November 1954.
82 Hansard, Fifth Series, *House of Lords Debates*, vol.190, col.306, 8 December 1954.
83 WAC, R1/90/5, G113, 'Report by Director of External Broadcasting'.
84 Ibid.
85 WAC, R1/90/1, G21, 'Report by Director of External Broadcasting'.
86 Ibid.

Chapter 8

1 Also present were: J. B. Clark, Director of External Broadcasting; Tangye Lean, Assistant Director of External Broadcasting; James Monahan, Controller European Services; Hugh Carleton Greene, Controller Overseas Services.
2 TNA: PRO, FO953/1640, PB1011/6, 'Governors' Dinner to Foreign Secretary', memorandum by Director of External Broadcasting, 8 December 1955.
3 Ibid.
4 TNA: PRO, FO953/1641, PB1011/17, 'BBC External Services', memorandum by Paul Grey, 10 April 1956.
5 TNA: PRO, FO953/1646, PB1012/6, 'BBC External Services', Grey to Stewart, 20 February 1956.
6 TNA: PRO, FO953/1641, PB1011/17, 'BBC External Services', 10 April 1956; FO953/1646, PB1012/6, 'BBC External Services', 20 February 1956. Grey noted that previously 'We have, of course, discussed the BBC services frequently and decided so far that we should leave well alone'. Ibid.
7 TNA: PRO, FO953/1641, PB1011/17, 'BBC External Services', 10 April 1956.

8 Khrushchev had been First Secretary of the Central Committee since September 1953 with Bulganin taking up the position of Chairman of the Council of Ministers (Premier) in February 1955.
9 The Austrian State Treaty, signed on 15 May 1955 by the occupying powers (Britain, Russia, France and America), allowed for the establishment of an independent Austrian Government on 27 July 1955. Allied troops withdrew on 25 October 1955. The July 1955 Geneva Summit Conference between the leaders of Britain, France, Russia and America met to discuss German reunification, disarmament, European security and enhanced economic and cultural relations.
10 The Soviets detonated an enhanced fission devise in August 1953. The deal to supply Soviet arms to Egypt was negotiated in September 1955. The Warsaw Pact was signed on 14 May 1955 by the Soviet Union, Albania, Bulgaria, Czechoslovakia, Hungary, Poland and Romania – the German Democratic Republic joined the following year.
11 TNA: PRO, FO953/1641, PB1011/17, 'BBC External Services', 10 April 1956.
12 TNA: PRO, FO953/1643, PB1011/54, 'Criticisms of the External Services of the British Broadcasting Corporation', memorandum by Cosmo Stewart, 20 September 1956.
13 Ibid., Grey to Lean, 21 September 1956.
14 Ibid., 'Criticisms of the External Services', 20 September 1956.
15 Ibid., PB1011/54, Grey to Lean, 21 September 1956.
16 TNA: PRO, FO953/1640, PB1011/13, 'The External Services of the BBC', by Sir Ian Jacob, 31 May 1956.
17 WAC, R1/92/3, G45, 'Report by Director of External Broadcasting', 25 May 1956. BBC broadcasts to Finland, Turkey, Persia, Israel and Greece were also affected positively by this reduction in jamming. Jamming stations in the Satellites, however, continued to operate.
18 Programmes to Poland, Czechoslovakia, Hungary, Rumania, Bulgaria, Albania and the East Zone of Germany were still attacked by local jammers although the Russian high-power, long-range jammers that supplemented these had been withdrawn. WAC, R1/92/3, G45, 25 May 1956.
19 WAC, R1/92/2, G27, 'Report by Director of External Broadcasting', March 1956; TNA: PRO, FO953/1640, PB1011/6, 'Governor's Dinner', 8 December 1956.
20 WAC, R1/92/2, G27, March 1956.
21 WAC, R1/92/6, G73, 'Report by Director of External Broadcasting', 18 September 1956.
22 WAC, R2/9/1, Board of Management meeting, 'USSR: Visit by BBC Officials', 12 March 1956; R1/24, Board of Governors meeting, 'Director-General's Report', 15 March 1956.

23 The other members of the Delegation were: R. T. B. Wynn, Chief Engineer; Frank Gillard, Chief Assistant to Director of Sound Broadcasting; A. E. Barker, Deputy Editor, News; Leonard Miall, Head of Talks, Television; S. N. Watson, Head of Television Section, Designs Department.

24 WAC, R1/92/3, G48, 'Report on Visit to the USSR, April/May 1956', undated, p. 5.

25 Ibid., p. 36.

26 Ibid., pp. 2 and 5.

27 WAC, R1/92/6, G73, 18 September 1956.

28 WAC, R1/92/3, G48, undated, p. 3.

29 WAC, R1/92/6, G73, 18 September 1956.

30 WAC, R1/92/3, G48, undated, p. 2. The majority of installations (25 million) were served by wire networks and consequently under censorship.

31 TNA: PRO, FO953/1640, 'The External Services of the BBC', 31 May 1956; FO953/1643, PB1011/54, Grey to Lean, 21 September 1956. Soviet Radio had been anxious to complete a formal agreement covering liaison between the two organisations, but this was resisted by the BBC delegation and subsequently a letter from Clark to Puzin was accepted as the basis of agreement. WAC, R1/92/6, G73, 18 September 1956.

32 TNA: PRO, FO953/1643, PB1011/54, Grey to Lean, 21 September 1956.

33 TNA: PRO, FO953/1640, PB 011/13, 'The External Services of the BBC', 31 May 1956.

34 TNA: PRO, FO953/1643, PB1011/54, Grey to Lean, 21 September 1956.

35 Ibid.; 'Criticism of the External Service', 20 September 1956.

36 WAC, R1/92/6, G73, 18 September 1956.

37 TNA: PRO, FO953/1643, PB1011/54, Grey to Lean, 21 September 1956.

38 TNA: PRO, FO953/1640, PB1011/13, 'The External Services of the BBC', 31 May 1956.

39 Ibid.

40 WAC, R1/92/3, G45, 25 May 1956. This report was based on 127 refugee interviews. The BBC had access to the RFE report under a reciprocal information sharing arrangement with the Americans.

41 TNA: PRO, FO953/1640, PB1011/13, 'The External Services of the BBC', 31 May 1956.

42 Ibid.

43 On the development of Khrushchev's thinking between the death of Stalin and the Twentieth Party Congress, and the internal political machinations of the period see, for example: Nikita Khrushchev, *Memoirs of Nikita Khrushchev, Vol. 2: Reformer, 1945-1964*, edited by Sergei Khrushchev, translated by George Shriver (University Park: Pennsylvania State University, 2006), pp. 201–21.

44 T. H. Rigby (ed.), *The Stalin Dictatorship: Khrushchev's 'Secret Speech' and Other Documents* (Victoria: Sydney University Press, 1968), pp. 23–91.
45 WAC, E40/151/1, *Rumblings in Hungary*, General News Talk by F. G. Rentoul, 30 June 1956.
46 WAC, R1/92/6, G73, 18 September 1956.
47 Johanna Granville '"Caught with jam on our Fingers": Radio Free Europe and the Hungarian revolution of 1956'. *Diplomatic History*, 29 (5), 2005, p. 820. Anne Applebaum, *Iron Curtain: The Crushing of Eastern Europe 1944-56* (London: Allen Lane, 2012), p. 481.
48 WAC, R1/92/6, G73, 'Report by Director of External Broadcasting: June to August 1956', 18 September 1956.

Chapter 9

1 Gyorgy Litvan (ed.), *The Hungarian Revolution of 1956: Reform, Revolt and Repression, 1953-63* (London: Longman, 1996), p. 57.
2 Brian Cartledge, *The Will to Survive: A History of Hungary* (Tiverton: Timewell Press, 2006), pp. 468–9.
3 From 1949 Budapest Radio was also known as Kossuth Radio after Lajos Kossuth, a Nineteenth-Century Hungarian political leader of the 1848 revolution. Both terms remained in common use during this period.
4 George Mikes, *The Hungarian Revolution* (London: Andre Deutsch, 1957), p. 80.
5 Ibid., p. 79.
6 Tony Judt, *Postwar: A History of Europe since 1945* (London: Heinemann, 2005), p. 318; Johanna Granville, '"Caught with jam on our Fingers": Radio Free Europe and the Hungarian revolution of 1956', *Diplomatic History*, 29/5 (2005), p. 825fn.; Gary Rawnsley, *Radio Diplomacy and Propaganda: The BBC and VOA in International Politics, 1956-64* (Basingstoke: Macmillan, 1996), p. 93.
7 Cartledge, *Will to Survive*, p. 469.
8 Applebaum, *Iron Curtain*, pp. 464–5.
9 Ibid., p. 473.
10 Applebaum, *Iron Curtain*, p. 478.
11 TNA: PRO, FO1110/781, PR1021/181, Macdonald to Grady, 23 December 1955.
12 WAC, R1/92/2, G56, 'Report by Director of External Broadcasting', March 1956.
13 WAC, E35/50/1, 'Hungary: Before Rakosi's Fall', H.C.Eur.S. to Hungarian P.O., 19 July 1956.
14 TNA: PRO, FO1110/781, PR1021/121, Note by Storey, 9 June 1955; Ibid., Macdonald to Overton, 22 June 1955; Ibid., Cope, Budapest, to Mason, 2 June 1955.
15 Ibid., Macdonald to Overton, 22 June 1955.

16 Ibid., Cope, Budapest, to Mason, 2 June 1955.

17 Ibid., Macdonald to Overton, 22 June 1955.

18 Ibid., PR1021/181, Grady to Storey, 18 November 1955.

19 Brian Cartledge, *The Will to Survive: A History of Hungary* (Tiverton: Timewell Press, 2006), p. 461.

20 Peter Unwin, *1956: Power Defied* (Norwich: Michael Russell, 2006), p. 112.

21 WAC, R1/92/6, G73, 'Report by Director of External Broadcasting', 18 September 1956.

22 WAC, E40/154/1, *More Hungarian Alarms* by F. G. Rentoul, 3 July 1956.

23 R. F. Leslie (ed.), *The History of Poland since 1863* (Cambridge: Cambridge University Press, 1980), p. 349.

24 Ibid., p. 350; Timothy Garton Ash, *The Polish Revolution: Solidarity* (London: Penguin, 1999), pp. 11–12.

25 WAC, R1/92/6, G73, 18 September 1956; E2/812/1, Macdonald to Foster, 16 November 1956.

26 Leslie, *History of Poland*, pp. 350–1.

27 WAC, R1/92/7, G91, 'Report by Director of External Broadcasting', 27 November 1956. These hour-long Radio Polskie programmes in September 1956 led to an innovative development at the BBC whereby the 'Polish transmissions were directly fed into Bush House [from BBC Monitoring at Caversham], so that commentators were able to speak with close knowledge of the atmosphere of the court'.

28 Cartledge, *The Will to Survive*, p. 464; Tony Judt, *Postwar: A History of Europe since 1945* (London: Heinemann, 2005), p. 314; Applebaum, *Iron Curtain*, p. 483.

29 Applebaum, *Iron Curtain*, p. 485; Cartledge, *Will to Survive*, p. 466. In a survey of 1,007 Hungarian refugees conducted in December 1956 by International Research Associates Inc. on behalf of the Unites States Information Agency (USIA) 40 per cent (the most popular choice) thought that the 'example of Poland' was the most important 'reason why people in Hungary were willing to attempt an uprising'. WAC, E3/907/1, 'Hungary and the 1956 Uprising: Survey Among Hungarian Refugees in Austria', February 1957, p. 31.

30 Tony Judt, *Postwar: A History of Europe since 1945* (London: Heinemann, 2005), p. 318; Granville, 'Jam on Our Fingers', p. 825fn.; Rawnsley, *Radio Diplomacy*, p. 93.

31 Eric Hobsbawm, 'Could it have been different?'. *London Review of Books*, 28(22), 16 November 2006, p. 3.

32 WAC, Programme as Broadcast, 'The BBC and the Hungarian Revolution', 23 January 1957.

33 WAC, PasB, 'The BBC and the Hungarian Revolution', 23 January 1957.

34 WAC, R1/92/7, G91, 'Report by Director of External Broadcasting', 27 November 1956.

35 *Highlight* was the predecessor of the *Tonight* programme; Alasdair Milne, *DG: The Memoirs of a British Broadcaster* (London: Hodder & Stoughton, 1988), p. 12.
36 WAC, R1/92/7, G91, 27 November 1956.
37 WAC, PasB, 'The BBC and the Hungarian Revolution', 23 January 1957.
38 WAC, R1/92/7, G91, 27 November 1956.
39 WAC, PasB, 'The BBC and the Hungarian Revolution', 23 January 1957.
40 Ibid.
41 In addition to the primary records kept at The National Archive, Kew, London, a significant number of Fry's telegrams during the uprising have been reproduced in: Eva Haraszti-Taylor, *The Hungarian Revolution of 1956: A Collection of Documents from the British Foreign Office* (Nottingham: Astra, 1995).
42 TNA: PRO, FO1110/873, PR10111/133, Memorandum by Foster, 19 October 1956.
43 WAC, E40/154/1, 'Telephone message from Miss Storey', 25 October 1957. Other information also communicated by Storey on 25 October from Fry's despatch was the prophetic analysis that the uprising appeared 'to have come as close to controlling Budapest as is ever likely'.
44 WAC, E40/154/2, 'Telegram No.429', Fry, Budapest, to Foreign Office, 25 October, 2.37 p.m.
45 WAC, E2/812/1, Macdonald to Foster, 16 November 1956.
46 WAC, E40/154/2, 'Telegram No.442', Fry, Budapest, to Foreign Office, 26 October 1956.
47 WAC, E2/812/1, Macdonald to Foster, 16 November 1956.
48 WAC, E40/154/2, 'Telegram No.442', 26 October 1956.
49 WAC, E2/812/1, Macdonald to Foster, 16 November 1956.
50 WAC, E2/812/1, 'The BBC and the Hungarian Uprising', Macdonald to DXB, 6 July 1965.
51 WAC, E40/154/1, untitled memo dated 24 October 1956.
52 Cartledge, *Will to Survive*, p. 470.
53 Laura-Louise Veress, *Clear the Line: Hungary's Struggle to Leave the Axis during the Second World War*, edited by Dalma Takacs (Prospero Publications, 1995), p. 350; Rawnsley, *Radio Diplomacy*, p. 89.
54 Cartledge, *Will to Survive*, p. 470.
55 Rawnsley, *Radio Diplomacy*, p. 91.
56 Rawnsley, *Radio Diplomacy*, p. 95; Cartledge, *Will to Survive*, p. 474.
57 WAC, E40/233/1, Message broadcast by Budapest Radio on behalf of the Revolutionary Committee of Radio Budapest, 30 October 1956.
58 Granville, 'Jam on our Fingers', p. 833; Peter Hennessy, *Having it so Good: Britain in the Fifties* (London: Allen Lane, 2006), p. 443.
59 WAC, E12/713/1, *Notes by Our Observer* by Anatol Goldberg, 3 November 1956.

60 WAC, R1/92/7, G 91, 27 November 1956.
61 Ibid.
62 WAC, Summary of World Broadcasts, 4 November 1956.
63 WAC, BBC Monitoring, Summary of World Broadcasts, 4 November 1956.
64 Cartledge, *The Will to Survive*, p. 481.
65 WAC, BBC Monitoring, Summary of World Broadcasts, 4 November 1956.
66 Rawnsley, *Radio Diplomacy*, p. 97.
67 WAC, BBC Monitoring, Summary of World Broadcasts, 4 November 1956.
68 Ibid.
69 11 and 13 November 1956, respectively. Rawnsley, *Radio Diplomacy*, pp. 99–100.
70 WAC, E40/154/2, 'Telegram No.738', Fry to Foreign Office, 16 November 1956.
71 WAC, E2/812/1, 'Hungarian Jokes', memorandum from ADXB to C.Eur.S., 16 November 1956; E40/154/2, 'Telegram No.776', Fry to Foreign Office, 20 November 1956.
72 WAC, E2/812/1, 'Hungarian Jokes', 16 November 1956.
73 WAC, E2/812/1, Macdonald to DXB, 6 July 1965.
74 WAC, E3/898/1, draft report on 'Listening in Hungary', 27 November 1957.
75 WAC, R1/92/3, G45, 'Report by Director of External Broadcasting', 25 May 1956.
76 Judt, *Postwar*, p. 318; Cartledge, *The Will to Survive*, p. 482.
77 There were five main audience studies conducted at the time for the benefit of western broadcasters. 1,007 Hungarians were interviewed in Austria by the New York firm, International Research Associates Inc., for the USIA in December 1956. Radio Free Europe conducted its own large questionnaire survey among refugees. 400 Hungarians were interviewed by an Austrian market research company at the end of 1956 which conducted a further study of 315 refugees for RFE in January and February 1957; 220 questionnaires were filled in for the BBC by Hungarian refugees in Britain. The US State Department also interviewed refugees in Europe and America. WAC, E3/898/1, 'Listening in Hungary', 27 November 1957; WAC, E3/907/1, 'Hungary and the 1956 Uprising: Survey Among Hungarian Refugees in Austria', USIA, 15 February 1957.
78 WAC, E3/898/1, 'Listening in Hungary', 27 November 1957. 'The lowest figure for listening to western broadcasts came from the 200 plus BBC administered questionnaires. It was 83% of the sample. The highest figure was 97% amongst the group of 315 Hungarian refugees interrogated for RFE in early 1957. Percentages in the three other main groups that provided information ranged from 90% to 96%.'
79 WAC, E3/907/1, 'Hungary and the 1956 Uprising', 15 February 1957. When asked how often they listened to foreign radio stations 67 per cent said that they

listened to the BBC 'frequently'. The equivalent figures for VOA and RFE were, respectively, 67 and 81 per cent.

80 WAC, E3/898/1, 'Listening in Hungary', 27 November 1957.

81 WAC, E3/907/1, 'Hungary and the 1956 Uprising', 15 February 1957. See also, WAC, E3/898/1, 'Listening in Hungary', 27 November 1957.

82 Rawnsley, *Radio Diplomacy*, p. 69.

83 WAC, E3/898/1, 'Listening in Hungary', 27 November 1957.

84 WAC, E3/907/1, 'Hungary and the 1956 Uprising', 15 February 1957. 84 per cent also said that they relied on foreign radio most for news of what was happening outside Hungary.

85 Ibid.

86 István Rév, 'Just Noise?', conference paper, *Cold War Broadcasting Impact*, Stanford University, 15 October 2004.

87 United Nations, *Report of the Special Committee on the Problem of Hungary*, General Assembly, Official Records: Eleventh Session, Supplement No.18 (A/3592), 1957, para. 100. The accusation was made in the *Hungarian White Book: The Counter Revolutionary Forces in the October Events in Hungary, Vol.2*, published by the Information Bureau of the Council of Ministers of the Hungarian People's Republic.

88 Rawnsley, *Radio Diplomacy*, p. 81.

89 WAC, E3/907/1, 'Hungary and the 1956 Uprising', p. 32. Within the largest cohort of Hungarians interviewed, 96 per cent believed that "the Hungarian people expected aid from the West, and from the US, in the uprising".

90 Ibid., p. 36.

91 In particular, see: Gary Rawnsley, *Radio Diplomacy*; Michael Nelson, *War of the Black Heavens: The Battles of Western Broadcasting in the Cold War* (London: Brassey's, 1997); Johanna Granville, 'Jam on Our Fingers'; Charles Gati, *Failed Illusions: Moscow, Washington, Budapest, and the 1956 Hungarian revolt* (Stanford: Stanford University Press, 2006); A. Ross Johnson, *Radio Free Europe and Radio Liberty: The CIA Years and Beyond* (Washington: Woodrow Wilson Center Press; Stanford University Press, 2010).

92 Gati, *Failed Illusions*, pp. 97–100. Emphasis in the original.

93 Nicholas Cull, *The Cold War and the United States Information Agency: American Propaganda and Public Diplomacy, 1945–1989* (Cambridge: Cambridge University Press, 2008), p. 132.

94 Johnson, *Radio Free Europe and Radio Liberty*, p. 80.

95 Ibid., p. 108; Nelson, *War of the Black Heavens*, p. 79.

96 A. Ross Johnson, 'Setting the Record Straight: Role of Radio Free Europe in the Hungarian Revolution of 1956', Open Society Archive, Central European University, September 2006, p. 39; Arch Puddington, *Broadcasting Freedom: The*

Cold War Triumph of Radio Free Europe and Radio Liberty (Lexington: University Press of Kentucky, 2000), pp. 103–4.

97 Johnson, 'Setting the Record Straight', p. 38.

98 Nelson, *War of the Black Heavens*, p. 74.

99 William Griffith, 'Policy Review of Voice for Free Hungary Programming, 23 October – 23 November 1956', 5 December 1956, in Csaba Békés, Malcolm Byrne, and János Rainer (eds), *The Hungarian Revolution: A History in Documents* (Budapest: Central European University Press, 2002), pp. 466 and 477.

100 Puddington, *Broadcasting Freedom*, p. 105.

101 Granville, 'Jam on Our Fingers', p. 826; Johnson, 'Setting the Record Straight', p. 15.

102 Puddington, *Broadcasting Freedom*, p. 105.

103 Nelson, *War of the Black Heavens*, p. 77.

104 TNA: PRO, FO1110/853, PR134/5, 'Report on Visit to Radio Free Europe, Munich' by Gregory Macdonald, February 1956. Macdonald was requested to 'see whether in my opinion the News operation was sufficiently objective'. Macdonald pointed out to his American hosts that 'my interest would expand beyond the news-gathering mechanism and the Newscasts in the various languages to related aspects of the output, such as Press Reviews and News Comment'.

105 TNA: PRO, FO110/853, PR134/5, Covering note on file by Penny Storey, 28 February 1956.

106 TNA: PRO, FO1110/853, PR134/5, 'Report on Visit to Radio Free Europe', February 1956.

107 Ibid.

108 Ibid.

109 Johnson, 'Radio Free Europe and Radio Liberty', pp. 105–7; Puddington, *Broadcasting Freedom*, pp. 103–4; United Nations, *Report of the Special Committee on the Problem of Hungary*, General Assembly Official Records: Eleventh Session, Supplement No.18 (A/3592), 1957, para. 131.

110 United Nations, *Report of the Special Committee on the Problem of Hungary*, General Assembly Official Records: Eleventh Session, Supplement No.18 (A/3592), 1957, para. 89.

111 Ibid., para. 2. Sitting on the committee were representatives of Australia, Ceylon, Denmark, Tunisia and Uruguay.

112 Ibid., para. 785. In addition to the BBC and FBIS sources, use was made of a publication entitled, 'The Hungarian Revolution and fight for Freedom in the Light of Hungarian Broadcasts'.

113 Ibid.

114 WAC, E12/713/1, 'UN Committee Report on Hungary', 20 June 1957.

115 Rawnsley, *Radio Diplomacy*, p. 92.

116 Ibid., p. 71.

117 WAC, PasB 'The BBC and the Hungarian Revolution', 23 January 1957.

Chapter 10

1 TNA: PRO, FO953/1644, PB1011/60/G, 'BBC's External Services', Cosmo Stewart, 26 October 1956.

2 TNA: PRO, CAB128/30 Part 2, CM(56) 73rd Conclusions, 'Oversea Broadcasting', 24 October 1956.

3 TNA: PRO, FO953/1644, PB1011/60/G, 'BBC's External Services', 26 October 1956.

4 TNA: PRO, FO953/1641, PB1011/17, 'BBC External Services', 20 February 1956.

5 Peter Partner, *Arab Voices: The BBC Arabic Service, 1938-1988* (London: BBC, 1988), p. 96.

6 TNA: PRO, FO953/1641, PB1011/17, 'BBC External Services', 20 February 1956.

7 Ibid.

8 Ibid. Note by Ivone Kirpatrick, 11 April 1956.

9 Ibid. Note by Anthony Nutting, 11 April 1956.

10 TNA: PRO, CAB130/119, GEN 542/6 (Final), 'Interim Report', August 1956.

11 TNA: PRO, FO953/1640, PB1011/12, Douglas Dodds-Parker to Grey, 24 May 1956.

12 TNA: PRO, FO953/1641, PB1011/20, 'Record of a conversation between the Secretary of State and Sir Ian Jacob about overseas broadcasting', 11 July 1956.

13 WAC, R1/92/2, G27, 'Report by Director of External Broadcasting', March 1956.

14 TNA: PRO, CAB131/17, DC(56)17, 'United Kingdom Requirements in the Middle East', 3 July 1956.

15 Tony Shaw, *Eden, Suez and the Mass Media: Propaganda and Persuasion during the Suez Crisis* (London: I.B. Taurus, 1996), pp. 4–5.

16 TNA: PRO, CAB131/17, DC(56)17, 3 July 1956.

17 TNA: PRO, CAB158/25, JIC(56)78, 'The Activities of Cairo Radio and their Impact on the Territories Towards which they are Directed', Report by the JIC, 23 July 1956.

18 TNA: PRO, CAB130/119, Committee on Overseas Broadcasting, GEN 542/6(Final) 'Interim Report', 1 August 1956. For the disagreement between the Foreign Office and the Colonial Office over these plans see, James Vaughan, *The Failure of American and British Propaganda in the Arab Middle East, 1945-1957: Unconquerable Minds* (Basingstoke: Palgrave, 2005), p. 202; TNA: PRO, CAB130/119, Committee on Overseas Broadcasting, GEN 542/1st Meeting, 'Oversea Broadcasting Policy', 12 July 1956.

19 Vaughan, *Unconquerable Minds*, p. 204.

20 TNA: PRO, FO953/1631, P1041, Stewart to Lodge, 8 May 1956. In addition, 7 hours of Persian programmes were broadcast and three and a half hours in Hebrew.
21 WAC, R1/92/3, G45, 'Report by Director of External Broadcasting', 25 May 1956.
22 TNA: PRO, FO953/1632, P1041/50, 'Copies of Weekly Letters sent by RIO, Beirut to Posts in the Middle East: Lists of articles translated into Arabic by RIO Beirut'; TNA: PRO, FO953/1630, P1041/17, 'Copies of Weekly Letters sent by RIO, Beirut to Posts in the Middle East: Lists of articles translated into Arabic by RIO Beirut'; TNA: PRO, FO953/1629, P1041/2, 'Copies of Weekly Letters sent by RIO, Beirut to Posts in the Middle East: Lists of articles translated into Arabic by RIO Beirut'.
23 WAC, R1/92/3, G45, 25 May 1956.
24 WAC, R1/92/2, G27, March 1956.
25 WAC, R1/92/3, G45, 25 May 1956.
26 Rawnsley, *Radio Diplomacy*, p. 24.
27 Vaughan, *Unconquerable Minds*, p. 207.
28 Anthony Nutting, *No End of a Lesson: The Story of Suez* (London: Constable, 1967), p. 10.
29 TNA: PRO, CAB130/119, Committee on Overseas Broadcasting, GEN 542/1st Meeting, 'Oversea Broadcasting Policy', 12 July 1956; CAB158/25, JIC(56)78, 23 July 1956.
30 WAC, R1/92/3, G45, 25 May 1956.
31 TNA: PRO, FO953/1640, PB1011/13, 'The External Services of the BBC' by Sir Ian Jacob, 31 May 1956.
32 Partner, *Arab Voices*, pp. 94–5.
33 WAC, R1/24, Board of Governors meeting, 'Director-General's Report', 19 July 1956; Asa Briggs, *The History of Broadcasting in the United Kingdom: Volume V, Competition* (Oxford: Oxford University Press, 1995), p. 119.
34 Vaughan, *Unconquerable Minds*, p. 202. The other three projects were VHF broadcasting facilities for the Arabian Peninsula; the strengthening of Radio Baghdad; clandestine broadcasting facilities.
35 TNA: PRO, AIR8/2062, Brook to C.A.S., 6 June 1956; TNA: PRO, CAB130/119, Committee on Overseas Broadcasting, GEN 542/2nd Meeting, 'Oversea Broadcasting Policy', 25 July 1956.
36 The BBC claimed that there were 1 million listeners to the service. TNA: PRO, CAB130/119, Committee on Overseas Broadcasting, GEN 542/1st Meeting, 'Oversea Broadcasting Policy', 12 July 1956; TNA: PRO, FO953/1641, PB1011/17. 'BBC External Services', 10 April 1956.
37 TNA: PRO, CAB130/119, GEN 542/1st Meeting, 'Oversea Broadcasting Policy', 12 July 1956.
38 Ibid., GEN 542/2nd Meeting, 'Oversea Broadcasting Policy', 25 July 1956.
39 Ibid.

40 TNA: PRO, FO953/1643, PB1011/44, 'The BBC External Services', 26 July 1956.
41 Ibid.
42 TNA: PRO, CAB130/119, Committee on Overseas Broadcasting, GEN 542/6(Final) 'Interim Report', 1 August 1956. The exact cost of the External Services and its various parts was very difficult to determine because of the arrangement with the Treasury 'whereby the external services are charged only with the additional cost incurred over that required to maintain the domestic services'; the cost of transmission 'which could only be assessed as a fraction, proportional to the time consumed, of the cost of maintenance and operation of the technical installation as a whole'. Accordingly, stated costs were rough estimates. See, TNA: PRO, FO953/1641, PB1011/17. 'BBC External Services', Appendix II: Costs of Services, memorandum by P. F. Grey, 10 April 1956.
43 Ibid.
44 TNA: PRO, FO953/1640, PB1011/13, 'The External Services of the BBC', 31 May 1956.
45 Briggs, *Competition*, p. 121; TNA: PRO, FO953/1643, PB1011/43/G, 'Record of a meeting with Sir Ian Jacob', Kirkpatrick to Rennie, 28 August 1956.
46 TNA: PRO, CAB134/306, GIS(46) 4th Meeting, 28 February 1946.
47 TNA: PRO, FO953/1643, PB1011/43/G, 'Record of a meeting with Sir Ian Jacob', Kirkpatrick to Rennie, 28 August 1956.
48 WAC, R34/1580/1, Suez Crisis: Historical I, DG's Desk Diary, 26 July 1956; Kyle, Suez, p. 134; David Carlton, *Britain and the Suez Crisis* (Oxford: Basil Blackwell, 1989), p. 35; Tony Shaw, *Eden, Suez and the Mass Media: Propaganda and Persuasion during the Suez Crisis* (London: I.B. Taurus, 1996), p. 108. Shaw notes that "Jacob had that day been involved in the entertainment of the young guest of honour, King Faisal of Iraq, who had expressed a desire to see the facilities of the BBC Arabic Service".
49 Kyle, *Suez*, p. 164.
50 Ibid., p. 189.
51 TNA: PRO, CAB28/30 Part 2, CM(56)59(3), 'Suez', 14 August 1956.
52 WAC, R2/9/2, Board of Management meeting, 'Suez Canal Crisis', 13 August 1956; WAC, R34/1580/1, programme note, 15 August 1956; The Conference was designed to pressure Nasser to reverse his course. On 23 August 18 of the 22 nations present agreed to a system of international control for the Suez Canal. See, Carlton, *Suez Crisis*, pp. 41–5, 47–8. The *Light Programme* was one of three domestic radio channels run by the BBC and is the equivalent of today's *Radio Two*.
53 WAC, R34/1580/1, programme note, 15 August 1956.
54 Sir Robert Menzies was eventually allowed to broadcast following the direct intervention of Eden who telephoned his former Permanent Secretary at the

Foreign Office, Sir Alexander Cadogan, now Chairman of the BBC Board of Governors, who in turn instructed Jacob to make the necessary arrangements. For a good account of this episode see, Shaw, *Propaganda and Persuasion*, pp. 114–16.

55 Briggs, *Competition*, 1995, p. 87.
56 Shaw, *Propaganda and Persuasion*, p. 121.
57 WAC, R1/92/6, G73, 18 September 1956.
58 Rawnsley, *Radio Diplomacy*, p. 43.
59 WAC, R1/92/6, G73, 18 September 1956.
60 Vaughan, *Unconquerable Minds*, pp. 212–13.
61 WAC, R1/92/6, G73, 18 September 1956. For Whitehall's publicity and propaganda themes during the Suez crisis see, for example: TNA: PRO, FO953/1633, P1041/75, Draft Directive on HMG's Propaganda in the Middle East for information of the East African territories, undated; WAC, R34/1580/1, 'I.C.E. Progress Report', undated; Ibid., I.C.E. briefing paper by Douglas Dodds-Parker, 11 October 1956; Vaughan, *Unconquerable Minds*, p. 214.
62 WAC, R1/92/6, G73, 18 September 1956.
63 Kyle, *Suez*, p. 247; WAC, R34/1580/1, 12 September 1956.
64 WAC, R1/24, Board of Governors meeting, 'Suez Crisis: Request for Broadcast by Leader of the Opposition', 13 September 1956.
65 TNA: PRO, CAB128/30 Part 2, CM(56)67(8), 'Oversea Broadcasting', 26 September 1956.
66 TNA: PRO, CAB130/120, Ministerial Committee on Oversea Broadcasting, GEN 554/1st Meeting, 'Oversea Broadcasting Policy', 9 October 1956. Other permanent members of the Committee were: Alan Lennox-Boyd (Secretary of State for the Colonies), David Heathcoat-Amory (Minister of Agriculture, Fisheries and Food), Charles Hill (Postmaster-General), Anthony Nutting (Minister of States for Foreign Affairs).
67 Ibid.
68 Ibid.; Philip Murphy, *Alan Lennox-Boyd: A Biography* (London: I.B. Taurus, 1999), p. 162.
69 TNA: PRO, CAB30/120, GEN 554/1st Meeting, 'Oversea Broadcasting Policy', 9 October 1956.
70 Kirkpatrick's figure of £8 million is in contrast with the cap of £11.8 million in 1956/57 imposed by the Cabinet for overseas publicity. See, TNA: PRO, FO953/1646, PB1012/3, Hillis, to Stewart, Foreign Office, 30 January 1956; TNA: PRO, FO953/1646, PB1012/6, 'BBC External Services', Paul Grey, 20 February 1956.
71 TNA: PRO, CAB30/120, GEN 554/1st Meeting, 'Oversea Broadcasting Policy', 9 October 1956.

72 TNA: PRO, CAB130/120, GEN 554/2nd Meeting, 'Oversea Broadcasting Policy', 18 October 1956.
73 TNA: PRO, FO953/1643, PB 1011/53, 'Foreign Office Liaison with the BBC Overseas Services', memorandum by Paul Grey, 24 September 1956.
74 TNA: PRO, CAB130/120, GEN 554/1st Meeting, 9 October 1956.
75 TNA: PRO, CAB128/30 Part 2, CM(56)73(4), 'Oversea Broadcasting', 24 October 1956.
76 TNA: PRO, FO953/1644, PB1011/60/G, 'BBC's External Services', 26 October 1956.
77 WAC, R34/1580/1, 'Draft Letter' from Douglas Dodds-Parker, 26 October 1956.
78 Briggs, *Competition*, p. 126.
79 The recommendations were for the elimination of services in four categories: (i) *Main Western European Countries*, French, Italian, Portuguese, Swedish, Danish, Norwegian, Dutch; (ii) *Commonwealth Countries*, Afrikaans, Bengali, Marathi, Hindi, Urdu; (iii) *Minor Western European Countries*, Greek, Finnish, Serbo-Croat and Slovene, Spanish; (iv) *Latin American Countries*, Spanish, Portuguese. In addition, while programmes to Germany 'should be reorientated so as to make Eastern Germany its principal target' the BBC should also consider 'whether the General Overseas Service does not offer some scope for reduction in its scale and for redistribution of the emphasis within it'. WAC, R34/1580/1, 'Draft Letter' from Douglas Dodds-Parker, 26 October 1956.
80 Ibid.
81 TNA: PRO, FO953/1644, PB1011/61/G, 'Draft letter to BBC', note of a telephone conversation, 26 October 1956.
82 Formerly, BBC Director of Administration.
83 Burke Trend noted on 26 October that the final version of the letter could "be prepared only after the Cabinet have taken a firm decision on policy". TNA: PRO, FO953/1644, PB1011/61/G, Trend to Rae, 26 October 1956; Ibid., note of a telephone conversation, 26 October 1956.
84 Keith Kyle, *Suez: Britain's End of Empire in the Middle East* (London: I.B. Taurus, 2003), pp. 347–50 and 380–5; The Sèvres Protocol as reproduced in, Hennessy, *Having It So Good*, pp. 435–6.
85 During the war Grisewood had been Kirkpatrick's deputy in the BBC's European Services.
86 Harman Grisewood, *One Thing at a Time: An Autobiography* (London: Hutchinson, 1968), p. 197.
87 WAC, R1/92/7, G91, 'Report by Director of External Broadcasting', 27 November 1956.
88 *Annual Report and Accounts of the British Broadcasting Corporation, 1956-57*, Cmd.267, October 1957, p. 15.

89 WAC, R34/1580/1, Record of a telephone conversation with Mr Paul Grey on the subject of 'appointment of liaison officer', 31 October 1956; Ibid., copy of 'draft letter' with covering note from Douglas Dodds-Parker to Sir Ian Jacob, 26 October 1956.

90 Briggs, *Competition*, p. 126.

91 Partner dates his arrival at Bush House as 2 November 1956.

92 WAC, R1/92/7, G91, 27 November 1956.

93 Briggs, *Competition*, p. 128.

94 Ibid.

95 Partner, *Arab Voices*, p. 111.

96 WAC, R1/92/7, G91, 27 November 1956.

97 *Broadcasting Policy*, Cmd.6852, HMSO, July 1946, para. 59.

98 TNA: PRO, FO953/1640, PB1011/16 'The BBC and its External Services', pamphlet by the BBC, 1956.

99 TNA: PRO, FO953/1643, PB1011/54, 'BBC External Services', Grey to Kirkpatrick, 2 October 1956.

100 TNA: PRO, CAB128/30 Part 2, CM(56)82nd, 'Suez Canal', 8 November 1956.

101 TNA: PRO, DEFE 5/78, COS(57)220, 'Part II of General Sir Charles Keightley's Despatch on Operations in the Eastern Mediterranean, November – December, 1956', 11 October 1957.

102 Ibid.

103 WAC, E1/631, AHEastS to HEastS, 12 January 1949.

104 Churchill Archive, Cambridge (CAC), UK. Sir Ian Jacob Papers. JACB 2/4, Poston to Jacob, 22 April 1957.

105 WAC, R1/92/7, G91, 27 November 1956.

106 TNA: PRO, FO1110/967, Memorandum by Oakeshott, 18 December 1956.

107 WAC, R1/92/7, G91, 27 November 1956.

108 WAC, R2/9/2, Board of Management meeting, 15 October 1956.

109 Ibid., 22 October 1956.

110 TNA: PRO, CAB130/120, GEN 554/7, 'Comments on Draft Report by the Committee', Memorandum by the Secretary of State for the Colonies, 21 November 1956.

111 CAC, Jacob Papers, JACB2/4, Sir Ian Jacob to Ralph Poston, 26 April 1957.

112 TNA: PRO, FO953/1640, PB1011/13, 'The External Services of the BBC', 31 May 1956.

113 WAC, R1/85/1, G5, 'Censorship in War', note by the Director-General, 20 December 1949.

114 For the orchestration of these plans see, Kyle, *Suez*, pp. 238–40.

115 WAC, R1/92/6, G84, 'Report by Director of Administration', November 1956; R2/9/2, Board of Management meeting, 'Passes for Entry to Greek and Arabic Sections', 17 September 1956.

116 WAC, R1/24, Board of Governors meeting 'External Services', 20 December 1956.
117 Lowell Schwartz, *Political Warfare against the Kremlin: US and British Propaganda Policy at the beginning of the Cold War*, (Basingstoke: Palgrave Macmillan, 2009), p. 203.
118 Briggs, *Competition*, p. 687. Professor Peter Wiles made the accusation and was, at the time a Fellow at New College, Oxford. Other critics included: Hugh Seton-Watson who was Professor of Russian history at the University of London; Professor Leonard Schapiro who was, in 1957, a lecturer at the London School of Economics and Political Science.
119 Schwartz, *Political Warfare*, pp. 200–7; David Wedgwood Benn, 'How the FO tried to stifle the BBC', *New Statesman*, 6 December 1999.
120 Schwartz, *Political Warfare*, p. 205.
121 *Overseas Information Services*, Cmd.225 (London: HMSO, 1957), para. 17.

Reflections

1 *Time and Tide*, 28 October 1950. Quoted in Briggs, *Competition*, p. 116.
2 *Broadcasting Policy*, Cmd.6852 (London: HMSO, July 1946), para. 60.
3 WAC, R20/53, 'Report of the Independent Committee of Enquiry into the Overseas Information Services', 27 July 1953.
4 TNA: PRO, FO953/1640, PB1011/13. 'The External Services of the BBC', Sir Ian Jacob, 31 May 1956.

Select Bibliography

Adamthwaite, Anthony, '"Nation Shall Speak Unto nation": The BBC's response to peace and defence issues 1948-58'. *Contemporary Record*, 7(3), 1993, pp. 557–77.

Aguilar, Manuela, *Cultural Diplomacy and Foreign Policy: German-American Relations, 1955-1968* (New York: Peter Lang, 1996).

Aldrich, Richard (ed.), *British Intelligence, Strategy and the Cold War, 1945-51* (London: Routledge, 1992).

—*The Hidden Hand: Britain, America and Cold War Secret Intelligence* (London: John Murray, 2001).

—'Putting Culture into the Cold War: The Cultural Relations Department (CRD) and British Covert Information Warfare'. *Intelligence and National Security*, 18(2), 2003, pp. 109–33.

Aldrich, Richard and Michael Hopkins (eds), *Intelligence, Defence and Diplomacy: British Policy in the Post-War World* (London: Frank Cass, 1994).

Applebaum, Anne, *Iron Curtain: The Crushing of Eastern Europe 1944-56* (London: Allen Lane, 2012).

Barman, Tom, *Diplomatic Correspondent* (London: Hamish Hamilton, 1968).

Békés, Csaba, Malcolm Byrne, and János Rainer (eds), *The Hungarian Revolution: A History in Documents* (Budapest: Central European University Press, 2002).

Black, John, *Organising the Propaganda Instrument: The British Experience* (The Hague: Martinus Nijhoff, 1975).

Briggs, Asa, *Governing the BBC* (London: BBC, 1979).

—*The BBC: The First Fifty Years* (Oxford: Oxford University Press, 1985).

—*The History of Broadcasting in the United Kingdom, Volume II: The Golden Age of Wireless* (Oxford: Oxford University Press, 1995).

—*The History of Broadcasting in the United Kingdom, Volume III: The War of Words* (Oxford: Oxford University Press, 1995).

—*The History of Broadcasting in the United Kingdom, Volume IV: Sound and Vision* (Oxford: Oxford University Press, 1995).

—*The History of Broadcasting in the United Kingdom, Volume V: Competition* (Oxford: Oxford University Press, 1995).

Browne, Donald, *International Radio Broadcasting: The Limits of the Limitless Medium* (New York: Praeger, 1982).

Bullock, Alan, *Ernest Bevin: Foreign Secretary, 1945-1951* (London: Heinemann, 1983), pp. 525–6.

Cairncross, Alec, *Years of Recovery: British Economic Policy 1945-51* (London: Methuen, 1985).

Carlton, David, *Britain and the Suez Crisis* (Oxford: Basil Blackwell, 1989).

Cartledge, Brian, *The Will to Survive: A History of Hungary* (Tiverton: Timewell Press, 2006).

Caute, David, *The Dancer Defects: The Struggle for Cultural Supremacy During the Cold War* (Oxford: Oxford University Press, 2003).

Clark, J. B., 'The BBC's External Services'. *International Affairs*, 35(2), 1959, pp. 170–80.

Colville, John, *The Fringes of Power, Downing Street Diaries 1939-1955, Volume One: September 1939-September 1941* (Sevenoaks: Sceptre, 1986).

Coplestone, Frederick, *A History of Philosophy Vol. 1: Greece and Rome* (London: Burns & Oates, 1961).

Cull, Nicholas, 'Book Review of *War of the Black Heavens: The Battles of Western Broadcasting in the Cold War* by Michael Nelson'. *Historical Journal of Film Radio and Television*, 20(1), 2000, p. 136.

—*The Cold War and the United States Information Agency: American Propaganda and Public Diplomacy, 1945-1989* (Cambridge: Cambridge University Press, 2008).

—*Public Diplomacy: Lessons from the Past*, CPD Perspectives on Public Diplomacy (Los Angeles, CA: Figueroa Press, 2009).

—'"Public Diplomacy" Before Gullion: The Evolution of a Phrase', *USC Center on Public Diplomacy*, undated. Available at: http://uscpublicdiplomacy.org/pdfs/gullion.pdf. Accessed 1 October 2013.

Cull, Nicholas, David Culbert, and David Welch, *Propaganda and Mass Persuasion: A Historical Encyclopaedia, 1500-present* (Oxford: ABC-Clio, 2003).

Defty, Andrew, '"Close and Continuous Liaison": British Anti-Communist Propaganda and Cooperation with the United States, 1950-51'. *Intelligence and National Security*, 17(4), 2002, pp. 100–30.

—'Co-ordinating Cold War Propaganda: British and American liaison in anti-communist propaganda, 1950–1951'. *Occasional working paper in contemporary history & politics, 5*, University of Salford, European Studies Research Institute, 2002.

—*Britain, America and Anti-Communist Propaganda, 1945-53: The Information Research Department* (London: Routledge, 2004).

Deutscher, Issac, *Stalin: A Political Biography* (London: Oxford University Press, 1949).

Dodds-Parker, Douglas, *Political Eunuch* (Ascot: Springwood, 1986).

Donaldson, Frances, *The British Council: The First Fifty Years* (London: Cape, 1984).

Esslin, Martin, 'The Listener in Occupied Europe and Behind the Iron Curtain', *London Calling*, 10 December 1953.

Fergusson, Bernard, *The Trumpet in the Hall, 1930-1958* (London: Collins, 1970).

Fletcher, Richard, 'British Propaganda since World War Two – A Case Study'. *Media, Culture and Society*, 4(2), 1982, pp. 97–109.

Foreign and Commonwealth Office, *IRD: Origins and Establishment of the Foreign Office Information Research Department 1946-48* (London: Foreign and Commonwealth Office Library and Records Department, 1995).

Fraser, Lindley, *Propaganda* (London: Oxford University Press, 1957).

Gaddis, John Lewis, *The Cold War* (London: Allen Lane, 2005).

Garnett, David, *The Secret History of PWE: The Political Warfare Executive 1939-1945* (London: St Ermin's Press, 2002).

Garton Ash, Timothy, *The Polish Revolution: Solidarity* (London: Penguin, 1999).

Gati, Charles, *Failed Illusions: Moscow, Washington, Budapest, and the 1956 Hungarian Revolt* (Washington: Woodrow Wilson Center Press, 2006).

Gienow-Hecht, Jessica and Mark Donfried, *Searching for a Cultural Diplomacy* (Oxford: Berghahn, 2010).

Gillespie, Marie and Alban Webb (eds), *Diasporas and Diplomacy: Cosmopolitan Contact Zones at the BBC World Service, 1932-2012* (New York: Routledge, 2012).

Granville, Johanna, '"Caught with jam on our Fingers": Radio Free Europe and the Hungarian revolution of 1956'. *Diplomatic History*, 29(5), 2005, pp. 811–39.

Greene, Hugh Carleton, *The Third Floor: A View of Broadcasting in the Sixties* (London: Bodley Head, 1969).

Greenwood, Sean, *Britain and the Cold War, 1945-1991* (London: Macmillan, 1999).

Grisewood, Harman, *One Thing at a Time* (London: Hutchinson, 1968).

Haigh, Anthony, *Cultural Diplomacy in Europe* (Strasbourg: Council of Europe, 1974).

Hale, Julian, *Radio Power: Propaganda and International Broadcasting* (London: Paul Elek, 1975).

Haley, William, 'The Next Five Years in Broadcasting', *BBC Yearbook 1948* (London: BBC, 1949), p. 7.

Hansard, 'Fifth Series'. *House of Commons Debates*, vol.425, col.1087, 16 July 1946.

Haraszti-Taylor, Eva, *The Hungarian Revolution of 1956: A Collection of Documents from the British Foreign Office* (Nottingham: Astra, 1995).

Heil, Alan, *Voice of America: A History* (New York: Colombia University Press, 2003).

Hennessy, Peter, *The Prime Minister: The Office and its Holders since 1945* (London: Allen Lane, 2000).

—*The Secret State: Whitehall and the Cold War* (London: Allen Lane, 2002).

—*Having it so Good: Britain in the Fifties* (London: Allen Lane, 2006).

Hill, Charles, *Both Sides of the Hill: The Memoirs of Charles Hill* (London: Heinemann, 1964).

Hixson, Walter, *Parting the Curtain: Propaganda, Culture and the Cold War 1945-61* (Basingstoke: Macmillan, 1997).

Hobsbawm, Eric, 'Could it have been different?'. *London Review of Books*, 28(22), 16 November 2006.

Jacob, Major-General Sir Ian, 'The European Service Holds The Mirror Up To British Opinion', by the Controller of the European Service, *BBC Yearbook 1947* (London: BBC, 1947), p. 16.

Jenks, John, *British Propaganda and News Media in the Cold War* (Edinburgh: Edinburgh University Press, 2006).

Johnson, A. Ross, 'Setting the Record Straight: Role of Radio Free Europe in the Hungarian Revolution of 1956' (Budapest: Open Society Archive, Central European University, 2006).

—*Radio Free Europe and Radio Liberty: The CIA Years and Beyond* (Washington: Woodrow Wilson Center Press; Stanford: Stanford University Press, 2010).

Johnson, A. Ross and R. Eugene Parta (eds), *Cold War Broadcasting: Impact on the Soviet Union and Eastern Europe, A Collection of Studies and Documents* (Budapest, New York: Central European University Press, 2010).

Johnson, Peter, *Reuter Reporter among the Communists, 1958-59* (London: Tagman Press, 2000).

—'Working as the BBC's German Service representative and news correspondent in West Berlin, 1965–1970', in Charmain Brinson and Richard Dove (eds), '*Stimme der Wahrheit*': *German-language broadcasting by the BBC*, Yearbook of the Research Centre for German and Austrian Exile Studies, 5 (Amsterdam: Rodopi, 2003), pp. 207–19.

Judt, Tony, *Postwar: A History of Europe since 1945* (London: Heinemann, 2005).

Kaufman, Victor, *Confronting Communism: US and British Policies Towards China* (Columbia: University of Missouri Press, 2001).

Khrushchev, Nikita, *Memoirs of Nikita Khrushchev, Volume 2: Reformer, 1945-1964*, edited by Sergei Khrushchev, translated by George Shriver (University Park: Pennsylvania State University, 2006).

Kirkpatrick, Ivone, *The Inner Circle: Memoirs of Ivone Kirkpatrick* (London: Macmillan, 1959).

Krugler, David, *The Voice of America: And the Domestic Propaganda Battles, 1945-53* (Columbia: University of Missouri Press, 2000).

Kyle, Keith, *Suez: Britain's End of Empire in the Middle East* (London: I.B. Taurus, 2003).

Lane, Ann, 'The past as matrix: Sir Ivone Kirkpatrick, Permanent Under-Secretary for Foreign Affairs'. *Contemporary British History*, 13, 1999, pp. 199–220.

—, 'Kirkpatrick, Sir Ivone Augustine (1897-1964)', in H. Matthew and Brian Harrison (eds), *Oxford Dictionary of National Biography* (Oxford: Oxford University Press, 2004), pp. 807–9.

Lashmar, Paul and James Oliver, *Britain's Secret Propaganda War* (Stroud: Sutton, 1998).

Latey, Maurice, 'Broadcasting to the USSR and Eastern Europe', *BBC Lunchtime Lectures 3rd Series* (London: BBC, 1964).

Lean, Edward Tangye, *Voices in the Darkness: The Story of the European Radio War* (London: Secker & Warburg, 1943).

Lee, John, 'British Cultural Diplomacy and the Cold War: 1946-61'. *Diplomacy and Statecraft*, 9(1), 1998, pp. 112–34.

Leslie, R. F. (ed.), *The History of Poland since 1863* (Cambridge: Cambridge University Press, 1980).

Litvan, Gyorgy (ed.), *The Hungarian Revolution of 1956: Reform, Revolt and Repression, 1953-63* (London: Longman, 1996).

Lord Carter of Coles, *Public Diplomacy Review*, December 2005. Available at: http://www.britishcouncil.org/home-carter-report. Accessed 1 October 2013.

Lucas, Scott, *Divided We Stand: Britain, the US and the Suez Crisis* (London: Sceptre, 1996).

Lucas, Scott and C. J. Morris, 'A Very British Crusade: The Information Research Department and the beginning of the Cold War', in Richard Aldrich (ed.), *British Intelligence, Strategy and the Cold War, 1945-51* (London: Routledge, 1992), pp. 85–110.

Maclean, Fitzroy, *Eastern Approaches* (London: Jonathan Cape, 1949).

Major, Patrick and Rana Mitter (eds), *Across the Blocs: Cold War Cultural and Social History* (London: Frank Cass, 2004).

Mansell, Gerard, 'Why External Broadcasting?: A Lecture', *BBC Lunchtime Lectures, 10th Series* (London: BBC, 1975).

—*Let Truth be Told: 50 Years of BBC External Broadcasting* (London: Weidenfeld & Nicholson, 1982).

Marett, Robert, *Through the Back Door: An Inside View of Britain's Overseas Information Services* (London: Pergamon Press, 1968).

Mayhew, Christopher and Lyn Smith (ed.), *A War of Words: A Cold War Witness* (London: I.B. Taurus, 1998).

Melissen, Jan (ed.), *The New Public Diplomacy: Soft Power in International Relations* (Basingstoke: Palgrave Macmillan, 2005).

—'Public Diplomacy', in Andrew Cooper, Jorge Heine and Ramesh Thakur (eds), *The Oxford Handbook of Modern Diplomacy* (Oxford: Oxford University Press, 2013).

Milne, Alasdair, *DG: The Memoirs of a British Broadcaster* (London: Hodder & Stoughton, 1988).

Murphy, Philip, *Alan Lennox-Boyd: A Biography* (London: I.B. Taurus, 1999).

Mytton, Graham, *Global Audiences: Research for Worldwide Broadcasting* (London: John Libby, 1993).

Nelson, Michael, *War of the Black Heavens: The Battles of Western Broadcasting in the Cold War* (London: Brassey's, 1997).

Nutting, Anthony, *No End of a Lesson: The Story of Suez* (London: Constable, 1967).

Nye, Joseph, *Soft Power: The Means to Success in World Politics* (New York: Public Affairs, 2004).

Pamment, James, *New Public Diplomacy in the 21st Century: A Comparative Study of Policy and Practice* (Abingdon: Routledge, 2013).

Partner, Peter, *Arab Voices: The BBC Arabic Service, 1938-1988* (London: BBC, 1988).

Pawley, Edward, *BBC Engineering, 1922-1972* (London: BBC, 1972).

Philby, Kim, *My Silent War: The Autobiography of a Spy* (London: Arrow, 2003).

Pirsein, Robert, *The Voice of America: An History of the International Broadcasting Activities of the United States Government, 1940-1962* (New York: Arno Press, 1979).

Puddington, Arch, *Broadcasting Freedom: The Cold War Triumph of Radio Free Europe and Radio Liberty* (Lexington: University Press of Kentucky, 2000).

Rawnsley, Gary, 'Media Diplomacy: Monitored Broadcasts and Foreign Policy'. *Discussion Papers in Diplomacy*, University of Leicester, June 1995.

—'Cold War Radio in Crisis: The BBC Overseas Services, the Suez Crisis and the Hungarian Uprising'. *Historical Journal of Film, Radio and Television*, 16(2), June 1996, pp. 197–219.

—'Overt and Covert: The Voice of Britain and Black Radio Broadcasting in the Suez Crisis, 1956'. *Intelligence and National Security*, 11, 1996, pp. 497–522.

—*Radio Diplomacy and Propaganda: The BBC and VOA in International Politics, 1956-64* (Basingstoke: Macmillan, 1996).

—'The BBC External Services and the Hungarian uprising, 1956', in Gary Rawnsley (ed.), *Cold War Propaganda in the 1950s* (Basingstoke: Macmillan, 1999), pp. 165–81.

—(ed.), *Cold-War Propaganda in the 1950s* (Basingstoke: Macmillan, 1999).

Renier, Olive and Vladimir Rubinstein, *Assigned to Listen: The Evesham Experience, 1939-43* (London: BBC, 1986).

Rév, István, 'Just Noise?', Paper presented at the Conference on Cold War Broadcasting Impact, Stanford University, 15 October 2004.

Reynolds, David, *Britannia Overruled: British Policy and World Power in the Twentieth Century* (London: Longman, 2000).

Richardson, General Sir Charles, *From Churchill's Secret Circle to the BBC: The Biography of Lieutenant General Sir Ian Jacob GBE CB DL* (Oxford: Brassey's, 1991).

Richmond, Yale, *Cultural Exchange and the Cold War: Raising the Iron Curtain* (University Park: Pennsylvania State University Press, 2003).

Rigby, T. H. (ed.), *The Stalin Dictatorship: Khrushchev's 'Secret Speech' and Other Documents* (Victoria: Sydney University Press, 1968).

Risso, Linda (ed.), 'Radio Wars: Broadcasting During the Cold War'. Special issue of *Cold War History*, 13(2), 2013, pp. 145–287.

Romijn, Peter, Giles Scott-Smith, and Joes Segal (eds), *Divided Dreamworlds?: The Cultural Cold War in East and West* (Amsterdam: Amsterdam University Press, 2012).

Schwartz, Lowell, *Political Warfare Against the Kremlin: US and British Propaganda at the Beginning of the Cold War* (Basingstoke: Palgrave Macmillan, 2009).

Scott-Smith, Giles and Hans Krabbendam (eds), *The Cultural Cold War in Western Europe 1945-60* (London: Frank Cass, 2003).

Seaton, Jean, *Carnage and the Media: The Making and Breaking of News about Violence* (London: Allen Lane, 2005).

Seaton, Jean and James Curran, *Power Without Responsibility: The Press, Broadcasting and New Media in Britain* (London: Routledge, 2003).

Selverstone, Mark, *Constructing the Monolith: The United States, Great Britain, and International Communism, 1945-1950* (London: Harvard University Press, 2009).

Shaw, Tony, 'Government Manipulation of the Press during the 1956 Suez Crisis'. *Contemporary Record*, 8, 1994, pp. 274–88.

—'Eden and the BBC during the Suez Crisis: A Myth Re-examined'. *Twentieth Century British History*, 6(3), 1995, pp. 320–43.

—*Eden, Suez and the Mass Media: Propaganda and Persuasion during the Suez Crisis* (London: I.B. Taurus, 1996).

—'Cadogan's Last Fling: Sir Alexander Cadogan, Chairman of the Board of Governors of the BBC'. *Contemporary British History*, 13(2), 1999, pp. 126–45.

—'The Information Research Department of the British Foreign Office and the Korean War, 1950–53'. *Journal of Contemporary History*, 34(2), 1999, pp. 263–81.

Short, K. R. M., *Western Broadcasting over the Iron Curtain* (London: Croom Helm, 1986).

Smith, James, *British Writers and MI5 Surveillance* (Cambridge: Cambridge University Press, 2013).

Smith, Lyn, 'Covert British Propaganda: The Information Research Department, 1947-77'. *Millennium*, 9(1), 1980, pp. 67–83.

Starck, Kathleen (ed.), *Between Fear and Freedom: Cultural Representations of the Cold War* (Newcastle upon Tyne: Cambridge Scholars Publishing, 2010).

Steinmetz, Willibald (ed.), *Political Languages in the Age of Extremes* (Oxford: Oxford University Press, 2011).

Stoner Saunders, Frances, *Who Paid the Piper?: The CIA and the Cultural Cold War* (London: Granta Books, 1999).

Tallents, Stephen, *The Projection of England* (London: Faber & Faber, 1932).

Taylor, Philip, 'The Projection of Britain Abroad, 1945-51', in Michael Dockrill and John Young (eds), *British Foreign Policy, 1945-1956* (Basingstoke: Macmillan, 1989), pp. 9–30.

—*Global Communications, International Affairs and the Media since 1945* (London: Routledge, 1997).

—*British Propaganda in the Twentieth Century: Selling Democracy* (Edinburgh: Edinburgh University Press, 1999).

Tokaev, Grigori, *Comrade X*, translated by Alec Brown (London: Harvill Press, 1956).

Tracey, Michael, *A Variety of Lives: A Biography of Hugh Greene* (London: Bodley Head, 1983).

Tusa, John, *Conversations with the World* (London: BBC Books, 1990).

—*A World in Your Ear: Reflections on Changes* (London: Broadside Books, 1992).

Unwin, Peter, *1956: Power Defied* (Norwich: Michael Russell, 2006).

Urban, George, *The Nineteen Days: A Broadcaster's Account of the Hungarian Revolution* (London: Heinemann, 1957).

Vaughan, James, 'Propaganda by Proxy? Britain, America, and Arab Radio Broadcasting, 1953-1957'. *Historical Journal of Film, Radio and Television*, 22(2), 2002, pp. 157–72.

—'"Cloak Without Dagger": How the Information Research Department Fought Britain's Cold War in the Middle East, 1948-1956'. *Cold War History*, 4(3), 2004, pp. 56–84.

—'"A Certain Idea of Britain": British Cultural Diplomacy in the Middle East, 1945-57'. *Contemporary British History*, 19(2), 2005, pp. 151–68.

—*The Failure of American and British Propaganda in the Arab Middle East, 1945-1957: Unconquerable Minds* (Basingstoke: Palgrave Macmillan, 2005).

Veress, Laura-Louise and Dalma Takacs (ed.), *Clear the Line: Hungary's Struggle to Leave the Axis during the Second World War* (Cleveland, OH: Prospero Publications, 1995).

Walker, Andrew, *A Skyful of Freedom: 60 years of the BBC World Service* (London: Broadside Books, 1992).

Wasburn, P. C., *Broadcasting Propaganda: International Radio Broadcasting and the Construction of Political Reality* (New York: Praeger, 1992).

Webb, Alban, 'Auntie Goes to War Again: The BBC External Services, the Foreign Office and the Early Cold War'. *Media History*, 12(2), 2006, pp. 117–32.

—'A Leap of Imagination: BBC Audience Research over the Iron Curtain'. *Participations*, 8(1), 2011, pp. 154–72.

—'The BBC Polish Section and the reporting of Solidarity, 1980-83', in Webb and Gillespie (eds), *Diasporas and Diplomacy: Cosmopolitan Contact Zones at the BBC World Service (1932-2012)* (London: Routledge, 2012), pp. 86–101.

—'Cold War radio and the Hungarian Uprising, 1956'. *Cold War History*, 13(2), pp. 221–38.

Webb, Alban and Catherine Haddon, '"An Internal Housekeeping Matter": Whitehall and the BBC Monitoring Service'. *The Political Quarterly*, 78(2), 2007, pp. 214–23.

Wedgwood Benn, David, *Persuasion and Soviet Politics* (Oxford: Blackwell, 1989).

Welch, David and Jo Fox (eds), *Justifying War: Propaganda, Politics and the Modern Age* (Basingstoke: Palgrave Macmillan, 2012).

Whitfield, Stephen, *The Culture of the Cold War* (Baltimore: John Hopkins University Press, 1996).

Wilford, Hugh, 'The Information Research Department: Britain's Secret Cold War Weapon Revealed'. *Review of International Studies*, 24(3), 1998, pp. 353–69.

Wythenshawe, Lord Simon of, *The BBC from Within* (London: Victor Gollanz, 1953).

Young, John, *Cold War Europe, 1945-91: A Political History* (London: Arnold, 1996).

Index

Adamthwaite, Anthony 4
Al Shaab 168
Aldrich, Richard 85
Alexander, Albert Victor (A.V.) 105
Allen, George 76
The American Forces Network 149
American wartime monitoring 84–6
in California 86
Foreign Broadcasts Information Service (FBIS) 85–6
Andropov, Yuri 143–4
Anglo-Egyptian Treaty 161
Annual Report and Accounts
in 1953 91
in 1956-57 175
Applebaum, Ann 41
ASIDE telegrams 55–6, 141, 166, 187, 203n. 13
Attlee, Clement 15, 28, 37, 96, 106, 108, 110
Austrian State Treaty 121, 220n. 9

Baghdad Pact's communication strategy, 1955 162
Barnes, George 44, 98–9
BBC Monitoring Service 81–8
the American FBIS' Daily Reports 154
BBCM in Caversham role 139, 155
in Caversham 139
Editorial Unit 83
Information Bureau 82–3
principles of professional monitoring 82–3
Reception Unit 82
Summary of World Broadcasts 154
US and UK co-operation in 84–8
volume of material to be monitored 84
BBC Transcription Service 92
Benes, Dr Edouard 36
Benn, William (Viscount) *see* Stansgate, Lord
Benton, Frank 84
Beveridge Report 14
Bevin, Ernest 19, 35, 38–9, 41, 76, 78, 95, 100, 103, 109–10
Black, John 5
Borsanyi, Gyula (Colonel Bell) 151
Both Sides of the Hill 5
Bottomley, Sir Norman 174–5
Bracken, Brendan 15
Briggs, Lord Asa 4–5, 20, 29, 82, 166, 173
British Broadcasting Corporation (BBC)
accommodating government attitudes, in programming 170
adult radio listeners in Europe 53
allocation of wavelengths and broadcast infrastructure 27
Annual Report and Accounts, 1956-57 175
approach to Iron Curtain audiences 71 (*see also* Central and Eastern Europe broadcast)
Arabic and Greek services, course hosted on radio communications 182
Aside and guidance telegrams, for Bush House 166
Attlee's announcement, no ininquiry into future of 194n. 25
audience in Czechoslovakia 36
audience size in Hungary, understanding 147–8
Bracken's view 15
British interpretation of events 1
broadcast to world, Hungarian nation's voice 144
Broadcasting Policy White Paper, 1946 165
broadcasting to East (*see* Middle and Far East broadcast)
challenging broadcasting crisis 139
changing Hungarian leadership within 142

character, reach and editorial practice of 2
Charter, Licence and Agreement 17–18
Cold War audiences, editorial effort for communicating 187–8
Cold War broadcasting 6–8
Committee on Overseas Broadcasting (GEN 542) 159
confrontation with government 157–8
content of overseas broadcasts, and government control 170–1
coverage of Hungarian uprising 155–6
Dodds-Parker draft letter for 173–4, 176
Drogheda Report recommendations 159–60
Eastern Services talks series 163
editorial affinity with listeners, in the Soviet sphere 187
editorial independence of 19–20, 181
enforcing governmental editorial control on 157
engaged in the activities with Advisory Committee 182
European Service 15, 17
events editorial interpretation, challenge for 142–3
expansion of 1–2
expenditure on overseas publicity 158
external and internal pressures 185
External Services (*see* External Services of BBC)
finance as determinant, of overseas broadcasting 186
flow of information, by BBCM and CRU 140–1
FO liaison officer in Bush House 157, 172–3, 175–6
FO telegrams, for reporting events 141, 166
front-line details use 142
GEN 542's Interim Report on 166
George Mikes, report from Budapest 134
government assistance in funding 21–4
government control over overseas broadcasting 20–5
Grant-in-Aid income, and rising expenditure gap 186
Hungarian section, announces Soviet control over Budapest Radio 146–7
Hungarian section, devoted to 'Writers' Revolt 135
information gathering 55
initial refusal to Menzies's, to broadcast 168–9
Jacob's analysis, of External Services 181
Kirkpatrick's analysis and suggestions, over government control of 171–2
Latey's commentary broadcast 147
letters received after the Europe liberation 186
licence fee revenue 21–2
Lloyd's view, lack of trust between government circles and 159–60
Lockhart's view, on funding and control over 185–6
Macdonald's analysis, on cultural differences between RFE 153
to maintain anti-Nasser sentiment, role of 168
message broadcast, received from Radio Budapest 145
monitored events closely, Hungarian section 136, 138–40
Monitoring Service 4
as the monopoly broadcaster 1
Morrison's committee 17
needs of censorship in war, Haley's view 181
obstacles to government control 165–6
overseas activities 1–2
overseas broadcasting, objectives of 165
overseas services, funded through parliamentary grantin-aid 194n. 9
political warfare and propaganda activities 13

post-war overseas broadcasting strategy 17–19
post-war relationship with British government 7–9
post-war reorganization of 17–18
'The Principles and Purpose of the BBC's External Services' 18
profile of listenership 16
publicity requirements, government demands 181
quoting virtually Budapest Radio 141–2
recommendations for services elimination, categories 232n. 80
relationship with government 4–9, 18–25, 182–3
report, about life in Hungary 154
and Report of the Drogheda Committee 113–16
role in managing expectations, of possibility of western intervention in Hungary 155
role played, in Hungarian uprising 154–5
Russian Service case, tension with government 183–4
services in the Cold War 75
services to foreign countries 15–17 (*see also* External Services of BBC)
source material for broadcast 5–6
against Soviet propaganda 37–8
Spanish and Portuguese Services 1
strategic realignment of 46–7
Suez crisis exposed, corporate obligations resting on 181
Wilson's role in Bush House 176–7
'Working Group' formation, on Soviet Union broadcasting 183
World Service 2–3, 5–6
Written Archive Centre 4
British government's overseas information services 5
The British Joint Intelligence Committee (JIC) 161
British public diplomacy 4
British Thought and the British Way of Life 162
Broadcast revolution, and Hungarian uprising
assistance by FO and British Legation 141
broadcasting crisis, faced by Bush House 139–40
changing nature of revolution, and events 143–4
the CRU role in 140
FO telegrams 142
radio, as cartographer of 138
Radio Budapest, as news source for Bush House 140–2
broadcasting
history of overseas 5
as an instrument of peace 1
Broadcasting Policy, White Paper 1946 2, 18, 23, 44, 97, 165, 177, 185
Brusak, Karl 136
Brussels Treaty 80, 95, 97
Budapest Radio 133, 155
from 1949 known as Kossuth Radio, after Lajos Kossuth 222n. 3
ceasefire and new government announcement by 143
news source, problem being main 141–2
as revolution cartographer 138
in Soviet hands 146
as voice of new Hungary 144–5
Bulganin, Nikolai 121, 123–4, 130, 159
Bush House
broadcasting crisis, faced 139–40
European service news room in 139
first occupied by the BBC European Services, in January 1941 193n. 2
offered listeners behind the Iron Curtain, interpretation of developments 138
relations with FO, on broadcasts to Soviet Satellites 135
relationship with Whitehall, discord over overseas services funding 160
telegrams reporting on events, copied to 141

White Paper on *Broadcasting Policy,* 1946 177–8
Butler, Lord Richard (R.A) 109–10, 170, 173–4, 183

Cabinet Committee (GEN 81) 17, 185
Cabinet's Colonial Information Policy Committee (CIPC) 62
Cadogan, Sir Alexander 105, 173, 183
Cairo Radio 161, 163–4
Caute, David 3
Cecil, Robert (5th Marquess of Salisbury) *see* Salisbury, Lord
Central and Eastern Europe broadcast 66, 100
audience profile 73–4
Communism in Practice 72
cultural rapprochement 120–6
difference between Yugoslavia and the Soviet satellites 68
editorial arrangements 74
format of transmissions 74
jamming issue 73
peculiarity of programmes 69
position of Yugoslavia and 68
positive publicity of Western democracies 69
in Serbo-Croat and Slovene 68
style of broadcasting 71–2
Tito/Cominform split 69
see also External Services of BBC; Russian broadcast
Churchill, Winston 14, 28, 110, 113, 218n. 71
Clark, John Beresford (J. B.) 31, 76, 87, 101, 113, 115–16, 124–6, 128, 131–2, 160, 162, 175–7
Cold War, battle of airwaves 150, 154
Cold War broadcasting, and international radio in Hungary 149, 152
Colombo Plan for Cooperative Economic Development 94
Colonial broadcasting 93–4
Colonial Information Policy Committee (CIPC) 62, 73, 83, 103–5, 107, 115
Colville, John 28
Committee on Anti-Communist Propaganda 105
Committee on Colonial Information Policy 43
Committee on Overseas Broadcasting (GEN 542) 154, 164, 166
Committee on Overseas Broadcasting (GEN 554) 170
Commonwealth Broadcaster's Conference, in Australia 172
Commonwealth Sigint Organisation (CSO) 211n. 73
'Communist Conflict in Hungary' 136
Condon, Richard 152
Co-operative European programming 97
Cripps, Stafford 102–3, 105, 108
Crookshank, Harry 20
Crowsley Park, reception centre for Monitoring 210n. 57
Cull, Nicholas 3
Cviic, Christopher 70
Czechoslovak coup 36

Daily Digest of World Broadcasts 83
Daily Monitoring Report 83–4
Davies, Ernest 112
Defence of the Peace Acts 54
Defty, Andrew 6
Denning, Lord Justice 71
Deutscher, Isaac 70
Director of Eastern Services (DES) 32
Displaced Person Camps, in Germany 58
Dodds-Parker, Douglas 159, 165, 170, 173, 182
Dodds-Parker's Committee on Overseas Broadcasting 165
Donfried, Mark 4
Drogheda Committee 110–16, 119–20, 158, 164, 186
Drogheda Committee Report 113–15, 159
Dulles, Allen 143, 151
Dulles, John Foster 169

East *vs.* West, in terms of access to information 54
Eastern Europe, problem of 35
Ede, James Chuter 105
Eden, Anthony 115, 164, 168–70, 173, 178, 180, 182
Egypt
acts of war, and issued ultimatums 174

Britain, Israel and France, engineering war against 158
broadcasting operation, as threat to British interests 161
events in, military coup in 1952 160–1
failure to comply, Anglo-French bombing of 174–5
fear of Egyptian radio's influence 163
links with Soviet Union 169–70
London Conference of Maritime Nations, to deal canal dispute 168
propaganda campaign, against the Western powers 161–5
'Psy-War' against 178, 181–2
Suez crisis, Egyptian perspective on 168–9
threat to Britain's key strategic interest 161
United Kingdom's policy, towards 157
Eisenhower, Dwight D. 29, 150–1
English-language General Overseas Service 3, 125
Esslin, Martin 94, 147
European Broadcasting Union (EBU) 100
European Recovery Programme (Marshall Plan) 71
External Services of BBC 4, 6, 27
aims and objectives of 34, 91–2
anti-communist stance 48–9
Arabic Service 33, 162, 164
audiences, lack of information 187
blueprint for reorganization, in Grey April paper 165
Britain's overseas publicity 38–9, 41
British influence overseas, constitutional significance 181
British Missions comments, reporting on 42
in Central and Eastern Europe 66–74
CIPC 'Three Year Plan' 105
Colonial Service 93–4
constitutional arrangements 34
cost of overseas information services 102–3
cost-benefit analysis, and Drogheda Committee setup 186
daily programmes to Eastern Europe 41
Drogheda Report recommendations, and overseas services abolition 159–60
Eastern Service 93
editorial principles for overseas broadcasting 45–6
engagement with audiences overseas, defining objective 186–7
extra-constitutional practices 32
Far Eastern Services 32, 93
in favor of British national interest 150
FO's liaison officer appointment for 172, 175–6
freedom of 33–4
full-scale programmes of refuting Soviet misrepresentations 44
government's demand, of cutting expenses 173
Grey April paper, review and conclusions 158–60
guidance by phone on day-to-day questions 32
imposing greater control, by government 174
Jacob and Kirkpatrick, role of 31
key role, to project British government's case to world 169
Kirkpatrick's suggestion for 171–2
Latin American Services 31–2, 93
Lennox-Boyd's view about 171
life, reporting on 42
limits of broadcast 188
Middle/Far East services, less expenditure 166
network of institutional and personal interfaces 32
news of events behind the Iron Curtain 42
North America Service 92
pattern of broadcasting overseas 41
platform, for promoting British interests in Middle East 180
Policy Review Committee for 165
post-war, designed for world at peace 186
post-war settlement of 167
programmes for India and Pakistan 93
quality and integrity of news 45

rebroadcasting of programmes 92–3
re-conceptualization of Britain's overseas information policy 40
reductions in budget 101–2, 104, 107–10, 157–8
in Russia 56–66
on Russia and communism 38–9
selection of broadcast items relevant to particular audiences 44
against Soviet propaganda 37–9
West Africa and the West Indies 93–4
Western Europe broadcasting, costing 166
Western Europe services, abolishment 157
Western Union broadcasting 95–100
Wilson's role in raising, conflicting government demands 176–7
see also Central and Eastern Europe broadcast; Middle and Far East broadcast; Russian broadcast; Western Union broadcasting

Foot, Robert 14
Foreign Broadcasts Information Service (FBIS) 85–6
Foreign Office telegrams 55–6, 141–2
foreign-language broadcasting 13
Foster, Peter 141
Fraser, Robert 103
Freedom Under the Law 71
Frost, Malcolm 85, 87
Fry, Leslie 141–2, 147
funding for BBC
activities of CIPC 103–5
cost of overseas information services 102–3
devaluation of sterling and 104
government assistance in 21–4
Grant-in-Aid funding 7, 21–3, 83, 110
Lockhart's view, on funding 185–6
Marshall Aid 102
operating estimate for 1950/51 and 1951/52 106–7
reductions in budget 101–2, 104, 107–10
relationship with Whitehall, overseas services 160
restrictions 106

Gaitskell, Hugh 108–10, 168, 170, 178
Gati, Charles 151
GEN 542's Interim Report 160, 166
General Overseas Service 92, 200n. 43
Gero, Erno 133–4, 137, 139, 142–3
Gienow-Hecht, Jessica 4
Goldberg, Anatol 58–9, 62, 94, 122, 125, 145, 183
Gomulka, Wladyslaw 138
Graham, David 62, 65–6, 70
Grant-in-Aid funding 7, 21–3, 83, 110
Greene, Hugh Carleton 60–4, 71–2, 182, 187
Grey, Paul 120, 127, 155, 158–60, 165–6, 175, 178, 183
Griffith, William 151–2
Grisewood, Harman 175
Gromov, Colonel-General 57
Gullion, Edmund 4

Hale, Julian 57
Haley, William 1–2, 14–17, 20–4, 29–32, 45, 83, 113, 178, 181
Hammerskjold, Dag 146
Hegedus, András 134, 142
Highlight (TV programme) 140
Hill, Charles (later Lord) 5, 170, 182–3, 185–6
Hillelson, Sigmar 81
History of Broadcasting in the United Kingdom 5
Hobsbawm, Eric 138
Hodson, Donald 72
House of Commons Select Committee Report, on Estimates 22
Hungarian Central Committee 139
Hungarian revolution, of 1956 137, 144
allegations against foreign broadcasters 149–50
BBC monitoring, of Petofi Club events 136
Budapest Radio, role in 144–5
Budapest Radio, Soviet captured 146
changing nature of revolution, and events 143–4
communism with Soviet face, criticism 135
dissolved ties with Warsaw Treaty 144–5

dominated broadcast output 139–40
events forcing the uprising 137–8
function performed by radio in 154–5
Gero's speech and impact 134
international broadcasting, role in Hungarians lives 149
interpretation to developments, BBC analysis 136–7
IRD suggestion, about Russian influence impact 135–6
Latey's commentary broadcast 147
Nagy's reform agenda 144
Petofi debate, about cultural and political freedoms 136
Poland, mass dissent on display in Poznan 137
political scene, priorities and direction of 134–5
radio, became cartographer of 138
Rakosi's, dismissal as PM 134, 137
recrudescence of Soviet authority, over Hungarian affairs 146–7
reforming demands, by Petofi Circle 133
rejection of Soviet control, over Hungarian affairs 134
removal of Moscow's influence, and advantages 138
replacement of Nagy with Hegedus 134
Soviet troops attack on Budapest 145–6
Hungarian Writers' Association 135
Hunyadi, Katlin 152

Index to the Daily Digest 83
Information Policy Department (IPD) 6
established in April, 1946 199n. 24
Information Research Department (IRD) 6
international broadcasting 4
International Trade Fair in Poznan, and riots 137
Irodalmi Ujsag 135
Iron Curtain 36, 40–2, 65, 68–9, 72–3, 78, 95
Isaacs, Gerald (2nd Marquess of Reading) *see* Reading, Lord
Italo-Abyssinian war, 1935 81

Jacob, Sir Ian 20, 39, 41–6, 48–9, 53, 58, 62–3, 70–1, 73–4, 76, 79–80, 87, 95–8, 103–5, 108–11, 113, 115, 119, 122, 126–30, 188
about Russian language service 40
agreed for, new line in publicity to Yugoslavia 69
on Americans establishing broadcasting stations 79
analysis, of BBC's External Services 181
on budget cuts 106–7
as Controller of European Services 27–8
criticisms about lack of consultation, for budget cuts 173–4
debate over broadcasts to Russia 128
development of policies and practices of government 29–30
editorial strategy for broadcasting over the Iron Curtain 129
'intelligence' needs of services 53–4
and jamming issue 65, 78
July 1946 directive for European Services 30–1
Latin-American Services 31–2
letter to, Peake's suggestion 202n. 12
medium-wave transmitter installation, in Middle East 164
meeting with Kirkpatrick, impact on overseas services 166–7
on money spent on information services 107–8
Nutting meeting with, about budget cut of External Services 157–9
overseas broadcasting management 29–30
paper for FO, 'The External Services of the BBC' 181
perception of role of BBC 30
Political Information Section 55–6
response to Nutting's proposals 173
sought advice of the Board of Governors, BBC unusual situation 170
supports funds increase, to build up a global service 166
Task of the Overseas Services of the BBC, paper by 67

thinking on Russian audience requirements 122, 126–9
visit to Commonwealth Broadcaster's Conference 172
jamming of BBC broadcasts 75–81, 122–5
in Central and Eastern Europe 73
estimate of 76–7
response to 76–8
in Russia 61–3, 76
US and UK co-operation 77–80
of Vatican Radio broadcasts 78
see also British Broadcasting Corporation (BBC)
Jenks, John 6
Jennings, Sir Ivor 163
Joint Intelligence Committee (JIC) 36
Jones, Arthur Creech 105

Kadar, Janos 143, 146
Keightley, General Charles 178
Kerensky, Alexander 59
Keynes, John Maynard 102
Khrushchev, Nikita 121, 123–4, 130–1, 133, 138, 143–4, 159, 162
Khrushchev's speech 131–2
Kirkpatrick, Ivone 22, 27–9, 31, 37–8, 40, 166–7, 171–2, 178
Kohler, Foy David 79
Kolarz, Walter 65, 70, 72, 94, 136, 140–1
Kossuth Radio *see* Budapest Radio
Kovacs, Bela 143
Kovacs, Istvan 146

Latey, Maurice 143, 147, 155, 176
The Law at Work 72
Lean, David 42
Lean, Edward Tangye 5, 42–3, 55–6, 68, 72, 96, 147, 157, 164, 173
Lean, Tangye 42, 55–6, 64, 68, 72, 96
Lee, Asher 53, 56
Lennox-Boyd, Alan 171, 180
Let Truth be Told 5
literary men, revolt of 135
Litterati, Gyula 152
Lloyd, Selwyn 159–60, 165, 168–9
Lockhart, Sir Robert Bruce 36, 185, 198n. 6
London Conference, Arabic translation transmission of 169
London Conference of Maritime Nations 168

McCall, Robert 43
Macdonald, Gregory 135, 141–2, 147, 152–3
Mackintosh, Malcolm 71
Macmillan, Harold 26, 119, 164, 182
Malenkov, Georgy 121, 130
Maleter, Pal 146
Manchester Evening News 14
Mansell, Gerard 5
Marett, Robert 5
Marquis, Frederick (1st Earl of Woolton) *see* Woolton, Lord
Martin, Kingsley 59
Mayhew, Christopher 38, 40, 43, 46, 60, 69, 96–7
Menzies, Sir Robert 168, 231n. 55
Michie, Allan 152
Middle and Far East broadcast 160
attempts to improve the reach, BBC in 163–4
BBC Arabic Service, reflecting British policy and concerns in 162
BBC/British government response, to Nasser's decision 162
BBC's External Services, slashing of expenditure on 164
British authorities, strategies to enhance prominence of UK policy 161
British publicity in, response to the hostile propaganda 163
Cairo Radio, most effective propaganda medium in 161, 163–4
low-powered VHF stations, in Persian Gulf 162
medium-wave transmitter installation in 164
nature of Britain's engagement in and criticisms faced 175
overseas broadcasting, objectives 165
radio, and international broadcasting role 161
Radio Baghdad, not operational 162
The Voice of the Arabs (VOTA) 161, 163

Whitehall reliance, on the BBC's services to 162
Whitehall's response, arms deal 162
Whitehall's 'Sovietisation' of the Middle Eastern propaganda war 163
Middle East Information Department (MEID) 32
Mikes, George 134
Mikoyan, Anastas 137–8, 143
Ministerial Committee on Overseas Information Services 26
Ministry of Radio Engineering Industry 126
Mirror of the West 162
Molotov, Vyacheslav 121, 138
Monitoring Report 84
Monitoring Service structure 210n. 45
Morrison, Lord Herbert 17, 23–4, 109–10, 185
Mosley, Gordon 72
Munnich, Ferenc 146
Murray, Ralph 39–40, 43, 72, 107

Nagy, Imre 134–5, 142–6, 150, 155
Nasser, Abdel Gamal 160–2, 168–70, 172
Near East Arab Broadcasting Station (NEABS) 179
Nelson, Michael 6
Nicholls, Jack 112
Noel-Baker, Philip 103, 105
North Atlantic Treaty 71, 99
Notes by Our Observer series 59, 145
Nutting, Anthony 111–2, 120, 157–9, 163, 173

Organisation for European Economic Cooperation (OEEC) 95
Overseas Information Service, White Paper on 184
Overseas Intelligence Department 35
Overseas publicity 24, 27, 38–9
aim of 67

Papp, Etele 139
Partner, Peter 158, 177
Peake, Charles 55
Peake, Sir Charles 55, 68
Peterson, Sir Maurice 60
Petofi Circle 133
Petofi, Sandor 136
Polish United Worker's Party (PZPR) 137
Political Information Section 55–6
Political Warfare Executive (PWE) 13, 19
Ponomareva, Nina 127
Poston, Ralph 179
Powell, Sir Allan 14–15
'Projection of Britain Overseas' 26
Public Opinion in Soviet Russia 65

radio 4
radio arms race 75
Radio Free Europe (RFE) 138, 148, 154
allegations against 150–1
broadcast, provoked expectations of assistance from West 152
cultural differences between the BBC and 153
editorial approach assessments, and public criticism 151
Macdonald's analysis, assumptions of 152–3
popular, as per USIA study 148
problems in running of 153
report, in January 1956 152
Radio Free Europe (RFE) report 6, 129, 148
Radio Liberty 6
Radio Madrid 149
Radio Moscow 138, 144
Radio Paris 149
Radio Polskie 137
Radio Vatican 149
Radio Vienna 149
Radiodiffusion Francaise 99
Rajk, Laszlo 72, 138
Rakosi, Matyas 134, 137
Ransome, Patrick 47, 61, 65, 67, 69, 93
Rawnsley, Gary 6, 163
Reading, Lord 115
Rennie, Jack 163
Rentoul, Ferenc 135–6, 139–40
Report on Broadcasting Policy, by GEN 81 17
Rév, István 149
RIAS (Radio in the American Sector, Berlin) 149
Royal Charter 2, 7, 14, 35, 53, 75
'Rumblings in Hungary' 136

Russian broadcast
abandonment of 66
barriers to regular broadcasting 57
Britain's communication strategy to Russia 57–8
critiques about 59
cultural rapprochement 120–6
effect of atmospheric conditions on short-wave propagation 64
effect of Soviet indoctrination 60
implementation of 'crash starts' 63–4
jamming of, impact 61–3, 123–5
political and cultural freedom 65
post-Stalin leadership 121–6
profile of Russian listeners 57–8, 60, 63–4
projection of Anglo-Russian friendship 57
purpose to 57
radio diplomacy between BBC and Soviet broadcasters 124–6
restructuring of programmes 127–32
serious challenges in 65–6
Soviet propaganda 56–8, 60, 62
tie-up with Soviet resources 63
variations in the pitch of 62
see also Central and Eastern Europe broadcast; External Services of BBC
'Russian Jamming' report, by J. B. Clarke 207n. 2
Ruthven-Murray, Barabara 47

Said, Nuri 168
Salem, Major Salah 168
Salisbury, Lord 111
Sargent, Sir Orme 37
Schwartz, Lowell 6
Selverstone, Mark 69
Sèvres agreement 174, 179
Sharq-al-Adna 161, 179
Shaw, Tony 6
Sherwood, J. 94
Short World Press Review 152
Slavonic Orthodox Church 64
Smith, Patrick 36
Special Survey of the Suez Canal Crisis 168
Spectator magazine 183
Stansgate, Lord 28
The State Treaty 136
Stephenson, Donald 32–3, 182, 187
sterling devaluation, consequences of 79, 102
Sterndale-Bennett, John 55
Stewart, Cosmo 127, 158, 173
Suez Canal Crisis 157–9
BBC Arabic Service, presenting British government's policies 177
BBC's Arabic Service, analysis of 162
Britain's post-Suez place in world 182
Bush House role, in giving voice to 169
Bush House's relations with Whitehall, in post-Suez context 183
Canal nationalization, debates in Whitehall 161, 164, 168
as cover for toppling Nasser 172
criticism fired from Whitehall during 180
deepening, and impact on BBC's services 169–70
disaster for British government 176
Eden's domestic television broadcast concerning 169
Eden's resignation and 180
Egyptian perspective on, by Salah Salem 168
exposed different appreciations, obligations resting on BBC 181
government's psychological warfare plans, as problem 178
not operational, Radio Baghdad at time of 162
Sharq-al-Adna refused to broadcast 179
threat to Britain's key strategic interest 161
The Voice of Britain disaster and 179
in Whitehall, an all-consuming crisis 168
Suez Canal nationalization, in July 1956 157, 160
Summary of World Broadcasts 83
Supreme Headquarters Allied Expeditionary Force (SHAEF) 15, 83
Suslov, Mikhail 143

Szabad Nep 133
Szabo, Laszlo 135

Tarjan, George 140–3, 156
Taylor, Philip 3
Thayler, Charles 79
Through the Back Door 5
Thury, Zoltan 152
Tildy, Zoltan 143
Titchener, Lanham 176–7
Tokaev, Grigori 59
Topic of Today 162
Treasury Grant-in-Aid
 see Grant-in-Aid funding
Trend, Burke 173
Tusa, John 5

UKUSA Security Agreement 85–6
United Nations' Special Committee Report, on the Problem of Hungary 153–4
The United States Information Agency (USIA) 148
United States Information Service (USIS) 80

Vansittart, Lord 59
Vansittart, Robert (Baron)
 see Vansittart, Lord
Vaughan, James 6
Venables, H. G. 66
Veress, Laszlo 143
Voice of America (VOA) 6, 73, 78, 80, 138, 148, 150–1
The Voice of Britain (VOB) radio 178–9
Voice of Free Hungary *see* Radio Free Europe (RFE)
The Voice of the Arabs (VOTA), from Cairo Radio 161, 163
Voice of the USA 63
Voices in the Darkness 5

Walker, Patrick Gordon 163
Wallinger, Geoffrey 70–1
War of the Black Heavens 6
Warner, Christopher 37–8, 40, 43, 46–8, 56, 60, 69–70, 72, 76, 95, 112, 202n. 12
Warsaw Treaty 121, 143–4, 220n. 10
wedge strategy 69
Western broadcasters 6
Western broadcasters, in Hungary
 allegations made against, by leadership 149–50
 audience studies conducted, for benefit of 225n. 77
 BBC, RFE, VOA 148
 cross-listening evidence of 149
 jamming impact on 148–9
western radios
 in Hungary 148–9
 transmitting in Russian 123
Western Union broadcasting 95–100
 planned co-operation between European broadcasters 99
 Western European Commentaries 98, 100
 see also External Services of BBC
Western Union Committee 96
White Paper
 based on the Drogheda Report 113–15
 on *Broadcasting Policy,* 1946 2, 18, 23, 44, 97, 165, 177, 185
 on *Overseas Information Service* 184, 186
Whyte, Colonel 85
Wilford, Hugh 6
Wilson, Duncan 176–7
Wint, Guy 169
Wooferton 208n. 15
Woolton Committee, in 1944 185
Woolton, Lord 15
A World in Your Ear 5
Writers' Revolt 135